# NEXT STOP: GUADALCANAL

**JULY 31:** *Tonight we are really off to the wars. The entire force got underway about 1630. D-Day is set for August 7, a week from today; Zero hour for 0830.*

*I have been going through a big stack of orders covering the complicated plans for attacking Guadalcanal-Tulagi. I am impressed by the complexity of an amphibious operation and will be much surprised if everything goes smoothly. This is really just a grand experiment and God had better be with us.*

*There is strong Japanese concentration in the New Guinea-New Britain region. They may embarrass us considerably . . .*

# GUADALCANAL REMEMBERED

## HERBERT C. MERILLAT

AVON BOOKS ◆ NEW YORK

# Acknowledgments

Fortunately, for research on a book of this kind, I live in Washington, D.C., with its uniquely rich resources in archives and libraries. I have been a frequent visitor to the Navy Yard, where both the Navy and the Marine Historical Centers are located. Brigadier General Edwin H. Simmons, USMC (Ret.), director of the Marine Corps Division of History and Museums, and his staff have been unfailingly helpful. Among them I want in particular to thank the director; Joyce E. Bonnett in the Archives; Evelyn Englander in the Library; Benis M. Frank in the Oral History Section; and Richard Hillman in Graphics, who prepared the maps of Guadalcanal.

At the Navy's Operational Archives, its director, Dean C. Allard, and Leslie Grover Kingseed and Michael Walker of his staff, have similarly been of great assistance and generous of their time in guiding me to pertinent materials. I am also much indebted to Brigadier General James Lawton Collins, USA (Ret.), Chief of Military History, and Charles W. Ellsworth, Jr., in the Army Center of Military History. At the National Archives, John E. Taylor has helped to guide me through the maze of recently declassified materials on radio intelligence in World War II. For published works bearing on the subject matter of this book the armed-forces libraries, Library of Congress, and Martin Luther King Library have been indispensable resources.

Several retired Marine Corps officers who served on the staff of the First Marine Division during the Guadalcanal campaign have kindly helped me with answers to specific questions, and I very much appreciate their assistance:

General Gerald C. Thomas (then division chief of staff), General Merrill B. Twining (operations officer), Lieutenant General Edward W. Snedeker (signal officer), and Colonel Sanford B. Hunt (signal assistant to the chief of staff).

My friends Nicholas Blatchford and Richard B. Freund have read the manuscript in draft and given wise and welcome advice. Another friend, Edward R. Weismiller, has been exceedingly generous of his time and exceptional editorial talents; I owe him special thanks. I am also much indebted to General Simmons and Benis Frank for their comments and suggestions. Richard B. Frank, now at work on a very detailed history of the Guadalcanal campaign, has kindly drawn on his own thorough research to save me from some errors. I also want to thank S. Fifi'i, in the Ministry of Foreign Affairs of the Solomon Islands, for providing recent information about Guadalcanal and the aerial map of Honiara. As with two earlier books, I am grateful to Allen T. Klots, executive editor of Dodd, Mead & Company, for his encouragement and for guiding this one to publication.

Despite the wealth of sage counsel and expert advice I must take full responsibility for any errors in fact and for debatable judgments. The book has grown out of an essentially personal exploration of the Guadalcanal campaign and its wider ramifications. It happens that I write this note exactly forty years after I was first asked whether I would be interested in joining the Marines as a combat correspondent.

H. C. MERILLAT

*Washington, D.C.*
*April 15, 1982*

# Contents

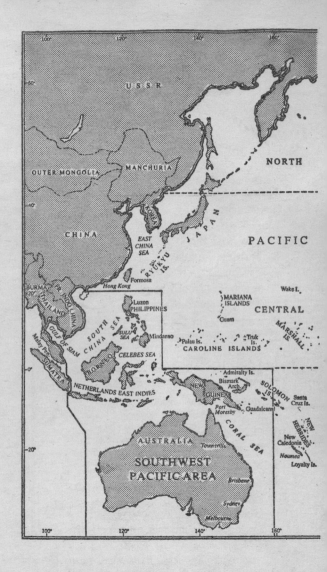

*General map of Pacific basin showing division between theaters of operation: Pacific Ocean Areas (subdivided into North, Central, and South) and Southwest Pacific Area, MacArthur's realm*

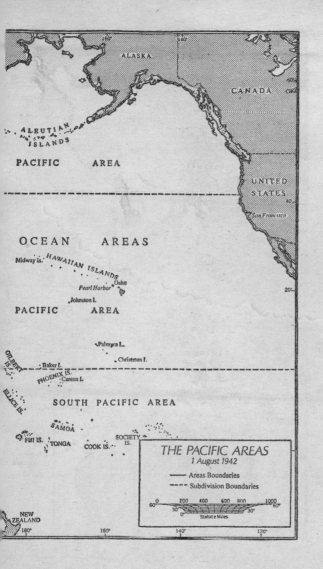

ALASKA

CANADA

ALEUTIAN
ISLANDS

PACIFIC        AREA

UNITED
STATES

San Francisco

OCEAN        AREAS

Midway Is.   HAWAIIAN ISLANDS

Pearl Harbor   Oahu

Johnston I.

PACIFIC        AREA

Palmyra I.

Christmas I.

Baker I.

GILBERTS

PHOENIX IS.   Canton I.

ELLICE IS.

SOUTH   PACIFIC   AREA

SAMOA

FIJI IS.   TONGA   COOK IS.   SOCIETY
IS.

NEW
ZEALAND

THE PACIFIC AREAS
1 August 1942

——— Areas Boundaries
- - - - Subdivision Boundaries

0   200   400   600   800   1000

Statute Miles

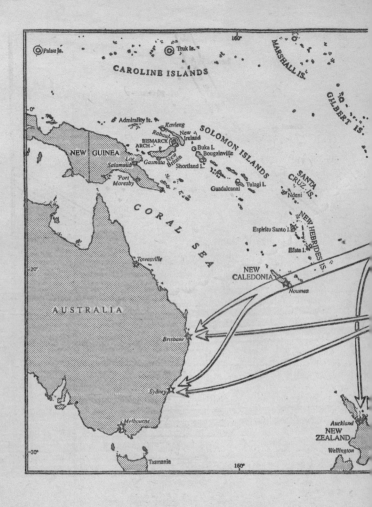

*Area of most places mentioned in the book and the line of communications between the United States and Australia–New Zealand*

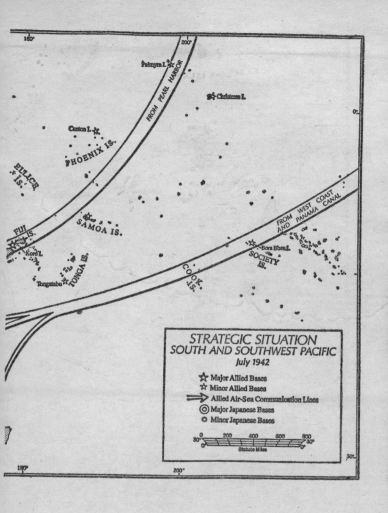

STRATEGIC SITUATION
SOUTH AND SOUTHWEST PACIFIC
July 1942

☆ Major Allied Bases
☆ Minor Allied Bases
➤ Allied Air-Sea Communication Lines
◎ Major Japanese Bases
○ Minor Japanese Bases

0   200   400   600   800
Statute Miles

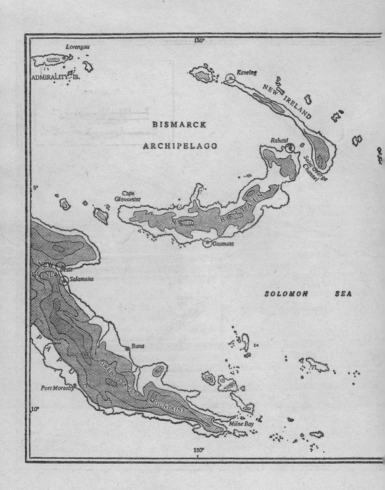

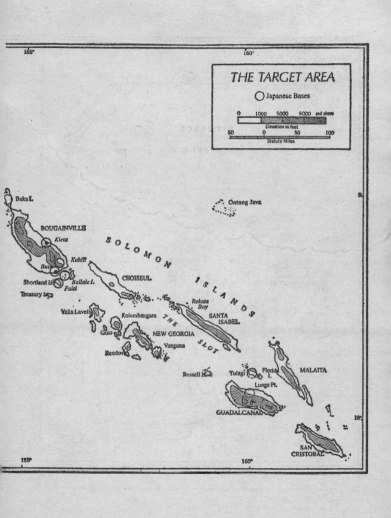

THE TARGET AREA

◯ Japanese Bases

0    1000   5000   9000  and above
Elevation in feet

50        0        50       100
Statute Miles

Buka I.

BOUGAINVILLE
*Kieta*

Kahili

Buin

Shortland Is.

Treasury Is.

Ballale I.
Faisi

Vella Lavella

Gizo

Rendova

Kolombangara

NEW GEORGIA

Vangunu

S  O  L  O  M  O  N   ISLANDS

CHOISEUL

Rekata Bay

SANTA ISABEL

T H E   S L O T

Ontong Java

Russell Is.

Tulagi

Florida I.

Lunga Pt.

GUADALCANAL

MALAITA

SAN CRISTOBAL

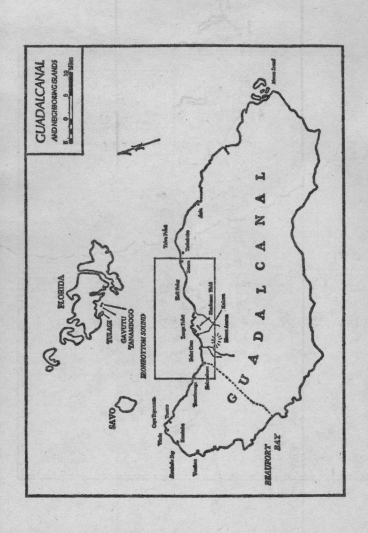

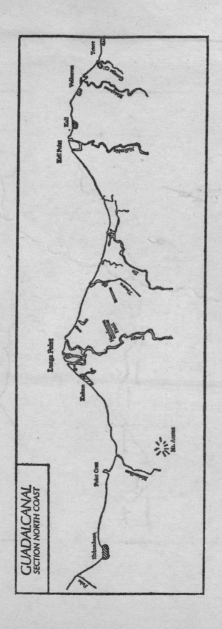

*Area where most of the fighting took place*

# Introduction

Assume that this page is a map of Guadalcanal. The space your thumbnail covers gives a rough idea of the size of the American beachhead during most of the long conflict there in 1942. The battle raged around and over those few square miles because they contained an airfield. That primitive airstrip became a magnet drawing fighting ships by the score, planes by the hundreds, and troops by tens of thousands, from both sides. The struggle to possess it became the turning point—and some would say, more arguably, the decisive battle—in the war between the United States and Japan.

In a sense, the Japanese lost the war the day they attacked Pearl Harbor. They then made it certain that the overpowering strength of the United States would be marshaled against them. Eventually they would lose, unless Americans grew dispirited by repeated local defeats and mounting losses, and by a German triumph in Europe. To speak, then, of decisive battles in a war whose outcome was never in much doubt is questionable. But there were major critical points at which Japanese defeat and American success would substantially hasten eventual victory. Midway, Saipan, and Luzon were among them.

Among them, too, Guadalcanal belongs. It was not just a turning point in the sense that from then on Japan would be on the defensive and the United States on the offensive. That much was as clear soon after the campaign as it was four decades later. The victory's greater significance only became apparent after the war. The hemorrhaging of Japanese air power—first in attempts to recapture the island,

and then in efforts to halt a further American advance based on that same island—had contributed enormously to the American victories that came later.

A Guadalcanal—a place where the tide in the Pacific war would be changed in a long, grueling clash—would have emerged somewhere, at some time, in the Pacific war. The clash happened to come upon, over, and around a beautiful, blood-soaked, TNT-torn, tropical island that few had heard of before the battle was joined. At various times high commanders on both sides had doubts that the place was worth the toll it was exacting. Indeed, its importance was open to argument. There were some on the American side who thought it would be wise to conserve scarce assets in the Pacific until the enormous reserves then building up at home could be brought to bear. But the island took on symbolic as well as military importance. The conflict became not only a passage at arms but a test of national will and an index of prestige.

Forty years have confirmed that the island campaign was both symbolically and strategically the turning point of the war. And now, four decades later, the time has come—if ever it is to come—for me to draw on personal notes which, I believe, throw new light on the campaign. To do so provides an occasion and a framework for looking afresh at the main decisions and events in a historically important struggle.

This new account is written from the vantage point of an officer—a civilian in uniform, press officer, and in-house historian for the First Marine Division—attached to the division staff that planned and directed the ground fighting during most of the campaign, someone who kept a detailed narrative of events on the island and, in later years, watched the story filled in more completely as new information and official histories became available.

My personal sources consist of two kinds of records: those of military operations and related actions as observed by or reported to me during the campaign; and notes of personal experiences and reactions. The two were mixed together. My green canvas musette bag gradually accumulated a stack of material: a running narrative, notes typed on foolscap, carbon copies of stories written by myself or others on the scene, handwritten entries in a diary, and jottings in a little black loose-leaf notebook and on odd bits of paper.

From that assortment I wrote an impersonal narrative of events, somewhat in the style of the usual unit history, which was published as *The Island* in 1944. So far as I have been able to find out, much of the material I drew on for that book has disappeared, probably destroyed in a periodic housecleaning at Marine Corps Headquarters. The diary and black notebook survive in my possession, with their mixture of operational and personal notes. In this new account the personal entries serve as a framework for reviewing, recounting, and commenting on larger events.

The book is, in effect, a heavily annotated diary. To daily entries are added extensive materials and remarks that explain, or correct, or enlarge upon personal records and recollections. If the comments (sometimes filling whole chapters) have turned out to be longer than the daily entries . . . well, few on the island at the time (perhaps no one, and certainly not I) knew of larger plans, decisions, and happenings that profoundly affected the local battle. I have assumed that readers will be more interested in a rounded account than in a limited view from the command post.

Several excellent histories have been written under the auspices or with the encouragement of the various armed services involved in the campaign. In these a reader can find blow-by-blow, unit-by-unit accounts of the fighting at sea, in the air, and on the ground. I have not attempted here another narrative of that kind. Apart from the personal passages, I have seldom gone into detail except where I think that earlier accounts have only touched on matters that deserve fuller attention, or where important new material has recently become available.

The book focuses mainly on the first four crucial months of the campaign, the period covered by my notes. Beyond that I have tried to give enough of Allied and Japanese strategic thinking to explain how and why a clash on an unknown island grew into a prolonged conflict that decided the future course of the war. I have taken the story beyond the four months to deal more briefly with the final victory on Guadalcanal, the island's conversion into a major Allied base for later operations, and the history of Guadalcanal since the war.

At Guadalcanal, as in the whole Pacific war, the U.S. Navy carried the main burden and heaviest responsibility. But air, sea, and ground forces, of all services, had to work in mutual support to win the local conflict and fight on across vast ocean spaces to the Japanese homeland. The symbiosis was strikingly evident at Guadalcanal. The United States had never before undertaken so ambitious a combined operation.

Marines on Guadalcanal were often critical, even bitterly so, of the Navy—usually, except for a few in the top echelons of the Marine command, for the wrong reasons. And naval officers often resented the acclaim lavished on marines for holding the island when the "silent service's" burden and losses were heavier but less visible to the public. Some high officers in each service thought those of the other too cautious and unaggressive. As to errors of omission and commission in high strategy, Marine officers came out relatively unscathed; they had no share in the larger decisions.

Perhaps someday a historian will analyze the campaign in terms of the training, experience, temperament, and doctrinal attitudes of four admirals—Frank Jack Fletcher, Robert L. Ghormley, William F. Halsey, and Richmond Kelly Turner. It would be an instructive and rewarding exercise to do so. In these pages I have only touched on desisions they made that are essential to an understanding of the campaign. There were other important naval commanders, above and below them in the chain of command, but these four, in charge locally, had the most direct impact on events at Guadalcanal.

On the twentieth anniversary of the Guadalcanal landings veterans of the First Marine Division received a message from Jacob Vouza, a brave and canny Guadalcanalese scout whose services had won their special admiration and affection: "Tell them I love them all. Me old man now,

and me no look good no more. But me never forget."
When I first read those words I thought I could adopt them
as my own. On reflection I would have to modify them.
As in any military service, there were too many who really
enjoyed killing, too many larceners, too many con artists
to let one "love them all." And could I say "me never
forget"?

I do forget, have forgotten, a great deal. Not in the
sense Vouza intended; I will always remember the First
Marine Division with admiration as a fighting force. But
much that happened on Guadalcanal is lost to memory.
Certain events and my reactions to those events seem
reliably fixed in my mind. But if, within minutes or hours
or at most a few days, I had not committed such things to
paper, I would now find the months on Guadalcanal a
blurred, dimly perceived landscape punctuated by a few
vivid beacons.

Lawyers, historians, and Internal Revenue Service agents
(among others who want to know just what happened
when) regard a record written immediately after an event
as the most reliable evidence of that event, so far as the
writer knows about it. As to reports of what others have
done, they can be no more accurate than the information
those others have supplied, and what they choose to tell
may be distorted. Official military action reports, like
others, depend on someone's recollection, more or less
accurate and honest.

As to the main events in the Guadalcanal campaign,
there is no doubt that they happened. Marines did land on
August 7, 1942. On the night of August 8–9 U.S. carriers
did withdraw from the area and Allied navies did lose four
cruisers in a surface battle. The U.S. Navy combat did
bring in major reinforcements on known dates. The first
combat air squadrons did arrive on August 20. Four major
Japanese counteroffensives were thrown back. And so on.

When we come to the details of these actions there are
and always will be many uncertainties. And when we try
to learn what went on in the minds of high commanders as
they laid plans, made crucial decisions, dealt with crises,
and directed their forces in combat, truth is even more
elusive.

Those who want to make their own explorations of the Guadalcanal campaign might well start with half a dozen accounts, written from varying points of view. Having digested those, they might educate their palates with selections from a dozen or more other volumes. By then they will be able to note the differences between one chef's concoction and another's. They will have learned to detect ingredients added in one place, missing elsewhere.

Navy, Marine Corps, Army, and Army Air Forces were all involved, in varying degrees, at Guadalcanal. Most writers on the campaign have had a primary interest in one or another of those services, or of a particular arm within that service. The very nature of their undertakings, and primary reliance on the records of the chosen arm, result in some distortion. Official and semiofficial histories have nevertheless been remarkably evenhanded.

I have had no connection with the Marine Corps since I resigned my commission in the Reserve a few years after the war. But my own wartime involvement undoubtedly colors what I have written in this book. That is bound to be so; quite apart from sentiment, I saw the campaign through the eyes of a junior staff officer at the command post of the First Marine Division. Recognizing my unconscious bias I have tried to control it—with what success I cannot say.

Before writing a summary report of any given ground action—say, the Battle of Bloody Ridge—for this book, I have usually compared at least six accounts, each having a valid claim to authoritativeness. There are always discrepancies among them, sometimes substantial. One may omit, or barely touch on an event or decision that seems important to another. Or it may plainly be wrong in some respect. In the last analysis a reader must decide for himself what has the ring of truth.

I have edited the entries in my personal diary to reduce them to manageable size, to omit much that is no longer interesting to me and must be of even less interest to others, and to improve phrasing that is inept or tediously repetitive. Afterthoughts and brief explanatory notes that do not appear in the original entries are placed in brackets.

Official figures on unit personnel strengths, casualties,

enemy plane losses, and temporary disabilities on account of disease or fatigue are frustratingly unreliable. Both American and Japanese records are incomplete, or difficult to piece together, and often conflicting. In this book I have usually given such statistics in round numbers.

By now the heroes (at least some of them) have been honored, medals awarded, memoirs written, myths established, and unit actions chronicled in considerable detail, although not always to the satisfaction of participants. There are some recent accretions to the store of knowledge; I have taken them into account. But here, above all, within the framework of personal recollections, I have tried to give readers (for some of whom Guadalcanal will seem as remote as Gettysburg or Waterloo) a more broadly brushed picture of events that swirled around the island, against a background of still larger events and decisions.

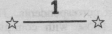

# 1

# Initiation

My own journey to Guadalcanal began with a chance encounter at the bar of the University Club in Washington, D.C., in April 1942. A friend had been commissioned as a major in the Marine Corps Reserve to help develop the public relations activities of the Corps. He was George Van der Hoef, a graduate of the University of Chicago who had served as a public relations official in several government agencies and was considered skilled at his trade. Van der Hoef was stout, round-faced, bright, imaginative, a firm believer in the worth of his calling, and afflicted with the most severe stammer I have ever encountered. He had been taken on as executive officer of the recently established Public Relations Division of the Corps.

Brigadier General Robert L. Denig, called back to service from retirement, was in charge of the division. Denig was an affable, rotund, balding man in his fifties, with a pixyish quality enhanced by an oriental tilt and narrowness of snapping brown eyes. "Togo" was his nickname. He often said later that he knew nothing about public relations when first assigned to his new job. In the small prewar Corps, dealings with what we now call the media were considered to be an adjunct of recruiting. The general took to his new duties with flair and became a beloved father figure for two generations of Marine publicists.

Van der Hoef was to be Denig's "idea man." He came up with the notion of assigning commissioned and non-commissioned officers to all major units. They would write about marines everywhere, but particularly about men on fighting fronts. Eventually the servicemen-reporters

8

were called combat correspondents. The NCOs, at least, were so dubbed. Those with commissions were called public relations officers (PROs)—a less glamorous title, smacking more of Madison Avenue than of the fighting front.

The idea, as it evolved, was to assist the civilian press in the field and to supplement war reporting of the usual kind with more detailed descriptions of what individual units were doing and, above all, what individual marines were doing. These personal items came to be called "Joe Blow" stories. Local newspapers were soon to develop a sharp appetite for them. Press, magazine, and radio coverage of this kind would be good for a reading and listening public thirsty for news of the war, at a more personal level than that of most war reporting. It would give Joe Blow's hometown a sense of participation and pride in local boys. It would be good for morale on the home front and of marines whose reportable doings would get recognition.

Not least, it would be good for the "image" (although I do not recall that the word was then in use in P.R. circles) of the Marine Corps. In the longer run, official combat reporters might provide some of the stuff of history, seen from the viewpoint of men involved in battle.

At the time of the encounter in the University Club, the idea was still in embryo. The P.R. Division was just beginning to recruit members for this new branch of the Corps. Officers and NCOs fully trained for combat who also had some experience with the working press seemed to be ideal for assignment as combat reporters. But there would be a risk in so using them, particularly when the aims and methods of the program were still unfamiliar: officers commanding line units in a Corps which boasted that everyone was a rifleman first and only secondarily a specialist would be inclined to switch such people, once in the field, to regular combat duty.

At the beginning of the new venture the Public Relations Division, backed by the commandant, was ready to commission, for duty of this novel type, some who had not gone through the training mill. They were civilians in uniform, like the major—and like me. Some would remain at Marine Headquarters or at important media centers around the country. Most would eventually go to combat zones.

Van der Hoef, having sketched the idea with appropriate P.R. persuasiveness, asked me if I would be interested in joining up as a staff sergeant. The Second World War, it will be recalled, was the last of our popular wars. That is, there were large numbers of young men who were willing, even eager, to serve in the armed forces against Hitler and Tojo. I was among them. In fact, at the time of the barside chat, I was about to be commissioned in the Naval Reserve. In that service, because of faulty eyesight, I would probably (in those early months of the war) be assigned duty as a communications officer. I told Van der Hoef I would think about it.

Five days later, again at the University Club, he returned to the subject. I more or less jokingly said that if he could make me an officer, as the Navy seemed about to do, I might be interested. I liked the idea of joining a small, elite service instead of getting swallowed up in the bureaucracies of the Army and Navy. Above all, the Marine job would give me an opportunity to write.

To my surprise, Van der Hoef said there was some possibility of a commission. He asked me to write him a letter setting out my personal history—education, experience, and the like. That was on a Monday. Tuesday I sent the letter. Wednesday morning George called to say that his boss, General Denig, would like to see me. I went over to Marine Headquarters in Arlington that afternoon and came away with the general's blessing on my application. There remained formalities of filing my papers, taking a physical examination, and getting the necessary waiver for my eyesight. I took the physical Friday and was pronounced fit, except for vision. By Saturday I felt that I was practically a Second Looey in the Marine Corps Reserve.

That same Saturday a Lieutenant Hibbard in the Navy asked me to come over to the Navy Department. I went. He offered me a job in Air Intelligence, was surprised to hear that I was not yet commissioned in the Naval Reserve, and suggested that I start as a civilian. Upon checking with the Bureau of Navigation, he learned it would be two or three weeks before I could be sworn in as an ensign.

It may be that a muddle about my name decided my fate. On May 8 BuNav informed the Director, Naval Officer Procurement, that my application had been approved and a commission as ensign would be forwarded within a few days. But "it is noted that the name of subject applicant appears on his application as Herbert Laing Merillat, whereas the birth certificate gives his name as Herbert Christian Merillat." The commission would not be delivered until this discrepancy was satisfactorily explained.* I had meanwhile told Mr. Hibbard that I was probably going to join the Marines. The Corps moved with exemplary speed. On May 13 I was sworn in as a second lieutenant in the Marine Corps Reserve. Five days later I was off to the wars.

General Denig tossed me a book of matches bearing the legend "Once a Marine Always a Marine," and wished me luck. I recall him leaning out of his office window in Marine Headquarters—thinking what thoughts, I wonder—as I staggered away, toting a bedding roll, field clothing bag, and assorted other gear. The next day I arrived, by train and bus, at New River in North Carolina.

Sergeant James Hurlbut, destined to be the first NCO combat correspondent in action, was with me. Jim had earlier served a hitch in the Marine Corps. Before going back into uniform he had been working with a radio station in Washington, and was full of ideas about more effectively using the airwaves in Marine public relations. Part of his job, for the moment, was to help me learn the ropes.

Our orders were to report to the First Marine Division, then in the rough encampment at New River that would soon be commissioned as Camp Lejeune. Commanded by Major General Alexander Archer Vandegrift, the division was made up of three infantry regiments (the 1st, 5th, and 7th Marines), and a regiment of artillery (11th Marines),

*The middle name "Christian" came from my father (Christian Clarence). But it seems my mother really wanted me named after her brother, Herbert Laing. I grew up signing my name with "Laing" in the middle. Having been reminded by BuNav of my "real" name (which I preferred) I began to encourage people to call me Chris. To this day friends and acquaintances are divided between those who call me "Herbert" (mainly prewar) and those who call me "Chris" (postwar).

each numbering roughly 3,000 officers and men. To the four basic regiments were added specialized "divisional" units of battalion size (about 900 in strength, with variations)—tanks, engineers, "pioneers," and others. Earlier in the year the 7th Marines had been detached and sent to help garrison Samoa.

That Sunday morning, May 17, Hurlbut and I found the advance echelon of the division, consisting largely of the 5th Marines, entraining for Norfolk. With considerable difficulty we convinced a perplexed division personnel office that we were supposed to go along. Nobody had ever heard of such creatures as a public relations officer and sergeant. After an overnight train ride on piles of assorted gear we embarked at Norfolk, amid the confusion that attends such occasions. Our transport was the *Wakefield*, the transatlantic liner *Manhattan* in prewar days. We crossed the Caribbean and Pacific, and landed in Wellington, New Zealand, on June 14. About eight weeks later we found ourselves landing, D-Day morning, on the beaches of Guadalcanal, and stayed on the island for four lively months.

So rapid a transmutation from Treasury Department lawyer, with a smattering of P.R. experience, into a veteran of Guadalcanal puzzled friends and acquaintances. How had Merillat had time for basic training, let alone officer's school? The answer was, he had not. I was indeed a civilian in uniform. The P.R. Division could be entirely confident that I would not be snatched away to lead a platoon into battle.

The only times I had fired a Colt automatic (my alloted sidearm) was on a range in Honolulu. There I had served a brief stint with the Treasury's Office of Foreign Funds Control soon after Pearl Harbor. Local authorities had passed the word that civilian officials should be ready to share in the defense of an island still fearful that the Japanese might return—this time to land. As part of my one-week "indoctrination" at Marine Headquarters, a sergeant in the P.R. Division had patiently taught me to strip and reassemble a Colt.

I was only slightly less green in the field of public relations. My training had been as a lawyer, and my first job had been to help draft tax legislation in the Treasury Department. Two assignments brought me somewhat into touch with press and radio. For several months in 1941 and 1942 I was assigned to keep the secretary informed of editorial and public opinion concerning tax and fiscal measures that the Treasury was proposing. Also, for several months, I had helped to explain to a largely uninterested public and press, and to gatherings of bankers (who *were* interested), the workings of Treasury Department controls over financial dealings with Axis nationals and their neutral fronts.

It was never entirely clear to me why I was picked for the assignment to the First Marine Division. That was considered a great plum by P.R. men who yearned for active field duty; the division was marked to be the first unit of its size in the Marine Corps ever to go into action. There were moments in the next few months when I would have been happy to yield the honor to someone else. I never thought, later, to ask Denig or Van der Hoef why they had picked me for this venture. And now both have departed this world.

Early in the voyage to New Zealand, after senior staff officers had palavered, I was assigned to D-1, the personel section of the division staff. The other three staff sections were D-2 (intelligence), D-3 (operations), and D-4 (supply). The senior D-1 officer with the advance echelon was Captain James C. Murray, and it was to his care I was committed. About my own age—that is, in his late twenties—the captain was a Yale graduate who had chosen a career in the Marine Corps. He was about six feet tall. Short-cropped sandy hair described an ellipse over a high forehead, above a long face that terminated in a strong chin. Like me, he wore glasses much of the time. Very young to hold a responsible divisional staff post, he was, as became clear in later weeks, highly regarded by the commanding general and his staff.

At first I took Murray's coolness personally, but came to learn that he was generally regarded as frosty by inferiors in rank. Aloof, reserved, introverted: the same adjectives have been applied to me. Between these twain the ice never fully thawed, although we were to share, in coming months, many experiences that would normally make for camaraderie.

Looking back, I realize that Murray was remarkably patient with my unknowingness, and helpful in getting me educated. In many respects, especially matters involving confidential discussions with the general, Murray himself was the public relations officer.

On the first day out at sea from Norfolk, Murray told me that I was to be the historian of this expedition. Here, at least, was a definite assignment, and one that I welcomed. I did not at the moment worry about how it fitted in with the comprehensive history-writing that the armed services might be planning. And I did not at the moment worry about how the assignment fitted in with other duties Denig & Co. might have had in mind in shipping me out. Until we got into action—half a year thence, as General Vandegrift had been led to believe—there would probably be little to do in the P.R. line. Our very presence in New Zealand was supposed to be a secret.

Perhaps Murray regarded me as a symbol of the publicity world against which he had a special grievance at the outset of the voyage. The Sunday we left New River for Norfolk a radio program in New Zealand announced that preparations were being made to receive American troops soon. A few days later it was announced that Vice Admiral Ghormley had set up headquarters in New Zealand as commander of an amphibious force. The captain was indignant. Publicity could rob the expedition of surprise and lead the Japanese to strengthen garrisons in the Southwest Pacific, or even to invade New Zealand immediately. "Someone in the Navy Department or the goddam New Deal" was responsible, said Murray. At one point he remarked that General Denig, my P.R. boss back at Marine Corps HQ, "doesn't draw five feet of water with General Vandegrift," which I took to be, in naval parlance, an expression of low esteem.

During the voyage I busied myself learning something of the organization of the Corps and its combat units, pored over field manuals and pamphlets on weapons and tactics, our own and Japanese. I picked up the rudiments of Marine jargon, which is basically navalese. A bed or substitute therefor is a "sack," floor or ground is "deck," ceiling "overhead," and latrine "the head." Rumor is "scuttlebutt" (named for the old shipboard water cask, later drinking fountain), rough wilderness that officers like to choose for training exercises is the "boondocks," field shoes worn there are "boondockers," and a marine's rifle is his "piece" or "weapon," but never, never his "gun."

Marine and Navy hierarchies quickly became evident. Of these, grading by rank was only the most obvious and familiar. Despite some difficulty in adjusting outward attitudes toward others according to the insignia worn on their collars or caps or sleeves, I was properly in awe of superiors. I would have thought it laughably unbelievable if told that nine years later I would be spending a year at the National War College in Washington, chumming it up with Army and Marine and Air Force colonels and Navy captains about to receive their first stars.

The mysteries of the Lineal List were much harder to grasp than those of openly emblazoned rank. Even within a given grade—say, of major, or colonel, or major general, or admirals of various degrees—line officers of the regular services carefully kept tabs on the standings of their peers in the List. Annapolis men had a clear guide for their initial status: their standing in the roll of graduates from the Naval Academy in a given year. For non-Annapolis officers—much more often found in the Marine Corps than in the Navy—the date of commissioning determined status. Upon promotion to a higher rank, relative status depended upon the date of promotion, and, when more than one was promoted at the same time, upon the order in which names appeared in the promotion list.

This hierarchy of numbers is essential in a well-ordered service. The senior line officer within the highest rank present is automatically in command. Particularly in battle it is important to know who succeeds to the mantle if the commander is knocked out. But status may also be used for pettier purposes. On the *Wakefield* we heard of majors and lieutenant colonels, crowded like lowly second lieutenants four or five to a cabin, who consulted the Lineal List to determine which was entitled to the choicest bunk. "He keeps his finger on his number,'' junior officers said of such.

R.H.I.P.—Rank Has Its Privileges—they said of all the higher officers. Having been warned by an advance man in New Zealand that liquor was scarce there, the brass aboard the *Wakefield* had four hundred cases put aboard as we went through the Panama Canal. I never knew for certain just what strata of officers were permitted to share in this benison. Certainly none trickled down to second lieutenants.

I began to learn what bound the Navy and Marine Corps together and what made them separate, distinct services—at least as a matter of law. Both, it appeared, were branches of the ''Naval Service.'' The heads of both reported to the Secretary of the Navy, who was their civilian chief. Under their respective heads (Chief of Naval Operations in the Navy, Commandant in the Marine Corps) each recruited, trained, equipped, organized, and administered its own people.

In practice the links were much stronger. There had to be close cooperation between the two in such matters as training and equipment. Moreover, having built up a given Marine combat unit, the commandant normally assigned it to the Navy for use in Fleet operations. Such units, whether landing parties at Vera Cruz or Marine divisions in the Pacific, were then under the Navy's operational control. At times, as in World War I, Marine units might be made available to the U.S. Army Chief of Staff, and would operate under Army commands. In fact, before the United States had entered World War II, a Marine brigade had been assigned to an Army command in Iceland.

It took us twenty-five days to make the trip from Norfolk to Wellington. For the first six days, along the east coast of the United States and across the Caribbean, a cruiser and four destroyers or subchasers escorted us through waters where German U-boats had been sinking an alarming number of ships that spring. Then we were three days in the Canal Zone, waiting for our turn to make the transit to Balboa. Only some of the brass were allowed to go ashore, on the important mission already noted. But two lieutenants stationed in the Zone came aboard to see friends, bearing ice cream and beer. The five second lieutenants in my cabin managed to get a share of the goodies.

For three nights and days out of Balboa a lonely old destroyer escorted us. Then the *Wakefield* was on her own, relying on speed for protection against submarines. On May 29 we crossed the equator, and the next day there was the usual horseplay as polliwogs—those who had never before crossed the meridian—were initiated as shellbacks, being doused with filthy water, having their hair shorn, and guzzling foul-tasting potions. The general officially announced what we already knew: our destination was Wellington.

The event during the voyage that was to have by far the biggest impact on us took place far to the northwest. On June 4 and 5, off Midway Island, the U.S. Navy intercepted a Japanese invasion armada and its powerful supporting forces. In that crucial encounter the enemy lost four aircraft carriers, the U.S. only one. As a result we would be in action much earlier than anyone aboard the *Wakefield* then suspected.

———————————————

*June 14.* We awoke in sight of land, of mountains rising steeply from the sea. After breakfast I went topside and soon could make out a city in the distance: Wellington. We met the *West Point,* née *America,* as we approached the harbor; apparently she was returning to the States from Australia.

At 1120 the first line was thrown to the dock. The Royal New Zealand Air Force band greeted us with snappy music and snappy marching. At one point they struck up "Beer Barrel Polka," and a few thousand Marines joined in the chorus. Everyone was in high spirits.

Local dignitaries, civilian and military, came aboard soon after the gangplank went down. About 1400 some press people came aboard. Hurlbut and I had been standing on the quarterdeck, watching the comings and goings. He spotted the correspondents. I dashed topside to see Captain Murray and arrange to meet them. I ran into him just as he was starting into the general's cabin, and he said "You may as well come along."

So, at last, I was admitted to the Presence, and was introduced to General Vandegrift and his chief of staff,

Colonel Capers James. They were affable and pleasant, and asked some questions that indicated they had been well aware of my presence. The gentlemen of the press soon arrived. Murray presented them to the general, who introduced me to them as "my public relations officer," which rather startled but pleased me.

---

"Startled" needs some explanation. I was indeed—my orders said so—public relations officer assigned to the First Marine Division. But I was not then, and never really became, "his" press officer in a personal sense. I was not yet used to a general officer's manner of speaking about "my division," "my artillery," "my planes."

General Vandegrift was, when I first met him, a balding man of middling height (5 feet, 8¾ inches, to be precise), blue-eyed, with regular features and a strong chin ending in a dimple. He was then fifty-five years old, and the jaw was somewhat softened by jowls. He spoke with the accents of his native Virginia. Colonel James was a forty-six-year-old South Carolinian, a graduate of The Citadel. Taller than the general, he had, like him, sparse sandy hair, but his face was less firm and commanding than that of the man whose strong right arm he was meant to be. James had served in some of the usual Marine between-the-wars campaigns and posts—in Santo Domingo, Nicaragua, and China.

In his long and distinguished career, culminating as commandant of the Corps, Vandegrift never, so far as I am aware, huckstered for publicity, for himself or for the Corps. When he was military secretary to the commandant, before becoming boss of the First Marine Division, "public relations" was among his assigned responsibilities. He did not, then or later, favor contrived publicity. He seems to have leant rather too far backward, and left publicity, associated at that time mainly with recruiting efforts, to junior officers.

Indeed, if Murray was accurately reporting the general's views ("General Denig doesn't draw five feet of water" with him), Vandegrift was, like most high-ranking Marine officers in 1942, suspicious of the new combat correspondent program. In the half year that followed our first

meeting in Wellington I saw him almost daily, simply
because our tents or other billets were close together. I
talked to him only when there seemed a real need, and he
was unvaryingly courteous. He was readily accessible to
the press on Guadalcanal. I am sure that any attempts at
press-agentry on my part would have been as distasteful to
him as to me. Fortunately, being PRO for the Marines on
Guadalcanal did not require puffery.

In Wellington I had some welcome duties, and some not
so welcome, as press officer for the division. All were
carried out under Murray's watchful eye. And I kept in
mind my assignment as inhouse historian or chronicler,
although there was not much to record at this stage. The
afternoon of the day we docked some of my cabin-mates
and I granted ourselves liberty and went ashore, had a
couple of drinks at the St. George Hotel and dinner at the
Grand—Wellington's two finest. One of my first acts was
to buy a diary, "Whitcombe's New Zealand Professional
Man's Diary for 1942," for five shillings sixpence. This
became one of several repositories for notes made as division chronicler, along with more personal musings.

Division HQ stayed aboard the *Wakefield* for four more
days, while troops and gear were unloaded. Most of the
5th Marines were headed for a camp near Paekakariki,
about thirty-five miles from town. New Zealand newspapers,
film units, photographers, and radio people began turning
up with requests to interview officers and "typical"
marines, to take their pictures, to see and photograph
troop arrivals at the Packakariki encampment which
New Zealanders had hastily built to receive their transpacific guests and defenders. As go-between I drew a
certain amount of lightning from staff officers worried
about security and annoyed at being bothered.

On June 19 division HQ moved ashore, to the Hotel
Cecil. The residents of this rather rundown hostelry had to
give way to the newly arrived Marine command. My own
"office" was behind the reception counter, where at least
the occupants could see who was coming and going. We
began meeting New Zealanders. Many hospitably invited
us to lunch, dinner, evenings-at-home, and on one notable
occasion I had a Sunday breakfast of oysters and beer.

At dizzyingly higher levels local VIPs and the general, with some of his staff, began making their calls and countercalls immediately after we landed. These were duly recorded in the Whitecombe's diary. One of Vandegrift's first calls was on Lieutenant General E. Puttick at New Zealand Army General Headquarters. As temporary defenders of the Commonwealth we would be under his command. On the 15th, from the naval attaché's office in the U.S. Legation, Vandegrift put through a call to his U.S. Navy superior, Vice Admiral Robert L. Ghormley, in Auckland. Apparently the admiral told the general there was no need to rush up to the northern city to report in bodily. But ten days later the admiral called back, asking Vandegrift to come to Auckland immediately. He flew up on the 26th.

---

*June 29.* Notes on the Auckland conference. [The diary does not indicate the source; undoubtedly it was Captain Murray.] The general reported to Admiral Ghormley on Friday the 26th and was told he would get some pretty shocking news. The news *was* a shock. Details later. The general flew back to Wellington Saturday afternoon, leaving Lieutenant Colonel Frank Goettge, the D-2 [intelligence officer] to collect intelligence data. On his return the general called Lieutenant Colonels Pate [supply officer], Thomas [operations officer], and Twining [assistant operations officer], and Captain Murray to give them a sketch of the plan for employment of the division. They worked through Sunday. Shortly an operation order will come out, ordering the 5th Marines to embark for "training exercises." Liberty trains will be cancelled, effective tomorrow the 30th.

Lots of action today. The division staff is busy. The orders for "maneuvers," came out. Two " Combat Groups" have been organized: "A" consisting of most of the troops now here, built around the 5th Marines; "B" will be the 1st Marines, reinforced, commanded by Colonel Clifton Cates (which will not arrive in Wellington until July 11). How *this* will stir up the scuttlebutt!

---

*July 2.* This morning I accompanied a New Zealand National Film Unit photographer and our own camera-wielders to get some shots of troops embarking for "training exercises." The first troop train got in from Paekakariki a little after noon. We got some pix of marines getting off the train, marching to the quay, and going aboard a transport.

Tension has been growing the past few days since the word got around that most of the marines now here will soon be starting on maneuvers. The whole town seems to know about it. The men this morning were a good deal grimmer than usual—fewer smiles, less horseplay. I think most of them are convinced they are going to see action, and soon.

---

A few days earlier a Film Unit photographer named Silk had stopped in at the Cecil. He wanted to arrange to send film directly to *Life* magazine by military air transport, and also to visit the Paekakariki encampment. He saw Captain Murray later in the day and got no encouragement on the airmail proposal. Murray told him he should take such matters up with me, and Silk remarked I had probably not been in "the Army" long enough to be of much help on his project. Reporting this conversation over dinner Silk added that Murray had said: "Merillat doesn't know anything." This was close to the embarrassing truth. But Merillat was learning a few things. Among them was the true destination of the embarking marines.

# The Big Picture

The reembarkation of the 5th Marines, little more than
two weeks after they had landed in Wellington, set the
rumor mills agrinding: Samoa was threatened, and we
were going to reinforce the garrison there; or we would do
the same for Fiji; or we were off to help save New Guinea;
or perhaps this was, as announced, simply to be a training
exercise, probably on New Zealand's South Island. The
general and his senior staff quite properly believed the real
plan should be kept secret. In those early July days only
half a dozen officers were supposed to know when or
where we were going into action. But secrets are seldom
as secret as the brass would like them to be.

July 4 was a gloomy, rainy day in Wellington, the
beginning of a long wet spell that would plague loading
operations. That day someone told me the division's real
destination. My notes do not identify and I do not now
recall the source of this fascinating information. Perhaps it
was Bob Barnes, a friend in the supply section, with
whom I spent much of the day; his boss usually knew what
was going on. More probably it was Captain Murray; later
diary entries suggest that he knew I knew. Memory simply
does not serve in this matter, as in so many others.

Having carefully refrained from writing down so secret
a piece of information, I cannot even be certain that both
Tulagi and Guadalcanal were named. As we now know,
the original orders from Washington specified, as targets
in the Solomons, only Tulagi and "adjacent positions."
Guadalcanal very soon came into the plans, certainly no
later than July 7.

In any event, I had no idea where Tulagi and Guadalcanal were. I headed for a public library, asked for an atlas, and, after considerable searching, found Tulagi in the lower Solomons—an island chain of whose very existence I had been unaware up to then. Nearby was a larger island, named "Guadalcanar" on the map.

Coincidentally, the name "Tulagi" had flickered across a great many people's minds in Wellington that Fourth of July. The *Dominion,* a Wellington daily, carried a story with a New York dateline. It expressed a hope that United States Marines would soon strike against Japanese outposts in the Pacific.

HOPE OF COMING U.S. THRUST
South Pacific Marines
INTENSIFIED RAIDS IN NORTH
(*Received July 3, 7 P.M.*)

New York, July 2.

Operations to seize Japanese-held bases, such as Rabaul, Wake Island, and Tulagi, are advocated by the military writer of the New York *Herald-Tribune,* Major Eliot. One of the signs which suggest that the United Nations may be getting ready to capitalize on the naval advantage gained in the Coral Sea and Midway battles is the recent American bombing of Wake Island, he says. The other signs include the intensified raids on the Timor and New Guinea areas.

"Bombing alone is not enough, because at best it can only prevent the enemy from using the bases," he continues. "What is needed is to drive the Japanese out of their positions and convert them to our own use. The only way to take positions such as Rabaul, Wake Island, and Tulagi, is to land troops to take physical possession of them."

The *Dominion*'s story ended with two paragraphs in bold type:

The newspaper adds: "It may also be significant that the censor passed the news of the arrival of the completely equipped expeditionary force of American Marines at a South Pacific port recently, as Marines are not usually sent to bases where action is not expected.

"It may well be that we are preparing to reap the fruits of the Coral Sea and Midway victories. Sooner or later the present stalemate in the South Seas will be broken on a battlefield of our own choosing."

This piece of journalistic speculation caused consternation in the division staff, particularly among those few who knew that the writer had named, among three enemy bases, one that we were about to attack. Had there been a leak in Washington?

Among Navy war planners in Washington, headed by Rear Admiral Richmond Kelly Turner, the Solomons had emerged early in 1942 as a possible target in a future counteroffensive. But a sustained attack of any kind seemed a remote prospect at that time. In the first few months of the year a more urgent task was to decide how much to invest in defense of what the Allies still held in the Pacific— holdings that had diminished with alarming speed early in 1942.

Immediately after the United States went to war in December 1941 top American and British leaders, political and military, met to discuss broad strategic plans and steps that might immediately be taken to carry them out. They confirmed their earlier agreement that the war against Germany should be given highest priority. Having overrun much of Europe the Germans threatened to annex the remainder, including Britain and Russia, and move into the Middle East. They might soon be in possession of all Europe's industrial plant and Persian Gulf oil.

The agreed Europe First strategy required that American aircraft, trained troops and fliers, munitions, and supplies of all kinds go mainly to bolster the Soviet armies and to build up Allied forces in Britain for a possible assault on continental Europe late in 1942. The buildup in Britain bore the code name BOLERO.

The Allies agreed that the war in the Pacific was to be, initially, a holding action. Forces fighting there must make do with whatever could be allotted to them at the beginning of 1942. By Allied agreement the vast Pacific theater of operations was placed under U.S. command. The U.S. Joint Chiefs of Staff divided it into two major areas: the Pacific Ocean Area under the Navy, with Admiral Chester W. Nimitz as commander-in-chief (CINCPAC,) and the Southwest Pacific Area (including Australia, New Guinea, the Philippines, and the Solomons), placed under the command of General MacArthur after he was brought out of the Philippines. Nimitz's domain was further divided into three subareas, of which the one that mainly concerns us here was the South Pacific. This area included, apart from vast tracts of salt water, New Zealand, New Caledonia, the New Hebrides, Samoa, and Fiji.

How much of the Pacific should a "holding action" try to hold? American and British leaders eventually agreed that, at the very least, an effort must be made to hold Australia; to do so meant that the continent's line of communications with the United States must be kept open. After the Japanese attack on Pearl Harbor the United States moved quickly to put defensive garrisons on a string of islands, widely separated in the broad expanse of the Pacific, running from the Hawaiian Islands southwestward toward New Zealand and Australia. Among them were Palmyra, Canton, Samoa, Fiji, and New Caledonia. This last, a French possession, was to be the principal advance base in the South Pacific.

American planners hoped that the line of island bases could protect the sea lanes between the Hawaiian Islands, the Panama Canal, and the U.S. west coast on the one hand, and New Zealand and Australia on the other. The bases would also serve as a ferry route for Army Air Force planes into the southern Pacific. The AAF proposed to hold its main "Mobile Forces" of heavy bombers in Hawaii and Australia, at either end of the route, and commit them when needed at intermediate points.

Each little island was protected by a garrison of ground troops and an aviation contingent. Each was highly vulnerable to a determined, carrier-backed Japanese attack. But U.S. planners hoped that local defenses, backed by bombers from the Mobile Forces, could at least repel raids and small-scale attacks. In the last analysis, as Midway demonstrated, defense would depend on quick support and succor by the Pacific carrier fleet.

West of the tenuous Allied line the Japanese had a similar string of bases, the outer defense perimeter of the Greater East Asia Co-Prosperity Sphere which the Japanese quickly seized after the outbreak of war. These bases included Wake, atolls in the Gilberts and Marshalls, the northern Solomons, New Britain, and the northern coast of New Guinea. The most formidable base in the southwestern Pacific was Rabaul, on the Australian-mandated island of New Britain. It was backed to the north by Truk, Japan's equivalent to Pearl Harbor, which the empire had acquired as a League of Nations mandate after the First World War.

Rabaul, seized from Australia in January 1942, became the chief Japanese bastion in that part of the Pacific, known as the "Southeast" Area to the Japanese. An excellent fleet anchorage at Rabaul and several nearby airfields were supported by other air and naval stations on New Britain and neighboring islands, including the northern Solomons. From the Rabaul complex the Japanese threatened both New Guinea and islands to the southeast on which the United States had a tenuous hold. Port Moresby, near the southeastern end of New Guinea, under the tail of that turkey-shaped land mass, was the prize the Japanese next sought. From it they would be able to threaten Australia's lifeline to the United States, and perhaps even invade the continent.

The Imperial Japanese Navy also moved down the Solomons chain. In May 1942 it seized Tulagi, capital of the British Solomon Islands Protectorate, which commanded a deep and capacious harbor. There the Japanese set up facilities for seaplanes—patrol craft, bombers, and Zero floatplane fighters.

Like their foe, Americans were steadily thickening and strengthening their outer perimeters during the first half of 1942. Admiral Ernest J. King was the officer chiefly responsible for the American effort. Appointed Commander in Chief, United States Fleet (COMINCH) soon after Pearl Harbor, he was the Navy's member of the U.S. Joint Chiefs of Staff, and their executive agent for conduct of the war in the Pacific Ocean Area—subject to agreed strategic plans. Aged sixty-three when appointed to the Navy's highest post, King was a demanding, determined, and brilliant officer. And he had it in mind, to the constant annoyance of American and British military colleagues who thought a Germany-first priority excluded anything but passive defense in the Pacific, to undertake "offensive-defensive" initiatives against the Japanese as soon as possible.

As King asked his Army counterpart for more and more troops and air contingents to garrison additional islands, the Army Chief of Staff, George C. Marshall, became increasingly concerned that the Pacific would draw off troops and AAF squadrons committed to BOLERO. American leaders still hoped to come to grips with the Germans on the continent of Europe before the end of 1942 or soon thereafter. Marshall asked King what general scheme of operations was guiding him in his repeated requests. On March 2 King replied that his aim was not only to protect communications with Australia but also to "set up 'strong points' from which a step-by-step general advance can be made through the New Hebrides, Solomons, and the Bismarck Archipelago." Among additional needed "strong points" he listed Efate (in the New Hebrides), Funafuti, and Tongatabu.

When the northwestward advance began, he added, the necessary amphibious troops would come chiefly from the "Amphibious Corps, Pacific Fleet." Although even King and his planners were not yet thinking specifically about Guadalcanal, they had Tulagi very much in mind. And they were clearly pointing to the First Marine Division, which was then taking shape in the boondocks of North Carolina.

In April Nimitz and King selected a commander for the South Pacific. For nearly two years Vice Admiral Robert L. Ghormley, a friend of Chester Nimitz from Annapolis days, had been in London as chief U.S. naval observer. There he had helped to arrange informal cooperation between the U.S. and Royal Navies in policing the Atlantic and in the exchange of technical information. It was a post that called more for skills of diplomacy than those of command. Reputed to be an able strategist, Ghormley was now thrown into one of the most difficult and frustrating commands of the war, in a part of the Pacific little known to American military or naval planners.

When Ghormley paused in Washington on his way to the Pacific, Admiral King told him he would have a "most difficult task" in the South Pacific: "I do not have the tools to give you to carry out that task as it should be." He added, without mentioning that his eye was already on the Solomons, that "in time," possibly as early as the fall of 1942, "we hope to start an offensive from the South Pacific."

Ghormley set up his headquarters in Auckland, New Zealand. He soon learned, from unfilled requests for construction equipment, base-building units, cargo-handling gear, and the myriad other things needed to prepare for operations, that King and Nimitz indeed did not have the required tools. He did not even have any ships except for those sent from time to time into his area—and their operations were controlled from Pearl Harbor.

In the encounter of carrier fleets off Midway in June, the Japanese had lost four flattops. They had also lost many of their best naval pilots; it was the beginning of a hemorrhage that would eventually prove fatal. Midway was a disaster for the Japanese more serious than that their enemy suffered at Pearl Harbor. Obsolescent battleships, too slow to accompany carrier task forces, could be spared; flattops could not. Midway resulted, for the time being, in a rough parity in shipborne air forces. What use the U.S. Navy would make of this temporary balance remained now to be seen.

On June 24, less than three weeks after the fateful engagement off Midway, Admiral King issued an alerting notice to his Pacific commanders. He told Nimitz and Ghormley to prepare for operations against the Santa Cruz Islands (about three hundred miles east of the Solomons), Tulagi, and "adjacent positions" in the Solomons. This was to be Task One in a planned drive toward Rabaul. Tasks Two and Three were to take other islands further up the Solomons chain and Papua (the New Guinea turkey's tail), and finally, New Britain and the Rabaul complex itself. On July 2 the Joint Chiefs of Staff issued a formal directive for the operations.

There had been a spirited dispute in high places as to who should be in charge. General Marshall, Army Chief of Staff, backed MacArthur's claims to be put in command of Task One. Tulagi lay on his side of the boundary between the Southwest and South Pacific. Moreover, operations in the Solomons ought, in the Army's view, to be coordinated, under one commander, with those in New Guinea in the combined drive against Rabaul. King replied, in a memo to Marshall, that Task One would be largely a naval operation, and the landing force—the First Marine Division—part of the Navy's South Pacific Amphibious Force. He insisted that the Navy be in command of Task One. Indeed, he said, the Navy should go ahead with the operation even if the Army in the Southwest Pacific (that is, General MacArthur's command) gave no support. Stung by the implication, Marshall replied that the Army would back the offensive with everything it had available, regardless of which service was in charge.

King and Marshall worked out their differences in a face-to-face chat. Marshall finally agreed with King's plan. They settled the problem of area boundaries ingeniously; the line between MacArthur and Ghormley was moved one degree of longitude to the west, bringing Guadalcanal and Tulagi within the South Pacific. The Navy's COMSOPAC (Ghormley) was to be in command for Task One, Mac-Arthur for Two and Three. The formal JCS directive of July 2 did not name Guadalcanal as an objective in the first phase. If it was in the Washington planners' thoughts at all, it was as an "adjacent position" to Tulagi.

Ghormley finished decoding King's advance warning notice of the forthcoming operation on June 25. He immediately summoned Vandegrift from Wellington. The next day, twelve days after he had arrived in New Zealand, expecting to have half a year to put his division into fighting trim, the Marine general received his stunning orders: he was to get ready to land in the Solomons on August 1, in less than five weeks.

Vandegrift's division was scattered around the Pacific. One regiment, the 7th Marines, his best-trained and -equipped unit, was on garrison duty in Samoa. Another, the 5th Marines, had just gone into its encampments outside Wellington. The remaining rifle regiment, the 1st Marines, was still at sea and would not arrive in Wellington until July 11; its youthful, recently recruited troops were particularly in need of further training. The whole division needed training to operate as a unit and to test newly received equipment.

Loading problems made it seem almost impossible for Vandegrift to meet an August 1 deadline for D-Day. The 1st Marines, their attached units, weapons, ammunition, equipment, and supplies would have to be unloaded from the ships that were ferrying them across the Pacific, then reloaded aboard attack transports and cargo ships according to the intricate patterns of "combat loading." Ghormley was even more pessimistic than Vandegrift about the August 1 target date.

The JCS directive told Ghormley and MacArthur to confer about the plans. The admiral flew to the general's headquarters in Brisbane. A few weeks earlier, when the victory off Midway made an early American offensive seem possible, MacArthur had proposed a direct assault on Rabaul, under his command. He could do the job, he said, with two aircraft carriers, a division trained for amphibious operations, and additional bombers, plus the Australian and American troops he already had. Now both he and Ghormley advised against the operation that the JCS had just ordered in the southern Solomons.

In a combined message to the Joint Chiefs, they recommended that Task One be postponed until it could be backed by more land-based air units and quickly followed by Tasks Two and Three. Their main argument for delay was that the two carriers (all that the Navy had so far promised) would be exposed to attack by land-based bombers from the Rabaul complex. The ships that carried assault troops to the lower Solomons would have to stay in the target area "from thirty-six hours to four days, outside the range of supporting air bases, exposed to continuous hostile attack." "The two commanders," they concluded, "are of the opinion, arrived at independently, and confirmed after discussion, that the initiation of the operation at this time, without a reasonable assurance of adequate air coverage, would be attended with the gravest risk. . . ."

In four days came Washington's reply. Three carriers, not just two, would definitely be available. The Army Air Force had promised support by its Mobile Force of heavy bombers stationed in Hawaii. The directive of July 2 still stood. The operation would proceed. Was anything "absolutely necessary," beyond the forces already listed as available? Thus challenged, Ghormley replied that he could make do with what he had been promised, provided MacArthur was given enough bombers to tamp down Japanese air power in the Rabaul complex.

Meanwhile the Japanese had not been idle. Late in June their naval forces began to move into Guadalcanal, twenty miles across the water from Tulagi. A unit of Special Naval Landing Forces (roughly the equivalent of U.S. Marines, but much more lightly armed) and two construction battalions were landed. Early in July they burned off the grassy plain behind Lunga Point and began to chop down palms in the adjacent coconut plantation. American reconnaissance planes, and British and Australian "coastwatchers" who had remained hidden on the island, reported these developments. Clearly the Japanese were beginning to build an airfield. Guadalcanal was no longer just a position "adjacent" to Tulagi; it had become the primary American target. And it had come to be of the most urgent importance to seize that field before the enemy began flying bombers and fighters from its coral surface.

# 3

☆ ——— ☆

# A Wobbly Watchtower

After the Joint Chiefs had delivered their thunderbolt to Vandegrift, via Ghormley, First Marine Division planners set to work. Their task was to convert a general directive into specific operational orders. Secretive and solemn, they closeted themselves in what they called the "Black Room" on the second floor of the Hotel Cecil.

Lieutenant Colonel Gerald C. Thomas was the chief of the planners. A Missourian and graduate of Illinois Wesleyan University, he had enlisted in the Marine Corps at the age of twenty-two, and had been given a field commission while fighting in France. Vandegrift had known him since they had served together in Haiti. The general had appointed him to be his D-3, or operations officer, in March 1942.

Jerry Thomas was not quite forty-eight years old when we landed in the Solomons, one of the most junior in age and rank among the division staff officers and regimental commanders on Guadalcanal. And he was, by common agreement, one of the brightest, most driving, energetic, and cool-headed. Thomas was not universally loved by his peers in the division; he stepped on a good many toes before the campaign was over. But he was certainly widely respected.

The D-3 was of medium height and build, with hazel eyes and long arches of black eyebrows. Dark hair came to a widow's peak over his forehead. He spoke with intensity and usually stuck close to the business at hand. He had a habit of thrusting out his chin, slightly to one side, when vigorously making a point.

The assistant D-3, Thomas's chief helper, was Lieutenant Colonel Merrill B. Twining, an Annapolis graduate. Brainy and handsome, he had a sardonic sense of humor, an abrupt manner, and a gift for the pungent phrase. His short chestnut hair was parted down the middle. At one time in his career in the Corps, "Bill" Twining had been editor of *The Leatherneck* magazine, and he had taken a law degree while stationed in Washington, D.C.

While the planners planned, intelligence officers were gathering what information they could about those unknown islands where we were expected to land early in August. Lieutenant Colonel Frank B. Goettge was the D-2 (intelligence officer). A big man, he looked like the football player he had been at Ohio State University, but had a gentler manner than his craggy appearance would have led you to expect. Like many of the senior officers, he had short-cropped, iron-grey hair and prominent dark eyebrows.

How many Japanese were in the Guadalcanal and Tulagi garrisons? How were they disposed? What weapons did they have? What were the beach and reef conditions at possible landing sites? What kind of terrain would the landing force find inland from the beaches? Information on these and other crucial matters was skimpy or nonexistent at Ghormley's headquarters and elsewhere in New Zealand. Goettge flew to Australia, hoping to learn more from MacArthur's staff and the Australians. He had some success, but intelligence of the enemy and terrain remained alarmingly scanty.

Australians had established an extensive coastwatching system in the Solomons. As the Japanese moved in during the winter and spring of 1942 some men—brave or stubborn or both—went into hiding, equipped with radios, on the principal islands. Their mission was to watch and report on what the enemy was doing. They were mostly plantation managers, traders, skippers of interisland vessels, gold miners, and civilian or armed-service officers. We will hear more of them later on. For Goettge and the planners back in Wellington they were at this time among the few sources of information about enemy activity in the target area.

Goettge found other old Solomons hands in Australia.

Having been sworn to secrecy they were pumped for all the information they could give about the lower Solomons. Goettge brought back eight to Wellington with him. They were assigned to go in with the combat units as advisers and guides.

The only available aerial photographs of the target area were helpful but far from satisfactory. Taken from a high altitude they showed exasperatingly large patches of cloud over some key terrain features. (Later on, in the fighting on the island, a battalion commander reported his position to the division command post as being "at such-and-such coordinates, under the cloud.")

Supply is less glamorous than operations or intelligence but is the indispensable basis of any military operation, as we were soon to have forcibly impressed upon us. It fell to Lieutenant Colonel Randolph M. Pate, the D-4 or supply officer, to supervise the damp and exhausting business of loading our ships. It was damp because, as I have mentioned, it rained almost incessantly those first two weeks of July. Our ships lay alongside stone-paved quays that turned into shallow lakes. Watersoaked cartons and bags of rations and other supplies disintegrated. Labels washed off. Crates were jumbled in disorder. Confusion and dankness became more critical when the last of the rear echelon, built around the 1st Marines, arrived on July 11. They had only ten days to disembark from their transpacific carriers, then load and reembark in their attack ships.

Wellington dockers' habits made them more a hindrance than a help. They insisted on their usual morning and afternoon tea breaks and refused to work late hours. No one could tell them that a crucial military operation—more than incidentally for the defense of New Zealand—depended on extra efforts. Even before our arrival their unloading of cargo ships sent on ahead had proceeded at glacial speed. Vandegrift ordered marines to do their own hoisting and hauling. When combat loading got under way early in July sodden and uncheerful troops had to work around the clock in eight-hour shifts.

Ghormley's staff had given division planners a roster of troop ships and freighters—APAs (Attack Transports) and AKAs (Attack Cargo Ships)—that would be available for the forthcoming operation. Colonel Pate's task was to see that these were properly combat loaded. In ordinary commercial loading, cargo is stowed in holds so as to make fullest and most efficient use of available space. Combat loading calls for stowing rations, equipment, weapons, ammunition, and other material in such a way that things most urgently needed in combat will come off first, in amounts required by the units aboard a particular ship. It calls for specialized and exacting skills, developed by the Marine Corps and Navy over years of planning and exercises. This was the first time the operation had been carried out on a large scale in readiness for actual combat.

Pate, a bespectacled man of slender build, looked more a scholar than a marine. He was worried when he found that space available for stowage was considerably too small to accommodate material that Marine doctrine prescribed for a division-sized landing. Vandegrift ordered that only what was needed "to live and fight" be put aboard. Prescribed amounts of ammunition and supplies were cut back. Personal gear would be left behind.

More and more press people, New Zealand and American, turned up at the Cecil, sniffing around for information about what was going on.

---

*July 6.* I took Tillman Durdin of the *New York Times* to the *American Legion* [on which part of the 5th Marines was embarked]. Colonel [Leroy P. Hunt], commanding the regiment, a personable veteran of World War I, took him in charge. Hunt gave up the whole morning to showing us around the ship, explaining the make-up of a "Combat Group" (a reinforced infantry regiment) and "Combat Team" (each built around one of the regiment's three battalions), showing him the equipment, and explaining the fundamentals of landing operations. One tidbit from Hunt: "The essence of combat loading is not to put the toilet paper on top of the ammunition."

*July 8.* The general stopped by to say that it would be all right for Durdin to have a marine uniform. Does this mean that he is going with us on our little jaunt? Captain Murray didn't like the news about the uniform and made some remarks about generals' hankering after publicity.

*July 11.* The rear echelon arrived today, which means thousands more marines in town and many more colonels around HQ. I took the photographers down to the docks about 1300 and we watched the ships come in. First the *Ericsson,* which pulled into Pipitea Wharf, then the *Barnett* and *Elliott.* The rank poured ashore to be greeted by the general [and the news that they would be leaving again in about ten days]. The photogs were busy and I hope we got some good shots.

*July 12.* I had dinner with Betty Burridge and family, then a short ride in the family car and a long walk through the hills. Very pleasant. It was good to be away from HQ for a short time. The atmosphere is rather disturbing since the new arrivals came in. I now have a roommate, aide to General Rupertus. [Brigadier General William H. Rupertus was the assistant division commander, a balding dapper man of middling height who sported a neat moustache.] The general, whom I had never seen before, accosted me today in my room and asked to see Lt. Powell. I said I would tell the lieutenant and asked, "What name shall I tell him, sir?" "General Rupertus," he replied. I hadn't noticed the star on his collar. Murray, who was standing nearby, looked aghast.

Powell is a first lieutenant. I thought I would be ousted from my bed (the only one in the little room) and relegated to the cot. Powell, however, uncomplainingly took the cot.

*July 14.* Francis McCarthy of United Press, Douglas Gardner of the *Sydney Herald,* and Chief Photographer Lane of the Navy arrived in town today from Auckland. Lane had come down to get some pictures of Marine activity here. It was pouring buckets, but we went down to the docks and he got some shots. The wharves are full of equipment unloaded from the ships that got in last week. Aotea Quay looks as though the Marines mean business.

At lunch, at the Waterloo, we ran into McCarthy, a tough-guy sort who seems to take Hollywood versions of newspapermen as his model. When he learned that the Marine camps were deserted he launched into a tirade against Gene Markey [Ghormley's PRO, then widely known as the husband of Hedy Lamarr] for letting them come down here when he knew that nothing was going on. Actually, plenty is going on. I'm surprised to find a newspaperman who doesn't see it. The bustle on the docks doesn't seem to interest him.

*July 17.* I spent most of the day censoring mail, then closed up shop. A man from one of the Wellington dailies, a Mr. M., dropped in this afternoon, apparently on a fishing expedition. His ostensible reason for coming was to ask if he could write a story on American forces in New Zealand, so long as he didn't identify any of them as marines. But he shifted ground so often and flung his net so widely that I gathered he was after a bigger catch than that. Mr. Paul, Director of Publicity in the government, had warned me M. is considered to be a bit tricky, and from what I have seen of him I am not inclined to trust him very far or help him much.

M. talked with Murray for a while, *sotto voce,* telling him that the man who had been responsible for releasing the announcement of marines' arrival in the South Pacific had been demoted. Murray said, good humoredly, "I want Merillat to hear that."

The captain [Murray] brought me up to date on recent happenings. Vandegrift had arrived in Auckland on the 15th, summoned thither by Ghormley. About half an hour after he had reported to Ghormley, Admiral Turner, who is to command the amphibious force in the coming landings, also arrived. Vandegrift had told Ghormley that, because heavy rains have hampered loading, he couldn't meet the original sailing date. He said he was prepared to omit the rehearsal in the Fijis. On his arrival Turner said that he too was in no position to keep to the original schedule. But a group of our officers had gone to the Fijis to find a site for the landing exercise and make the necessary arrangements with the government there. Turner decided to go ahead with the rehearsal. We are to leave July 21.

There is one serious hitch: Turner said he had picked the

*McCawley* [an APA] as his flagship and told Vandegrift and his staff to embark in her. We had previously planned to be on the *Hunter Liggett* [the only transport in our group that was fully manned and commanded by the U.S. Coast Guard]. Our staff doesn't like the *McCawley:* inadequate radio communications; not enough space for office equipment and reproduction apparatus; staff crowding out some of the ship's combat strength.

Colonel Twining and Major McKean have not yet been able to get off from Noumea for their reconnaissance of X [I had not yet written down the names of our objectives].

---

The two officers finally managed to get to Tulagi and Guadalcanal in a B-17 from Port Moresby. But they had only a brief glimpse of the beaches and airfield. Japanese Zero fighters from Tulagi jumped them over Guadalcanal and their Flying Fortress had to speed away in a twenty-minute running battle.

On the 19th the general summoned regimental and battalion commanders to tell them about the division's mission. His staff went through the intelligence estimate and operations order. Vandegrift had been told, on his first visit to Auckland, that his third infantry regiment, the 7th Marines, would not be released from Samoa to take part in the landings. But the 2nd Marines, one of the Second Marine Division's regiments, were to join us in the Fijis en route to the Solomons.

General Rupertus was to command the forces landing on Tulagi and its neighboring islets, which formed the seaward side of Tulagi Harbor. He would have, initially, the 1st Raider Battalion and 1st Parachute Battalion (sans parachutes), which were also to join us in the Fijis, and one battalion each from the 2nd and 5th Marines. About four thousand officers and men would be committed to the Tulagi area.

The selected beach on Guadalcanal—Beach Red—was about three miles from the airfield, which the Japanese were hurrying to complete. Combat Group A, consisting of the 5th Marines, Reinforced (less the battalion sent to Tulagi) would land first and secure a beachhead. Combat Group B (the 1st Marines, Reinforced) would pass through them and strike toward the southwest to get behind the airfield. The landing force on Guadalcanal would total roughly eleven thousand officers and men.

The 2nd Marines would constitute the division reserve. Turner's plans called for sending that regiment, after Tulagi and the airfield had been seized, to occupy another island, Ndeni in the Santa Cruz group, some 350 miles to the east of Guadalcanal. We will hear much more of that scheme later.

In those last frantic days in Wellington one of the least pressing problems confronting the division staff was what to do with the PRO. On which transport should he be embarked? I urged that I be put aboard the command ship *McCawley* with the general and his staff. Where else would the division historian be able to observe the whole unfolding story? But I wound up on the *Hunter Liggett*. There the senior Marine officer aboard was Colonel Pedro del Valle, commanding the 11th Marines, the division's artillery regiment. "Don Pedro" was the very picture of a Marine colonel. He was a tall, sturdily built man with a strong Spanish face, black eyebrows, and grey-black hair. He had been appointed to Annapolis from Puerto Rico, from a family proud of many military branches in its family tree.

By the end of the third week of July the First Marine Division was as ready as it could be, in the circumstances, to sally forth. Equipment and supplies on the attack transports and freighters had been cut far back from what "the book" said was necessary for the forthcoming operation. Some skimpy information had been collected about the target. Troops, badly in need of training together and of physical conditioning after weeks at sea, were on board their ships. Adequate naval and air support had been assumed, and plans drawn for naval gunfire and aerial bombing in the landing phase. Complicated operational plans had been quickly drawn up for WATCHTOWER—the code name for the Tulagi-Guadalcanal operation. The admiral in command of the ships and men of the Amphibious Force had just arrived in New Zealand. Those commanding the various task forces involved—convoy, escort and screening ships, carrier groups—had not yet had an opportunity to put their heads together.

The First Marine Division's final report on the operation, submitted a year later, was to say: "The decision of the United States to attack was based upon larger reasons unknown to this headquarters, reasons of the most compelling nature, it must be presumed, for seldom has an operation been begun under more disadvantageous circumstances." When we left Wellington the division command did not yet fully know just how disadvantageous those circumstances would prove to be.

---

*July 22.* This morning our convoy filed out to sea: eight transports, four cargo ships, five cruisers, seven destroyers. It is a perfect day, with a brilliant sun in a cloudless sky. We steamed through the Heads of Wellington Harbor in Indian file. Just before noon the convoy and escort took up cruising positions. Three cruisers lead us, then come the twelve troop carriers and freighters, four abreast in columns of three, with two more cruisers bringing up the rear. Destroyers dart around the edges.

One of my new roommates keeps us amused with caustic observations on the Marine Corps, particularly the "Old" M.C. of which reservists hear so much from the regulars. The Old M.C., he says, was nothing but a gun club. If you could shoot fairly straight and looked pretty in a uniform you could be a marine. The whole outfit of 13,500 couldn't have stormed Sparta, Georgia, at the outbreak of the war. [Actually, the Marine Corps had grown to nearly 66,000 before Pearl Harbor.] All in fun, of course, but a reminder that the Old M.C. was quite inadequate for the job to be done by the New.

Another crack [an old one, but new to me]: "I used to think 'Semper Fidelis' meant 'Faithful Forever,' but now I know it means 'I've got mine; how are you doing?' "

---

We were headed, initially, for Koro Island in the Fiji group. There we were to rendezvous with the naval forces that would support the Solomons landings, and with other Marine units that would be attached to the division. And at Koro we were to rehearse the landings: go down the cargo nets into landing craft which would assemble, cross the lines of departure, head for the beaches, and go ashore with the support of naval gunfire and bombing by carrier planes.

---

*July 23.* I saw Col. del Valle today, to speak for a berth in a landing craft on D-Day. He seems more favorably inclined to the idea of a press officer and historian than most of the old-timers do. He suggested I go ashore with his HQ and stick close to it until the general arrives. I read del Valle's "Estimate of the Situation," a well-written and interesting document, and learned a good deal about what we are headed for. The 11th Marines will go in about two hours after the first wave—a good time from my point of view.

*July 24.* Heavy seas. I spent most of the day in my sack. I did, however, call on Col. del Valle and spend an hour going over the operations order for the rehearsal. After I had read those mimeographed pages the colonel showed me a paragraph in the Field Manual, emphasizing that orders should be as simple and general as possible. The implication, I gather, is that this one had too much detail.

*July 25.* More heavy seas and heavy sacking.

*July 26.* A beautiful day, and an eventful one. I was on the signal deck at 1330 when a lookout spotted seven ships on the horizon. The seven grew to twenty-one. We were all thrilled at this access of naval strength. Among the newcomers an aircraft carrier was the center of liveliest interest. But that was just the beginning. Within an hour ten more ships were sighted, and at their center another carrier. Then eight more ships, including a third flattop, came into view. It was an impressive sight as these four forces joined—a rendezvous at sea I'll never forget. And Bob Barnes had wanted to play bridge through it all!

Tonight all hands are busy cleaning their weapons, storing away their green winter uniforms, and packing their musette bags. Scuttlebutt has it that we'll have a dry run tomorrow; if not then, surely the next day. We seem to be easing along at a few knots, which leads us to think we are getting close to the Fijis.

---

It was, indeed, the most powerful invasion armada the United States had ever put to sea up to that time. The Navy had committed three of its four carriers to support the landings: the *Enterprise, Saratoga,* and *Wasp.* But, as we will shortly see, it was a limited and half-hearted commitment.

---

*July 28.* When I awoke this morning we were still under way, but soon arrived off Koro. Just after 0900 came the order to stand by to lower boats. A moment later came the order to lower, and in no time the ship was stripped of its landing craft: T-boats [the standard Higgins boats, from which troops vault over the side after they hit the beach] and ramp boats. Most of them dashed toward the ships from which the first wave was to head for the beach. Groups assembled and crossed the line of departure.

But there seemed to be a hitch. The story gradually came out. A bad beach; no troops to land except those absolutely necessary. Then, no troops are to land at all. Then, troops will get into boats, but will merely circle their ships and reembark. Then, no more personnel will even get into boats. Karl Soule [the photographic officer, attached to D-2] and I, trying to find a place in the boats, bumped into Col. del Valle, in full battle array. He muttered: "It's impossible to land on that beach. Coral!" And he stormed topside.

An unhappy incident occurred today. Two first lieutenants in the cabin next to mine were seeing which could draw his pistol quicker. Frontier stuff. They not only whipped their Colts from the holsters but clicked the triggers. A .45-caliber bullet tore through a cabinmate's body. Tonight after chow the colonel gave officers a lecture on playing with firearms. One officer is out of commission, he said, and another probably will be, for a different reason.

*July 29.* Soule went over to the *McCawley* this morning with del Valle and some others. I asked if I could go along, to see Murray and find out what in hell I am supposed to do. I got, however, a firm refusal. The colonel came up while I was talking to his exec about hitching a ride. Del Valle said: "The boat is very small and I daresay you had better not go. Now that's that." That was indeed that.

After noon chow, however, I learned that I had been ordered to transfer to the *McCawley*. Col. del Valle brought the word. I got my gear together, piled into a Higgins boat, and made the move. My greeting was warmer than I expected. The ship's troop adjutant was about to stick me in the "bull pen" on the superstructure with thirty other lieutenants when Murray rescued me. He said I could bunk in his room, where there are now six of us. The ship is terribly crowded but the chow is definitely superior. A pile of material has accumulated in the War Diary. I spent the evening going over operations orders for our venture in the Solomons.

Lt. Jones [the victim of the previous day's gunplay] died today—a sad business.

*July 30.* Today we were to have more of the rehearsal, with bombing and naval gunfire. H-hour [when the first landing craft were to touch the shore] was set for 1000. Gunfire was to cover the beach for five minutes before the first wave landed. Admiral Turner changed H-hour to 1030, but the word didn't get around fast enough; a wave of boats was already on the way in. Some were on a newly selected beach at 1030, so there could be no gunfire. It has not been an encouraging exercise. But there is usually a good first night after a bad dress rehearsal; maybe everything will be all right when we really get into action.

Hurlbut is stranded on the *Hunter Liggett*. I wish I could put him in a place where he would feel more useful.

*July 31.* Tonight we are really off to the wars. The entire force got under way about 1630. Our next stop is Guadalcanal. It still seems unreal to me. D-Day is set for August 7, a week from today; Zero hour for 0830.

I have set about in earnest to write the division history from the time we left New River up to now. I have been going through a big stack of orders covering the complicated plans for attacking Guadalcanal-Tulagi, and have been through the file of secret dispatches for this month, gleaning items of interest. I am impressed by the complexity of an amphibious operation and will be much surprised if everything goes smoothly. This is really just a grand experiment and God had better be with us.

There is a strong Japanese concentration in the New Guinea–New Britain region. They may embarrass us considerably.

*August 2.* A United Press correspondent [Robert Miller] and Acme photographer [Sherman Montrose] came aboard today. They say more than a dozen press people have come out from Pearl Harbor with the fleet and are scattered on ships all through the force. They have their troubles, too, and say that no one tells them anything, unless they happen on to a cooperative Navy PRO.

*August 4.* The atmosphere is getting a little tense. An ensign from the *Enterprise,* assigned here to help direct air support, says the carrier expects "something to come in" tomorrow. Yesterday they thought a submarine was contacted, but it turned out to be a school of fish—we hope.

I have been so busy that I haven't had time or energy to write many other things—a letter to the family, a report to General Denig, a ready-made story about the landings, based on plans. I must try to collect my wits and pound the stuff out.

Yesterday I had a talk with Murray, mostly about Hurlbut. First, I suggested that he be transferred back to Washington (as he has wanted) where he would be able to use his experience with radio; then mentioned that I thought he ought to be commissioned; then asked if he could be transferred to the *Neville* to cover the Tulagi landings. Net results: (1) no transfer to Washington likely—if HQ there thought he should be in the field, he should stay there; (2) very likely a commission for him, but in a line company, not in P.R. work; (3) no transfer to the *Neville*.

---

The most dramatic and fateful development during our approach to the Solomons was known, at the time, only to a very few officers, not including me. It deserves close scrutiny.

While we were off Koro, Vice Admiral Frank Jack

Fletcher, commanding the whole expeditionary force, summoned its top commanders to his flagship, the carrier *Saratoga*. This was the first and only time all of them met to talk over the operation on which we were embarked. While their staff officers and subordinate commanders gathered for discussions elsewhere on the ship, the principals met with Fletcher in his wardroom.

Those assembled included Rear Admirals Turner (commanding the Amphibious Force—the convoy, its escort of cruisers and destroyers, and embarked troops); John S. McCain (commanding land-based air forces, of all services, in the South Pacific, and responsible for air reconnaissance in that area); Leigh Noyes and Thomas C. Kinkaid (each commanding one of the carrier groups, Fletcher having retained direct command of the third); V. A. C. Crutchley, RN (a British admiral, assigned to the Royal Australian Navy, who was in charge of the combatant ships in the escort, and Turner's second in command); and General Vandegrift (commanding the Landing Force).

The only two of these gentlemen whom I ever saw during the campaign—apart from Vandegrift—were Turner and McCain. "Kelly" Turner had been the Navy's chief war-plans officer through 1941 and early in 1942, when the decision to advance up the Solomons toward Rabaul was first made. A tall man, with thick black eyebrows and short grey hair, he wore round, steel-rimmed glasses. His schoolmasterish appearance was deceptive. Turner was a driving and driven man, hard-cussing and hard-drinking, demanding, highly intelligent, with a notable memory and eye for detail; as we will see, he was also a frequent irritant to Marine and Army commanders. McCain, who became a firm believer in giving all possible support to the defenders of the airfield on Guadalcanal after it had been seized by Americans, was a feisty short man who looked old before his time. A prominent jaw and nose gave him a certain resemblance to Popeye the Sailor.

There was one conspicuous absentee at the conference off Koro: Vice Admiral Ghormley, superior in rank to all those present, and in command (nominally at least) of all forces in the South Pacific. For reasons about which we can only speculate, he did not fly up from Auckland. In an unpublished account of his stewardship as COMSOPAC Ghormley had only this to say: "I was desirous of attending this conference, but found it impossible to give the time necessary for travel with possible attendant delays."

At the time Ghormley was busy moving his headquarters from Auckland to Noumea. He was also embroiled in some diplomatic squabbles. The Free French government of New Caledonia had been resisting U.S. demands that all overseas communications, including official messages, be subject to U.S. military censorship; there were solid reasons to suppose that supporters of the Vichy government were sending out military intelligence—an intolerable situation for Americans as WATCHTOWER got under way. In addition, Ghormley was engaged in some stiff exchanges with authorities in New Zealand, whose prime minister had learned of WATCHTOWER on a visit to MacArthur, and had made a public statement that there would soon be military action against the Japanese.

Nevertheless, it is hard to understand why—if indeed he did—he gave such concerns priority over his responsibilities as U.S. commander in the area where the first American offensive was about to begin. Perhaps there were other reasons, such as uncertainty as to just what those responsibilities were, for his decision to stay away from the conference in the Fijis. Ghormley was represented by his chief of staff, Rear Admiral Daniel J. Callaghan.

Fletcher had attained the rank of vice admiral only a few days before the gathering on the *Saratoga*. Nimitz had wondered at times whether his Annapolis friend was sufficiently aggressive to hold major carrier-force command. Fletcher had been in command of the abortive effort to relieve the American garrison at Wake Island in December 1941. His relief force, built around the *Saratoga*, had paused for one crucial day to refuel, some 500 miles short of Wake, while the Japanese were beginning their second, and successful, assault on the island outpost.

Responsibility for the relieving force's delay, and for its subsequent retirement without attacking the Japanese ships at Wake, has been much investigated and debated. The temporary high command at Pearl Harbor, still reeling from the attack of December 7 and awaiting th arrival of a new chief, vacillated. Should it safeguard scarce carriers, or seek an engagement with the Japanese ships supporting the invasion of Wake? Counsels of caution prevailed. Fletcher probably had little to do with the crucial decisions. But many Navy and Marine officers, justly or not, felt he should share in the responsibility.

In any event, Nimitz and King, whose doubts about Fletcher were even stronger, had hesitated to commit to Fletcher's charge the ships sent into the Coral Sea in May. They would have preferred to give the job to Halsey. But Halsey was not available; he was then taking Doolittle's raiders toward Tokyo. With considerable reluctance, COMINCH and CINCPAC left Fletcher in command for the Coral Sea operation. There the U.S. Navy had sunk one small Japanese carrier and had turned back an enemy invasion fleet headed for Port Moresby; but it had lost the big carrier *Lexington* to Japanese bombs and torpedoes.

After that engagement Nimitz, weighing the results, decided that Fletcher had done well. He urged King to promote Fletcher to vice admiral and award him the Distinguished Service Medal. King refused to do either. Again in May, when tipped off that the Japanese Combined Fleet was soon going to attack Midway, Nimitz had doubts whether he should appoint Fletcher to oppose them. He asked Fletcher to appraise his own war record, in writing. He decided that Fletcher's "full and manly account of his stewardship" was satisfactory, and put him in command of the carrier forces for the Midway battle.

Fletcher had lost a carrier both in the Coral Sea and off Midway. This, it seems, was a sensitive point with him. Not an aviator himself, he had heard grumblings from naval air officers—suggestions that he had not sufficiently heeded their advice, that a trained airman could have avoided those losses. A new and younger breed of air-trained, air-minded naval officers grumbled throughout the war that not enough of their kind were given high commands.

Nimitz, however, decided to put Fletcher in charge of the "Expeditionary Force" for WATCHTOWER. But to hold that command, Fletcher must have the rank of vice admiral. Rear Admiral Leigh Noyes, his Annapolis classmate, stood three all-imortant numbers ahead of him in the Navy List. Unless Fletcher, even though he had had more combat experience, held higher rank, he could not be Noyes's commanding officer. Again Nimitz urged the promotion upon Washington, this time with success. And thus it was that Fletcher had three spanking new stars on each collar point when he summoned subordinate commanders to the meeting on the *Saratoga*.

Fletcher was outranked by Vice Admiral Ghormley and nominally under his command in the South Pacific Area. But the command relationships were curiously muddled. Ghormley's responsibilities were ambiguously defined from the time he reported to CINCPAC on his way to New Zealand. The only naval task forces over which he would have authority would be those that arrived in his area from time to time. Nimitz told him he would assign them to Ghormley in "broad terms in order that sufficient initiative may be left to the Senior Task Force Commander," who would be named by Nimitz. Ordinarily, he added, there would be little need for "amplification" by Ghormley, but he was to "exercise such direction as [he] may consider necessary when changed or unforeseen situations arise."

Ghormley carefully spelled out his own interpretation of this directive: he was not to interfere in a task force commander's mission unless circumstances, presumably not known to Nimitz, "indicated that specific measures were required to be performed by the Task Force Commander." In that event, he would issue the necessary orders.

We come to the command arrangements for WATCHTOWER. Transmitting the Joint Chiefs' directive of July 2 to the Pacific commanders, King's message said, "it is assumed that Ghormley will be made Task Force Commander at least for Task I, which he should command in person, in the operating area." The "operating area" included New Caledonia and the New Hebrides. Ghormley responded to this part of his instructions by moving from Auckland to Noumea late in July. Nimitz seemed to modify King's instructions in a dispatch sent to Ghormley five days later, telling him that he would exercise "*strategic* command in person" [emphasis supplied].

The line between "strategy" and "tactics" is not easily defined. All would agree that allocation of forces—a certain number of ships, planes, troops, supplies, and the like—to a theater of operations or a major command is a strategic decision. All would agree that when forces thus disposed come to grips with the enemy (are in actual *contact*), tactics takes over. There is a large grey area in between. When the war was over Ghormley himself said that at the Naval War College the term "strategic command," while never really "pinned down," was taken to mean that the strategic commander "exercised a general overseer's function, and that he did not inject himself into tactical situations except in completely extraordinary circumstances." Let us leave the matter there for the moment; it will arise in more acute form later on.

The day before the conference off Koro, Turner wrote Fletcher a letter. He said, among other things, that he hoped to unload the transports off Guadalcanal-Tulagi by the end of the second day. But the cargo ships would take longer—from three to six days: "We will need air protection during this entire period."

It was against such a background that the admirals and the general gathered in Fletcher's wardroom on the 26th. As we should expect, reports from those present differ as to just what was said. No official record was kept. There is no doubt about what most stuck in the mind, and craw, of Vandegrift and Turner. As the general later recalled, Fletcher asked Turner how long it would take to put the marines and their supplies ashore. Turner replied that it would take about five days. The expeditionary force commander then said he would pull the carriers out in two days.

Vandegrift and Turner protested vigorously. The general pointed out that this was not a small-scale in-and-out landing of the old familiar type but a major operation to seize and hold an objective that was sure to be bitterly contested. Air cover was essential; even a limitation to five days would involve great risks. Turner's chief of staff, Captain Thomas G. Peyton, recalled the meeting as "one long bitter argument" between Fletcher and Turner. The new vice admiral, he said, kept implying that the operation "was largely Turner's brainchild and mentioning that those who planned it had no real fighting experience." Fletcher criticized the haste and lack of thoroughness in planning, lack of opportunity for the task force to train together, and inadequate logistic support. "My boss [Turner]," said Peyton, "kept saying, 'The decision has been made. It's up to us to make it a success.'"

According to Kinkaid, who later called the mood of the meeting "animated rather than stormy," the main point in dispute was the length of time the carriers would stay: "Fletcher insisted that two days was all that could be risked—because of both the submarine danger and the risk of Japanese shore-based air attack." Callaghan, Ghormley's representative at the conference, apparently had little to say. But he took notes, and they are one of our sources of information about what happened at the meeting. Of fourteen specific operational points he recorded, the first six dealt with problems of refueling the carriers and other ships. As to the early withdrawal of the carriers, he noted, with an appropriate exclamation point: "Task Force must withdraw to South from the objective area (i.e., general advanced position) within two days after D day!"

# 4

# The First Days

The island that loomed black in the brief predawn grey on August 7, and took on shape and features as the sun climbed, is about ninety miles long and thirty miles across at its widest. As geologic age is reckoned, it is young. Thrusting up from the sea, volcanoes carried with them deposits of coral and other marine organisms that had built up along their rising edges. Eventually a spine of mountains, rising to 8,000 feet, was extruded. It stretches along the southern side. From those heights the jumbled earth descends toward the northern edge, first as lesser peaks and foothills, then, nearer the coast, splaying out in ridges of more recently lifted coral and other sea-bred debris, and finally, along the northern shoreline, becoming a band of alluvial soil washed down from the high ground by the island's many rivers.

From the northwestern tip at Cape Esperance to the Matanikau River (about twenty-five miles as a plane flies, considerably longer by a track that followed the indentations of the coast), eroded coral ridges come close to the beach. But there is enough flat land here and there to plant coconut groves. Three miles east of the Matanikau the coastal strip broadens markedly. Here, in the north central plain, British and Australian copra producers had established their largest plantations. And here, just east of the Lunga River, the Japanese were building their airfield. Where palms had not been planted the plains were covered with high, tough kunai grass. River edges in the plain and ravines among the coral ridges inland are choked with dense rain forest. Interlaced crowns of towering trees form

51

a canopy through which the sun, or searching eye or
camera of a reconnaissance pilot, rarely penetrates. Under-
neath, on the dank jungle floor, grow ferns, vines, low
scrub, and other flora of a tropical rain forest.

Assuming that the Japanese would have beach defenses
in the Lunga area, around the airfield, division planners
had decided to put five reinforced battalions ashore east of
the Ilu River, about three miles from the airstrip. Then the
marines were to move quickly westward to the Tenaru
River the first day.

Here I must pause to say something about place names.
As already noted, the division had only primitive and
inaccurate maps for the landings. The only available aerial
photographs were inadequate. Information provided from
memory by former residents of the region turned out sometimes to be faulty when it came to features like streams
and hills of crucial interest to military planners. On the
first maps and on others developed after the landings
certain place names became fixed.

One stream that was to figure importantly in the campaign was named, on our maps, the Tenaru River. The
stream was locally known as Alligator Creek, and what we
called the Ilu was really named the Tenaru. To complicate
the nomenclature, maps later developed by the U.S. Army
correctly name the Tenaru but call Alligator Creek the Ilu,
and these are the names used in the Army's official monograph of the campaign and in the detailed postwar map
made by the Defense Mapping Agency. Most postwar
writing about Guadalcanal has adopted the Army usage. I
have here used the names that appeared in our operations,
orders, maps, and reports.

From the deck that August morning the most prominent
feature to be seen inland, beyond the airstrip, and short of
the cordillera towering behind, was a massive foothill—
really a complex of interlocking ridges—called Mount Austen. Some old Guadalcanal hands who were advising the
Marine command about key terrain features said that this
imposing height was two or three miles inland. Accordingly, the operations plan directed one regimental combat
group, built around the 1st Marines, to push Southwestward from Beach Red to seize Mount Austen.

From the first glimpse in full daylight CACTUS (the code name for Guadalcanal) struck me as an island of great beauty. It has made the same impression on many others. But it must be noted that the island has not had this quality in the eyes of all beholders. The vision of many, we must suppose, has been colored by unpleasant memories of what went on there. To many marines and others it was a stinking hole—until, having moved on to other islands in the Solomons or Bismarck Archipelago, some began to look back on it as a tropical paradise.

Samuel Eliot Morison, author and editor of the classic account of the naval fighting in *The Struggle for Guadalcanal*, visited the island soon after the Japanese finally abandoned it. To him, or perhaps to one of his assistants who earlier visited the island, the dappled effect of grassy ridges among forested ravines and slopes had a "leprous" appearance. They detected fetid smells wafting out to sea, unlike those from any other island. It may be true that if a ship had happened to come in close to shore at certain times and places, when Japanese bodies still lay unburied, the smell of rot and death could be detected. Morison even coined a word to express his distaste for the place: "fecaloid."

Another chronicler of the naval struggle has said: "The climate is abominable; the heat, humidity, and torrential rains are never-ending. . . ." It was indeed often wet. Downpours sometimes hurt our operations, sometimes the enemy's. Both sides cursed them. Monsoon rains started in earnest during the third month of the campaign. Even then there were brilliant blue days when the sun sopped up wetness from airstrips and dried out gear. It was the rain forest, where the sun seldom reached, that men who patrolled or fought there remember as eternally dank. "Rainy" and "dry" seasons are relative terms in describing the Guadalcanal climate. There can be heavy downpours at the best time of year (from April to September) and there can be dry patches at the worst.

The climate is much like that of Washington, D.C., in high summer—oppressively hot and humid, and dangerously so for foot-slogging men in tough denims, toting weapons, ammunition, packs, and other impedimenta across ground exposed to a scorching sun. Heat exhaustion was a widespread problem, especially among new arrivals. In the medical record of the First Marine Division forty-six cases of heat prostration are reported. The figure includes only men treated in the division hospital during a four-month period, and does not cover Army sufferers. The much larger number of those who carried on without hospital treatment will never be known.

A casual visitor who stayed in the coconut groves of the northern coastal belt, without much exertion, might think that wartime reports had maligned the climate. Daytime temperatures there do not often rise above ninety degrees Fahrenheit, and the nights are pleasantly cool. It so happens that there is a fairly objective test for judging the scenic beauty and climatic mildness of the island: for years it has been a regular port of call for Australian cruise ships touring the South Seas.

---

*August 7*. Dog-day at last. We got up about 2 o'clock, laughed and joked as usual, ate an enormous breakfast, and set about getting ready to go over the side. I felt a little tense, I suppose, but the day was starting pretty much like any other aboard the ship since we left Koro. About 0500 I went topside with Captain Murray. We were already off Guadalcanal and could make out its dim outline to starboard. The outline of another island—Savo, I suppose—appeared on the port side. A bit later we could make out Florida. H-hour, for the landings on Tulagi, was set for 0800. Z-hour, for hitting Beach Red on Guadalcanal, was to be 0910; they were fast approaching.

General Quarters sounded about 0530. I was left on the top deck with the United Press man, Bob Miller, and Wing Commander Dale, the Australian who was to help guide the 5th Marines when they got ashore. We cursed the sparks spouting from the *McCawley*'s funnel; thought surely they must be seen ashore, but there was no sign of activity there. The minutes flew by, and I felt the tension grow as the big moment approached. Soon after 0600 a light flashed dead ahead; a cruiser had catapulted a scouting plane, but at the time I couldn't imagine what it was.

Then the show started. A cruiser sent a salvo of 8-inch shells screaming toward the island. Then came a steady rain of shells, with the blast of naval guns, the light of shells as they streaked toward the shore, the far off boom of explosions on the island in our eyes and ears. No answer from the shore. Soon we could see red tracers from carrier planes, strafing targets on the island. As dawn began to light the scene we could see the planes diving and wheeling, and palms, and clouds of debris and smoke sent up by shells and bombs, and fires in the coconut groves. A fuel dump was hit, sending flames and black smoke high.

The transports started lowering boats, supplies, and equipment. I was to go over the side at 0900. There was still no sign of activity on the island. Just before I started down the cargo net, with the chief of staff and party in the advance CP [Command Post], we got a message from a plane saying there was no troop movement toward Beach Red. We bounced over the surface and landed about 1000, to find a busy scene but reports of no opposition, no casualties. I got off to a good start by losing my balance and sitting down in the water as I jumped over the side of the Higgins boat.

---

During our approach to the beach Colonel Twining, assistant operations officer, had his field glasses focused on the scene ashore. "There goes the signal from Hunt's boys," he announced. "Landing unopposed." And so, happily for the marines, it turned out to be. One battalion of Hunt's 5th Marines had been the first to land, and begun to feel its way inland and toward the Tenaru. The mission of the 5th Marines was to secure the beachhead while the 1st Marines, who landed later in the morning, passed through them to strike out toward Mount Austen. The 1st did not get very far that first day. Behind the coconuts and a grassy field inland from the beach they ran into a tangle of tropical growth along a feeder of the Ilu that ran roughly parallel to the shore. And Mount Austen (or "Grassy Knoll," as it was called in operations orders and maps) proved to be much farther inland than the planners had been told.

The most vexing problem of the first day was congestion on the beaches. Huge piles of material began building up. The scene was chaotic. Marines and Navy began exchanging recriminations. The Navy's chief complaint was that not enough marines had been detailed to work the beaches. The Pioneers, the main unit assigned to the job, was too small and too scattered. Boats full of supplies had to lay to offshore because there were not enough space or enough men to unload them. Since the landings were unopposed, Turner asked, why not put those idle combat troops to work?

Vandegrift replied that until he knew when or where he might run into Japanese resistance, he could not detach men from combat units to move the dumps inland. A landing force is at its most vulnerable before it has occupied, and set up defenses for, a substantial beachhead. Preinvasion intelligence had estimated—quite wrongly, as it turned out—at least 2,500 enemy troops on the island, and they had not yet showed their hand. Both Navy and Marine commanders had a good point. It was later agreed on all sides that, before the next amphibious operation, plans must be made for more adequate working parties on the beaches.

The first visible Japanese reaction came in the sky. Air raiders arrived in the middle of the afternoon. High-altitude bombers attacked the shipping in the strait. They made no hits. Then dive-bombers attacked, hitting the stern of one destroyer. To the great relief of groundlings, neither flight had gone after the huge piles of material on the congested beach. For both raids Turner's ships had ample warning, which gave them time to get under way and dodge. Coast-watchers up the Solomons chain toward Rabaul had seen the enemy flights and flashed the word by radio.

General Vandegrift and the remainder of division headquarters came ashore at four o'clock, having spent most of the day aboard the *McCawley* trying to keep in touch with proceedings on both Guadalcanal and Tulagi, separated by twenty miles of water.

---

*August 8.* We bivouacked beneath the coconut palms last night, south of the Ilu's branch. We seemed completely cut off from everyone, but some found us. The general held court beneath a palm tree and heard the reports of his regimental commanders—Colonel Cates of the 1st Marines and Colonel Hunt of the 5th. Everyone seemed frustrated at not having any contact with the Japs. Unfair of them to take to the hills. The general remarked, ''I'm beginning to doubt whether there's a Jap on the whole damned island.''

There was rifle firing all night, as marines shot at each other, shadows, cows, and coconuts, but I haven't yet heard of any skirmish with Japs. We moved on this morning. The staff and retinue in jeeps and trucks chugged along the beach through lines of marines and unbelievable mountains of supplies and equipment. They paused now and then as the general and staff conferred with officers. We crossed the Ilu all right, although the general's jeep got stuck and held us up a few minutes. Just east of the Tenaru we saw the 5th Marines lining up to move west. Bob Miller and Montrose (the photographer) went with a patrol. Colonel Goettge said I couldn't go, apparently on the theory that I didn't belong in an advance scouting party.

We soon crossed the Tenaru and settled down a few hundred yards the other side—our second temporary CP. Not long after that someone told me that an air raid was due in about ten minutes. This was the first I had heard of it. I rushed up to the beach to watch the show. And what a show it was. I didn't see the Jap planes at first, but a sky full of flak from our transports told me they were there. Then I saw them. They swooped in from the east, unbelievably low, and swept along the lanes of transports. Antiaircraft fire from the ships was terrific. Jap planes plunged in flames—one, two, three, so many I lost count. One ran the gauntlet and started out to sea, toward the west. A fighter dived on him and sent him flaming into the sea. There was so much smoke and flame in the transport area that I thought surely many of our ships must have been hit. But as the stuff lifted I saw that apparently only one ship was burning. [This was the transport *Elliott*, which later sank, taking with her much of the equipment of the 2nd Battalion, 1st Marines.]

---

In their torpedo-plane attack the Japanese lost, by their own admission, seventeen ''Betty'' bombers, and quite possibly the toll was more. Our surface ships brought most of them down with intense antiaircraft fire. Carrier fighters played a walk-on role in this particular engagement; the day before eleven of them had been lost while intercepting the two raiding formations.

Meanwhile, as my notes for the 8th indicate, marines had pushed on to the airfield. The 5th Marines, moving along the shore, were sluggish in the opinion of Vandegrift and his staff. Several officers—the general and Goettge among them—claimed to have reached the airfield ahead of the regiment's patrols. Cates's 1st Marines, having been switched from their original target of Mount Austen, swung west and crossed the southern edge of the airfield. By nightfall, the prize was in our hands. The 1st Marines were at the Lunga and the 5th had crossed, overrunning the main Japanese encampment to the west. Clearly the defenders had decamped hastily, leaving behind quantities of food, equipment, and supplies. All was unscathed except for the damage caused by our naval shelling and bombing the morning of the landing. Nodding toward the ridges and forest to the south and west, the general remarked, "It looks like Nicaragua all over again."

Matters were quite different on Tulagi and its neighboring islets. There the Japanese garrison, well dug in, resisted fiercely—literally unto death. On that side of the water, Company B from the 1st Battalion, 2nd Marines (commanded by Captain E. J. Crane) made the first landing of the entire operation. Its mission was to occupy a point of land on Florida Island that commanded Beach Blue, where the main assault force was to land on Tulagi a few minutes later.

Tulagi Island is about two miles long, running from northwest to southeast. A ridge about 300 feet high runs down the island's spine, interrupted by a lower saddle of hilly ground near the southern end, then rising again to a promontory called, from its altitude, Hill 281. That end of the island was the seat of the resident commissioner for the British Solomon Islands Protectorate. The residency sat atop one of the lower hills in the saddle. There was a playing field nearby, on flat ground at the foot of Hill 281.

Simple wharves and jetties jutted into the harbor on the northern side.

The 1st Raider Battalion, which was to make the first landings on Tulagi, was commanded by Lieutenant Colonel Merritt A. Edson, of whom we will hear much. He was a Vermonter, forty-five years old at the time of the Guadalcanal campaign. "Red Mike" was, as his code name implied, a redhead, and he was blue-eyed. His normal voice, which could become a rasping bark in the heat of combat, was so soft and low that you leaned toward him to hear him. His lips often smiled when his eyes did not, as though he had a clever but not really funny joke on the Japanese, or they on him. Edson had enlisted in the Marine Corps Reserve during World War I, had been commissioned as a second lieutenant in 1917, and had served in France for more than a year, mostly after the armistice. He was one of the most aggressive of the Marine commanders in the Guadalcanal campaign.

Beach Blue, where the 1st Raiders landed, was on the seaward side of the island, closer to the northern than to the southern tip. Landing boats grounded on coral outcroppings offshore and Edson's men had to wade in. They met no opposition. The raiders then swung southeast, on either side of the central ridge, almost unopposed until they reached the saddle. There they ran into heavy Japanese fire. A battalion of the 5th Marines followed them ashore. While part of the battalion cleared scattered Japanese out of the northwest end of the island, the rest joined the raiders. Together they threw a line across the island, bent around the playing field and Hill 281. At this line they dug in for the first night and threw back several Japanese counterattacks that issued from a ravine at the foot of Hill 281.

Meanwhile the 1st Parachute Battalion was trying to take the little island of Gavutu. That island and Tanambogo, connected by a causeway, held the main installations of Japan's primitive naval and air base. Taken by surprise at dawn on August 7, the garrison in the Tulagi area had watched their flying patrol boats and Zero float-planes sink in Gavutu's harbor as U.S. carrier planes bombed and ships bombarded.

Gavutu is dominated by a small hill. The Japanese had honeycombed it with defensive caves. From these, and from a similar network on Tanambogo, 500 yards across the causeway, they poured heavy fire into the parachutists as they approached in landing boats. Our bombing had torn chunks out of a seaplane slip, where the parachutists had hoped to land. They had to scramble over a dock higher than their boats, and took heavy casualties. A second effort was put off until the next day.

Tanambogo proved to be an equally hard nut. Company B of the 2nd Marines, it will be recalled, had temporarily occupied a neck of land on Florida to guard the approaches to Beach Blue. Withdrawn from that spot, they were ordered to take Tanambogo. They arrived at Gavutu near dusk on the first day. Enemy fire swept the connecting causeway, blocking access by that means. Captain Crane's Higgins boats tried to land on Tanambogo. Only two reached the shore. Naval shelling had fired a fuel dump on the islet. Flames silhouetted the little landing party and the marines pulled out under heavy fire.

Reports of the fighting on Tulagi and its neighbors reached the division CP, set up under a palm tree on Guadalcanal, about midnight of the first day. General Rupertus sent a message saying there had been fierce fighting on his side of the water, and heavy casualties—22 percent among the 1st Raiders, 50–60 percent [fortunately, a substantial overestimate] among the parachutists. He asked for reinforcements. Vandegrift sent Captain Murray out to the *McCawley*, to try to persuade Admiral Turner to release a battalion of the 2nd Marines. That regiment, we will recall, had been earmarked for a later landing on Ndeni in the Santa Cruz Islands, one of the Joint Chiefs' specified objectives in their directive for Task One. To the general's surprise and satisfaction, Turner released two battalions.

In the small hours of the second day the transports bearing the two battalions moved from the Guadalcanal side to the Tulagi. By the middle of the morning one had landed on Tulagi and the other—the 3rd Battalion—on Gavutu, to launch another assault on Tanambogo. Having gained the top of Gavutu's hill on D-Day, parachutists destroyed the defenders the next day. They had called for charges of TNT and blasted cave emplacements one by one. Meanwhile the 3rd Battalion, 2nd Marines, succeeded in getting a lodgment on Tanambogo. It took them two days to clean out the islet's cave defenses. On Tulagi the whole of 2–5 (2nd Battalion, 5th Marines) had joined the raiders in taking Hill 281 and reducing the main stronghold near the playing field. Sniping continued for several days, but Tulagi was securely in Rupertus's hands.

For the first time American troops had encountered Japanese strongly dug in on the defensive. They learned that, in such a posture, the enemy would fight to the death. Of about 450 Japanese on the three islands (some estimates say 1,000) only twenty were captured—five of the Special Navy Landing Forces, and fifteen labor troops. Before the action was over little Tulagi and its tiny neighbors fairly groaned under the weight of U.S. Marines, who outnumbered the defenders about nine to one (or five to one, depending on the estimate of Japanese strength you accept). If, as it turned out, the 2nd Marines were not wholly necessary to reduce enemy strongpoints there, at least most of them were ashore and under Vandegrift's command, not afloat under Turner's. Those battalions would be badly needed and much used in the coming battles on Guadalcanal.

Both sides learned important lessons from the vicious fighting in the Tulagi group. General "area" bombardment by naval shells and bombs was ineffective against cave defenses. To give effective support, ships should move in close and pound specific targets. For their part, the Japanese learned to dig even deeper. During the rest of the war U.S. forces assaulting islands in the central Pacific would find formidable defenses of connecting caves and heavily reinforced concrete emplacements; they would also find the same do-or-die spirit.

When the sun set on August 8, D + 1, the situation seemed fairly well in hand. We occupied the chief prize, the airfield on Guadalcanal. On the Tulagi side some fighting lay ahead, but there was no doubt the islands were ours. At sea, too, things had gone well. Three Japanese air raids had exacted some losses: destroyer *Mugford* hit in the stern, another destroyer, *Jarvis,* more severely damaged (and eventually lost with all hands to a Japanese bomb as she tried to go back to base), and the transport *Elliott* ablaze in the channel after a bomber had crashed into one of her holds. But much worse damage had been expected from land-based air and the Japanese had paid heavily for their attempts. Three American carriers were unscathed; the air raiders had not even found them. They had lost twenty-one Wildcat fighters, through accident or enemy action, but the number was not unexpectedly large. All in all, the first two days had been very satisfactory.

That night the sky fell.

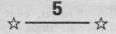

# Peril on the Sea

*August 9.* I will never forget last night. We bivouacked
beneath the coconut palms just west of the Tenaru, about
200 yards from the beach. I stretched out on my poncho
and blanket. About 10 or 10:30 it began to rain, first in a
drizzle, then in torrents. Soon the blanket was soaked, I
was soaked, my gear was soaked. I lay there in my puddle
trying to sleep while the rain poured down. Lightning was
almost continuous. There was a peculiar chain thunder
which at first I took for ack-ack. I imagined a Jap plane
skimming back and forth over our position. After midnight
I *did* hear a plane.

Then, at about two in the morning, the real show started.
Bright flares drifted down over the beaches and nearby
waters. Terrific explosions and great flashes out toward
Savo seemed to be right on the shoreline. At first I thought
we were being bombed, then I realized it was a naval
battle. The big guns roared out at sea, and it sounded as
though the entire Japanese and American navies were tan-
gling out there. Now and then there was a heavier explosion with billowing orange flames and smoke. For half an
hour the booming continued, gradually receding, and we
could hear it occasionally throughout the night, far away
by then.

Frayed nerves made us ready to believe any rumor.
D-2's phone rang repeatedly, announcing another alarm
each time: a flare had been dropped off Tulagi; one had
drifted down over Beach Red; one had been dropped over
Lunga Point. A plane droned overhead. A sergeant from
the 11th Marines called to say that Japs were landing on

Beach Red. Colonel del Valle was reported to be sending out a patrol to investigate. Things subsided a bit and I tried to catch a cat nap.

I was awakened by much bustle and clatter around the command post, and firing to the north. The Japs, we heard, were trying to land on the beach north of us. Security was quickly organized to hold a line at the CP. Earlier there had been heavy small-arms fire to the south and west (intramural, as it turned out) and it wasn't hard to imagine that the Japs were closing in. I couldn't take it seriously, for some reason [largely naivete, I suppose], but got out my watersoaked pistol to help keep the CP inviolate! It turned out that some of our Higgins boats, running along the shore to move supplies to Kukum, had been fired on from the beach. They returned the fire in a nasty mood. A spirited inter-marine fight had developed. That was the assault on the CP!

We don't know the outcome of the sea battle, but at any rate the Jap ships didn't get in to shell us or to land troops.

---

The aircraft we had heard droning over our beachhead were floatplanes from Japanese cruisers. Some of the officers on our own ships, patrolling the entrances to the sound on either side of Savo, had heard them too. Some had even seen their running lights. But everyone jumped to the comfortable conclusion that they were our own planes. Japanese scouts had, for more than an hour, been reporting the positions of our combat ships and transports and the courses our screening forces were taking on patrol.

On the day of our landings Vice Admiral Gunichi Mikawa, commanding the Japanese Eighth Fleet with headquarters at Rabaul, had hastily assembled seven cruisers— five heavy, two light—and led them south. Allied reconnaissance planes had picked up parts of his force while it was still off Bougainville far to the north—too far for our commanders to be certain where they were heading. One of the snoopers from an airbase in Australia identified two of the ships as seaplane tenders. Admiral Turner decided that they were headed for the north side of Santa Isabal Island, whence they would launch torpedo-plane attacks the following morning. He had asked Admiral McCain for

special air searches over the most direct route of approach
to Guadalcanal, down the center of the Solomons chain.
He did not know, that fateful night, that the searches were
not carried out.

What Turner did know was that Fletcher was pulling his
three carriers out of the area. At sundown on the 8th the
carrier commander had asked Ghormley's permission to
withdraw. Without waiting for an answer, he had headed
southeast from his patrolling position southwest of Guadalcanal. Fletcher was leaving even sooner than, at Koro
Island, he had threatened to do; he had stayed only thirty-
six hours after the first gun was fired.

Left without any air support Turner had to think of the
safety of his convoy and their screen of men-of-war. When
he got the news of Fletcher's departure those ships were
disposed in several groups: a cluster of cargo ships off
Tulagi, another cast of Lunga Point, and three screens of
fighting ships patrolling the approaches to the islands. The
least hefty of the three (one U.S. and one Australian light
cruiser, with two destroyers) was guarding the eastern
gateway. Three U.S. heavy cruisers and two destroyers—
the Northern Force—were plying the passage between Savo
Island and Florida/Tulagi. Three more heavy cruisers (two
Australian and one American) and two destroyers formed
the Southern Force, whose beat was between Savo and the
northwestern tip of Guadalcanal.

In the crisis he now faced Turner summoned Admiral
Crutchley and General Vandegrift to his flagship for a
conference. Crutchley, a red-bearded British officer detailed to the Royal Australian Navy, was in general command of the entire three-force screen and in direct command
of the three-cruiser group guarding the channel between
Savo and Guadalcanal. Summoned by Turner he pulled his
flagship *Australia* out of the screen and felt his way across
the dark waters to the *McCawley*. Vandegrift, trying to
find the flagship in a Higgins boat, finally reached it
shortly before midnight. There Turner broke the alarming
news of Fletcher's departure. Turner said his ships, left
"bare-assed," must leave in the morning. Vandegrift asked
that, before a final decision was made, he have a chance to
talk with his assistant division commander at Tulagi. Un-

loading on that side had gone slowly because of the heavy fighting. Vandegrift wanted to make sure that enough had got ashore for the marines to survive. Aboard a mine-sweeper he headed for a rendezvous with Rupertus off Tulagi. He learned that the supply position was indeed bad. Unloading was speeded up and Turner agreed to stay until the next afternoon.

Meanwhile Crutchley, after the midnight conference with Turner, decided not to rejoin his Southern Force. Instead, he would attach his cruiser to those in the eastern screen, a decision of which he neglected to inform either Turner or the captains of the other ships then slowly ploughing the waters between Savo and Guadalcanal, a channel that Mikawa's seven cruisers and one destroyer were fast approaching. The Japanese admiral had already launched two floatplanes. For an hour and a half they cruised at will over the unsuspecting Allied ships.

Mikawa led the column in his heavy cruiser *Chokai*, followed by four others of like heft, then two light cruisers and a destroyer. Among them they boasted sixty-two torpedo tubes, ready to launch the fast and deadly Japanese missiles, and seventy-two naval guns, half of which were of 8-inch caliber.

At 0138, three miles away from his prey, Mikawa's flagship fired the first spread of torpedoes and the admiral ordered "all forces to the attack." Soon the waters teemed with "Long Lances" speeding toward their unsuspecting targets. Floatplanes dropped flares to light up the Allied formations. Japanese guns began to speak. The Australian heavy cruiser *Canberra* was the first victim. Holed by torpedoes and racked by shells before she knew what was happening, she was soon aflame, dead in the water, and out of action. (She was sunk the next morning on Turner's orders.) U.S. heavy cruiser *Chicago*'s turn came next. A torpedo tore a huge hole in her bow. She staggered away to the west, not knowing where the attack had come from. Within six minutes Mikawa had disposed of the Southern Force. He swept on to deal with the Northern Force.

Even the hot, brief encounter a few miles to the south, obscured by rain squalls, and the strings of flares, left officers in that screen puzzled as to what was causing all the commotion. They soon learned the harsh facts. Japanese searchlights sought out the American ships. At 0148 Mikawa's flagship launched torpedoes and followed with salvoes from her 8-inch guns. In the confusion of battle Mikawa's cruisers formed into two separate columns, one on each side of the Americans. Thus sandwiched, our ships were doomed. The *Quincy* was the first to succumb. About 0230 her stern reared high in the air and she slid beneath the sea. The *Vincennes,* torpedoed several times, battered by shells, and ablaze, followed her into the depths a quarter of an hour later. The *Astoria* suffered a lingering death amid flames, floodings, and explosions; she sank at midday.

Within half an hour from the time the shooting had started it was over. At 0200 Mikawa decided to gather his scattered ships and withdraw. The explosions we later heard on the island, the mushrooming flames we later saw, came from stricken ships as fires reached their ammunition magazines and fuel tanks, and from one last distant encounter between the departing Japanese and a picket destroyer, *Ralph Talbot,* which was badly mauled.

Mikawa supposed that the U.S. carriers, already some two hundred miles away, were still nearby. He expected bombing attacks at sunrise, and wanted to put much water between his ships and Guadalcanal before then. He did not go after the helpless transports and cargo ships, huddling nervously off their anchorages. By his failure to do so Mikawa gave up an opportunity to bring the whole Allied offensive to a quick and disastrous conclusion. The Ghost of Fletcher Absent had saved the day—or the night, which had been calamitous enough.

The Japanese sped away almost unscathed. An American submarine got a measure of revenge for the humiliating naval defeat; it torpedoed and sank one of Mikawa's cruisers on the 10th, as she headed home to New Ireland.

For those frequent occasions when a mud-crawling soldier feels put upon, the British Army has a saying: "It's worse at sea." At times, it is indeed. There are no foxholes on ships. In that one night off Savo Island the American and Australian navies lost 1,023 dead—more than the First Marine Division would lose in four months of fighting. Hundreds of seamen leapt into the sea—oily, sometimes fiery, debris-littered, and much favored by sharks. Fortunately there were many survivors. Most of those rescued were moved immediately to other ships without coming ashore.

Marines on Guadalcanal and Tulagi did not know what happened out there. It must, most of us thought, have been a victory for our side, for the enemy had not come in to shell us, our supply-choked beaches, or the ships that had brought us. Some survivors, burned, cut up by flying steel, haggard from their ordeal, were seen ashore. That gave pause to the few who saw them. Some days passed before even the top Marine officers learned the sad truth.

Except for the loss of the *Canberra*, whose sinking was not concealed in Australia, the U.S. Navy did not acknowledge the losses suffered in the Battle of Savo Island until sixty-five days had passed. In August, naval communiques spoke darkly of the need to expect some losses in an offensive against the Japanese, but kept the real damage secret until October 12. Admiral King later said that silence was necessary to keep the enemy guessing as to how much hurt he had inflicted.

The duty officer on King's flagship, stationed in the Navy Yard in Washington, awakened the admiral in the small hours of August 12 and gave him Turner's message reporting the action off Savo. King read it in disbelief. "That, as far as I was concerned," he later said, "was the blackest day of the war. The whole future then seemed unpredictable." At the end of a long inquiry into what had gone wrong at Savo the Navy decided that so many officers had been at fault in one way or another that no one should be singled out for censure.

The invasion force's second serious wound that night was self-inflicted. I have already mentioned Admiral Fletcher's decision to withdraw his three carriers. As the sun was setting on August 8, the day after the landings, he radioed a message to Ghormley:

Fighter-plane strength reduced from 99 to 78. In view of the large number of enemy torpedo planes and bombers in this area I recommend the immediate withdrawal of my carriers. Request tankers sent forward immediately as fuel running low.

Without waiting for an answer the expeditionary force commander, with his three flattops and attendant vessels, steamed away from the south corner of Guadalcanal. Not immediately hearing from Ghormley, Fletcher turned back toward the island once. But when Ghormley's permission to withdraw came at 3:30 in the morning, he again headed southeast. Meanwhile fragmentary reports had reached his task force of a surface action of some sort off the landing area. Later on the 9th Ghormley reported the withdrawal to Nimitz: "Carriers short of fuel proceeding to fueling rendezvous." By then Fletcher was receiving, and passing on to Ghormley, reports of heavy Allied losses in the Battle of Savo Island.

As one reason for pulling out, Fletcher's famous message cited the reduction in his fighter-plane strength from ninety-nine to seventy-eight. That was neither an unexpected nor a crippling loss. He still had more Wildcats than he had had at the beginning of the Midway battle. He also pointed to "the large number of torpedo planes and bombers in the area." That was hardly a surprise to anyone, including his superiors who had ordered the operation. Torpedo-planes and bombers had indeed attacked transports and cargo ships and their combat escort, causing remarkably little damage. Japan's "sea eagles" had not even located the carriers, which were themselves unscathed although their air groups had taken losses.

To his message Fletcher added a request that tankers be "sent forward immediately as fuel running low." Analyses of the actual fuel situation at the time of the withdrawal show that the task force's supplies were adequate for several more days of operations. While the need for refueling—a continual and legitimate concern of every naval task force commander operating in the Pacific—would soon arise, it could presumably have been met by refueling in shifts without pulling out all three carriers at once. In later years Fletcher was to say that inadequacy of fuel was not the reason for his withdrawal, although he naturally would have welcomed an opportunity for bringing up the levels.

When Ghormley, however, reported the withdrawal to Nimitz, he ignored the other reasons given by Fletcher and said simply that "carriers short of fuel proceeding to fueling rendezvous." In his unpublished account of his stewardship as COMSOPAC, Ghormley enlarged on the point. Whether or not Fletcher should have stayed longer was a question of judgment: "All knew that the enemy could arrive in force and catch our Task Force short of fuel. That had to be considered very seriously. When Fletcher, the man on the spot, informed me he had to withdraw for fuel, I approved. He knew his situation in detail, I did not."

But Ghormley knew that Fletcher had decided, even before he reached the combat area, to pull out in two days. Admiral Callaghan, Ghormley's chief of staff, came back from Koro with a report on the conference. Ghormley sent Fletcher a message as the Allied armada approached Guadalcanal. It started out firmly enough: "Am informed you plan to withdraw carrier support from Tulagi area prior to Dog plus 3 days. Necessity exists of providing continuous fighter coverage for that area."

Then the note of firmness ends. Instead of saying, "You know your mission; carry it out," Ghormley suggested "for your consideration" some improvisations for air cover when the carriers left. These included leaving two fighter squadrons on Guadalcanal if the field was ready; or flying belly tanks from the carriers to rear bases where they would be fitted to fighters there which could then fly to Guadalcaual; or using the carriers as landing strips for short-legged Marine planes from an escort carrier, to enable them to reach the island. Nothing came of these plans.

In later years, answering criticism of his decision, Fletcher offered other reasons for his withdrawal. There had been warnings of Japanese submarines coming into the area—hardly an unexpected development. The Navy had only four carriers left and new ones would not be rolling out of American shipyards for nine more mouths—a fact well known to the Joint Chiefs of Staff when they ordered the Solomons operation.

Another justification Fletcher later invoked is more interesting. In May, before the Battle of Midway, Nimitz had given the two top carrier-force commanders—Fletcher and Spruance—a special letter of instruction:

> You will be governed by the principle of calculated risks which you shall interpret to mean the avoidance of exposing your force to attack by superior force without good prospect of inflicting, as a result of such exposure, greater damage to the enemy.

This can be roughly translated as follows: don't risk your carriers against any target but other carriers or major warships, and then only if you have a better chance of sinking them than they have of sinking you; don't expose your carriers to attack from land bases, which cannot be sunk or even knocked out for more than a few hours.

Perhaps Nimitz had in mind criticisms that had been leveled at Fletcher after he had led his carriers into action in the Coral Sea earlier in May: that he had brought his carriers close to Tulagi to launch raids against minor Japanese ships; and that he had sent his bombers against a light Japanese carrier when two big ones—unbeknownst to him at the time—were nearby.

In any event, Fletcher invoked his "special instruction" of May 28 as an overriding order not to expose his carriers to land-based air attacks in August—an order which, apparently, he did not regard as superseded by the Joint Chiefs' directive to seize and occupy specified targets in the Solomons. He seems to have felt free—perhaps even obliged—to keep the risks to his carriers to a minimum, regardless of effects that their withdrawal might have on the broader mission assigned to him

Spruance told his flag lieutenant, before Midway, that Nimitz had also given him a secret verbal instruction, not committed to writing: Spruance was not to lose his carrier force; if things went badly, he was to withdraw and allow the Japanese to take Midway. "They can't hold it, and we can get it back later," Spruance explained. Was there some similar private instruction to Fletcher before WATCH-TOWER? Something along these lines: we want those islands, but we don't want them so badly that you should risk the loss of your carriers. Fletcher's behavior would be somewhat more comprehensible if he had been under such orders, but nothing of the kind has yet come to light. Moreover, things had not gone at all badly at Guadalcanal up to the time Fletcher decided to pull out all three of his carriers.

There were strong arguments against undertaking the Guadalcanal venture. Ghormley and MacArthur, among others, had marshaled them when they first learned of the Joint Chiefs' directive of July 2. Among the strongest was the peril of exposing the Navy's few remaining carriers to land-based air attack long enough to get troops and their supplies ashore and their own land-based air cover established. The Joint Chiefs understandably might have decided that the risks of failure or unacceptable losses outweighed the possible gains. But the Joint Chiefs, fully aware of the risks, had nevertheless ordered that the operation be carried out.

In taking a decision that jeopardized the whole venture Fletcher in effect rewrote his superiors' orders. And his decision can hardly be called "tactical." No unforeseen disaster or unexpected threat had developed that would justify the "man on the spot" in abandoning his orders to carry out the assigned mission: "to seize, occupy, and defend Tulagi and adjacent positions," as his own operations order stated it. He only did, at Guadalcanal, what he had decided to do before the fighting even began.

Rumblings of disapproval were heard in higher quarters. By August 23 Nimitz was openly critical. Ghormley had reported fully on the defeat at Savo Island. Commenting on the report, Nimitz called the simultaneous departure of all the carriers on the 8th "most unfortunate" because "it left the unloading APs [transports] and AKs [cargo ships] without air cover." Moreover, the carriers' absence "permitted the enemy to make a clean getaway without being subjected to carrier air attack during the early daylight hours." Four days later Nimitz remarked to King that for two weeks after Savo "none of the many small groups of Japanese ships that operated in the close waters between Tulagi and Guadalcanal was attacked by either carrier air groups or by our surface ships, in both of which our forces were superior at the time.'' Meanwhile, he added, the Japanese had ''had time to assemble powerful forces.'' Fletcher's days as a commander of carrier task forces were drawing to a close.

The U.S. carrier groups continued, after their withdrawal on August 8–9, to roam the waters southeast of the Solomons. They filled the classic role of a ''fleet in being,'' keeping their enemy counterpart at a cautious distance from the embattled island, until one side or the other should find an occasion propitious for forcing the other into a ''decisive battle.'' Though few marines were aware of it, they had reason to be grateful for the American carriers' distant prowling. The flattops on both sides, so long as they lasted, would provide distant cover for the movement of supplies and reinforcements to Cactus. Twice, while so employed during the Guadalcanal campaign, the opposing carrier forces would approach and attack each other. But the textbook ''decisive battle,'' a strategic idea beguiling to both side: would never take place. The Guadalcanal operation, and the whole Pacific war, would turn out to be more complicated than that.

# 6

☆ ——— ☆

# Twelve Days in Limbo

In the afternoon of August 9 the last of our ships departed. The convoy's escort was sadly depleted; four cruisers and one destroyer now rested on the sea bottom and another cruiser, the *Chicago*, limped by with a big hole in her bow. As the sun set behind the mountains no friendly ships hovered offshore and no friendly planes patrolled the skies. We were on our own.

On the 10th the division headquarters moved to a new command post, meant to be permanent. Colonel Thomas and one of his assistants had picked out the site—a thicket of scrubby trees on the landward side of a low coral outcropping. At the northwest edge of the airfield, it was roughly in the center of the perimeter that was being organized.

That morning Vandegrift assembled there his regimental and battalion commanders. They got orders to do what must urgently be done: move those hummocks of supplies from the shoreline to dumps within our thinly held perimeter; set up defenses along the beaches east and west of Lunga Point and as far inland as meager numbers allowed; complete the runway.

The Japanese had massed alarming strength, including embarked troops, in and near Rabaul some 650 miles to the northwest. The Marine command supposed that if they threw any substantial assault force against us, it would swarm across the beaches close to the airstrip. Beach defenses were organized: batteries of the 11th Marines' 75-mm. and 105-mm. artillery so placed, south of the airstrip, that they could fire on any threatened segment of

74

the line; mutually supporting emplacements of machine guns along the water's edge, backed up by 75-mm. half-tracks (antitank vehicles running partly on wheels, partly on tractor treads) and mortars. Our cargo ships had landed little barbed wire, but marines salvaged some from plantation fences and strung it across the most likely avenues of enemy approach. As for the vulnerable southern or landward side of the perimeter, there were neither men nor weapons for a continuous defense line. Specialized units like the Engineer, Pioneer, and Amphibian Tractor Battalions retired to bivouac areas south of the airfield after their daily labors and became the nighttime defenders of that sector.

Beach defenses were organized from the mouth of the Tenaru in the east along the outlets of the Lunga River to a point west of Kukum, where the Japanese had built a primitive operating base for small craft. At each end of the beachfront—along the Tenaru in the east and up to the first ridge inland from the coastal strip in the west—the defense line ran about a mile inland. The long southern sector ran south of the airfield. As I have mentioned, this was loosely held, manned by contingents of company size (that is, of about 200 men each) in outposts with gaps in between. The line of defended beach was about five miles long. At its thickest point the defended area was about two and a half miles wide.

All in all the cordon thrown around the airstrip embraced an area of ten or eleven square miles. Most of that modest acreage can be seen in a photograph taken by a Navy plane on D-Day. Guadalcanal is about the same size as Delaware, but not the same shape. It was as if we held one of the resort towns along the Delaware Bay and the rest of the coastline was open to landings by anyone who had ships to get there. And the Japanese had such ships.

Colonel Thomas, the D-3, had drawn up the defense plan as we approached the Solomons. General Vandegrift had warned him that Admiral Turner had bizarre ideas about proper defenses: station detachments of marines at various points along the coast. Thomas's mind was fixed, if the admiral's was not, on the need to concentrate available forces to hold the airstrip, the piece of real estate that was the main target of the whole venture. He delayed showing Turner the defense plan until the day of the landings, when the admiral's mind was otherwise occupied. Turner could do little but assent, but it turned out that he had by no means given up his own scheme for dispersing units along the northern shore.

By August 13 working parties had cleared the landing beaches of supplies, and engineers had completed the runway to a length of 2,600 feet. By the 18th it had been extended to 3,778 feet. Captured Japanese equipment made both tasks possible. Japanese trucks helped haul things from the landing beaches to dumps. Without Japanese road rollers, earth-moving equipment, wheelbarrows, and a little rail line along the runway fitted with fill-moving cars, the airstrip could not have been so quickly completed; little Marine engineering equipment had been landed. Without Japanese rice bags of woven straw, gun emplacements could not have been built; sandbags had not been landed.

Contact with the outside world was tenuous. Navy and Marine operations plans had called for a naval radio station to be put ashore at Guadalcanal. In the scramble to clear out, equipment and supplies for the radio station were not landed. Again, captured booty saved the day. Not knowing how to read Japanese instructions, a Marine technician named Ferranto tinkered patiently with a Japanese transmitter. After five days it went on the air, with about 500 watts power. "This was the first time we had reliable communications with the outside world and it was a great boost to all of us" was the understated comment, years later, of the division signal officer, Major Edward W. Snedeker. Much other communications equipment, for internal use within the perimeter, sailed back to Noumea with the departing convoy. One acute shortage was in field telephone wire. To avoid any wasteful use, Snedeker personally parceled it out.

In those early days and for many years thereafter Marine and naval commanders wrangled about the degree of scarcity in food and other supplies. Within the first week the division quartermaster reckoned there were rations for only five days, and Vandegrift so reported to Turner and Ghormley. This alarming report undoubtedly did not take into account captured Japanese rice, tinned meat and fish, and other provender. Turner, by this time back in Noumea, replied that skippers of cargo ships told him they had put ashore food for more than fifty days—a gross exaggeration on the optimistic side. Other figures appear in various reports. Perhaps an accounting more closely reflecting the true state of affairs was that given in the division's final report, submitted almost a year later: as of August 15, it said, there were on hand seventeen days of regular field rations, three days of Type C rations, and ten days of captured Japanese food.

The conflict in statistics will never be fully settled. The fact is that there were alarming shortages, particularly in a situation where it was uncertain when additional cargoes could be brought in. Marines lived on two skimpy meals a day during the first six weeks. (Some units came to like this time-saving schedule for chow lines, and kept to it even when food became more plentiful and the two meals could be much heartier.) No one starved on Guadalcanal or Tulagi. No Americans, that is; in the later part of the struggle, Japanese troops were to starve by the hundreds. But no one grew fat, either, and weight losses of twenty to thirty pounds were common.

In what may be called the third round of writing about the Guadalcanal campaign, many years after the event, some accounts, seeking to "correct" earlier ones, have tried to give the impression that the Marines never lacked for anything they really needed. A biography of Turner, for example, comments that "the major essentials of battle— adequate men, rations, aircraft, bullets, bombs and aviation gasoline—were always present on Guadalcanal," adding the bland qualification "although the reserve stores rode the sine curve rollercoaster with distressing speed." Again, speaking of the initial landings: "The navy got a very large percentage of the Marines' logistic support out of the holds and on to the beaches." But they "did not get 100 percent of the logistic support ashore and that was the least they would have to do to accomplish their mission and satisfy the Marines."

Turner gave his biographer a number of juicy items suggesting that Marines had been extravagant in their de-

mands and wasteful of precious cargo space. In a letter
written two weeks after the landing Turner spoke of the
"vast amount of unnecessary impedimenta" the Marines
had brought along. A transport skipper reported that on the
second day of the landings, some fancy cheese broke out
of a melted carton, and commented in his ship's war diary:
"Weapons, ammunition, prime movers, and canned rations are more worthwhile than fancy groceries during the
first days" of such an operation. Again, in mid-December,
in the last phase of the campaign when the Army had taken
over command, the commander of a transport division
reported that "the straw that nearly tipped the balance was
the box of cargo that broke open in #3 hold and displayed
the contents as tennis rackets and tennis balls." Turner's
biographer cites this last report as an indication that "the
Marines occasionally contributed to the logistics problems
at Guadalcanal." It would be pleasant to think that some
enterprising unit, Marine or Army, four months after the
struggle started, did get ashore the wherewithal for a game
of tennis, which would have been about the first recreation
available apart from an occasional swim in the Lunga or
the sea, cribbage, checkers, and the usual range of card
games.

Statements like those just quoted give an absurdly skewed
picture of the supply situation on Guadalcanal. In a sense
the contention is both unseemly and irrelevant. Few Marine officers would continue to think, when the heat of
battle had passed, that the naval amphibious force had not
done about as well as it could after those first frantic days.
The early withdrawal of the carriers, the loss of cruisers
off Savo, the resulting scramble in the convoy to unload
what it could and clear out, set all plans awry. And few
naval officers in a position to know the facts would hold
that there were not many occasions when acute shortages
in many categories gave good grounds for fears that we
could not hold on.

The main fault—if fault it was, at a stage in the war
when much had to be done on a makeshift basis—was in
grossly inadequate preparation for speedy logistical backup.
The United States was simply not ready to support a major
operation for the seizure, holding, and rapid development

of an air and naval base open to heavy enemy counterattack. Both the Navy and Marine Corps learned important lessons about supply in the Guadalcanal operation, and applied their hard-won wisdom in later campaigns. It was the misfortune of marines and naval forces in WATCHTOWER to be laboratory animals.

Of all the shortages the isolated landing force faced during the early days the most dangerous was the complete lack of air cover, beginning at sunset on August 8, ending only late in the afternoon of the 20th. The Japanese quickly realized that they had almost complete freedom of the local seas and skies. I say "almost" for our antiaircraft batteries, once they were emplaced, forced the bombers to keep to altitudes higher than 20,000 feet. But the Imperial Navy soon established a daily routine of bombing raids, usually about noon, and occasional naval shellings, by day and night.

A particularly exasperating affront was daytime visits by submarines (I-boats) which could, with impunity, surface offshore and lob an occasional shell into the Lunga perimeter. Among the nighttime visitors were planes that droned back and forth over our position, dropping flares or bombs from time to time, doing little damage except to the nerves of exhausted men who yearned to sleep. All such menaces were given nicknames. The impertinent submarines were known collectively as Oscar. A single-engined nocturnal sky visitor, usually a Zero floatplane, was Louie the Louse. A two-engined night bomber was Washing-machine Charlie, so called because of the distinctive clanking rhythm of the plane's motors.

An incident on August 12 brought home in a most vivid personal way our vulnerability during the Twelve Days. At the division CP we knew roughly what had been happening on Tulagi and its neighboring islands, twenty miles away across the sound. Vandegrift had talked with Rupertus aboard the *Neville* the night of August 8–9, and they were in radio contact. But we wanted a more complete account of the fighting there, and Captain Murray, as personnel officer, also wanted, I suppose, records of casualties. The general decided to send a small party across by boat. Murray was the senior officer of the group. Another member of the party was Sheffield Banta, a feisty bantam cock of the "Old" Marines. He had been division sergeant major, recently promoted to the warrant-officer rank of Marine gunner, in the personnel section. Richard Tregaskis, Robert Miller, I, and the boat crews were the others. Tregaskis was the hugely tall correspondent for the International News Service who had landed with us. He was soon to win fame as the author of *Guadalcanal Diary*. Bob Miller was the United Press correspondent.

When this group set out from the primitive naval operating base at Kukum the morning of August 12 we didn't know what we might run into. Our little flotilla consisted of two Higgins boats and a tank lighter loaded with drums of fuel for boats at Tulagi.

We had hoped to start about dawn and get to the other side before Japanese bombers came over. But the boats were late. We didn't shove off until nearly 0900. It was a beautiful day, with calm seas and bright sky, and near-perfect visibility for planes and ships. My boondockers got soaked when I was climbing aboard, and I took them off to dry. The boat carrying Murray and me turned out to be an old tub that couldn't work up a speed of more than eight knots.

For an hour and a half the three boats chugged along without incident. Then we spotted a big, low-flying plane coming up the channel from the southeast. We hadn't seen an American plane for nearly four days and we assumed the worst. As the plane swept in low, headed directly for us, we grabbed our weapons (in my case a futile Colt .45), and one of the crew manned the machine gun.

The tension broke when we spotted stars on the wings. It was a U.S. Navy amphibian patrol plane, a Catalina piloted by Admiral McCain's aide. It was the first American plane to land on the airfield, which the pilot pronounced usable by fighters.

When it was almost over us the big plane veered off toward Lunga. As if to reassure us a school of dolphins, good omens for sailors, played about our boats for several minutes. Then, about eleven, we saw something in the water, almost dead ahead, a bit to port, between us and Tulagi. Murray called to me: "Take a look, Merillat. Is that a sub?" Spray on my spectacles and field glasses made it hard to be sure, but clearly *something* was there. It was perhaps 5,000 yards off. [But I am a poor judge of distances at sea; others who witnessed the scene placed the object closer. Admiral Murray's fleet did a sharp right turn, running back toward Guadalcanal.] By this time I could all too clearly see a submarine, and it was making for us. Any doubts about its identity ended when two shells burst one or two hundred yards from us. Ranging shots, they were.

The desperate burst of speed was too much for our creaky engine. It clanked and groaned and hissed, as clouds of steam and smoke poured from the housing. We decided to abandon our boat and move to another, if we could. Our coxswain signaled frantically to the others.

I crouched behind the gunwale, watching the sub coming toward us and thinking that there were only two possible outcomes: we would be hit and sunk, or we would be taken prisoner. I don't recall having a preference. Contrary to the old saw, my life did not flash before me. I was thoroughly absorbed in the moment.

The encounter had not gone unobserved on Tulagi. From high points on the island marines could see both the submarine and us. In fact, before we came into sight, they had spotted the intruder. At 0947 Rupertus had radioed to Vandegrift: "Enemy submarine surfaced and plied back and forth about 8000 yards off south coast of Tulagi." Then, at "1030 (approximate)" he sent another message: "Our boats observed; E Battery fired on sub; sub observed our boats and fired on them; . . . E Battery laid fire ahead of sub and then scored straddle."

Samuel B. Grifith, II, then a lieutenant colonel and executive officer of the 1st Raider Battalion, was among those watching. "In moments," he wrote in *The Battle for Guadalcanal,* "it became evident to each of the spectators that he was witness to the most dramatic of all imaginable scenes: a literal race between life and death." When smoke and steam began pouring from our engine, he said, and the boat slowed to a wallow, there were agonies of disappointment on Tulagi. " 'Jesus, her engine's conked out!' a marine said in a choking voice. He was crying."

Finally the other Higgins boat, seeing that we were helpless, pulled alongside. We threw in our gear—I leaving behind canteen, boots, pistol belt, and glass case—and then scrambled in ourselves. "Our boat," Tregaskis later wrote, "swung over next to the crippled one and we bumped gunwales, pulled apart and smashed together again. . . . The crew of the other craft fell, slid and vaulted into our boat." Of my own leap he said that "the ordinarily quite . . . dignified young man, jumped over from the other boat and landed, a disordered collection of arms and legs, on the bottom of our boat. He was wearing white socks."

I, for one, felt better for some foolish reason—perhaps because we were all in the same boat, as it were, and a sound one. We raced on to the east, watching the gunfire from the sub and the shore battery. We could see spouts around the I-boat. Finally it submerged. Watchers on Tulagi saw the Japanese gun crew scramble away from the deck gun and pile into the conning tower. One of the 75-mm. howitzer shells seemed to score a hit. We later learned the submarine was not sunk, for it made an odd report of the incident to its headquarters.

In the Higgins boat we shouted with relief, and joked and laughed at the letup in tension. At noon we arrived on Tulagi, feeling lucky to be alive. Intact except for a swollen hand and scratched knee, I wangled a pair of boondockers from the quartermaster and started the day's work—to get detailed reports of the fighting from officers and men who had been in action there. Among other things I saw my first dead Japanese, his corpse enormously bloated under the tropical sun, like a grotesque balloon in a Macy's parade.

That night, when we had completed our rounds, we slept at Carpenter's Wharf, the dock where we had landed. A submarine—probably the same one—had surfaced again several miles off Tulagi in the middle of the afternoon. Rupertus arranged that we leave at 0430, to be well on our way before sunrise. Some time after we had stretched out in a dockside shack a lanky figure loomed up in the dark. It was Dick Tregaskis. He leaned down to whisper about a concern that was on the minds of all of us: our underwater friend might rise to greet us on the return trip.

Tregaskis has written about his lying awake for hours, worrying about this possibility. Then it came to him that we might ask the amphibian plane that had landed on Guadalcanal in the morning to come fetch us: "I stepped over the sleeping officers in the shack, waked one who would know [undoubtedly Murray], and asked if the PBY could be called on to ferry us back."

Murray told Dick that the PBY had already left the island. Then Tregaskis suggested that we postpone our return trip until there was air cover. He was told we were carrying back dispatches and could not wait indefinitely for escort planes. As it turned out, no planes arrived at Henderson Field for eight more days.

In the early morning gloom we set out. The tank lighter, its cargo of fuel unloaded, now carried the few Japanese prisoners who had been taken in the Tulagi area. They huddled against the ramp in the bow of the craft, while MPs in the stern kept weapons trained on them. I wondered whether the prisoners expected to be shot at sea and dumped over the side. The two boats slid away from the dock and hugged the dark shape of Florida for the first stretch of our trip. We were nervous when lights flashed across the strait—probably gunfire. Indeed, a Japanese submarine did shell the Lunga perimeter early that morning. But we broke away from Florida and, throwing up sheets of spray, headed "home." We arrived at Kukum without incident, at 0830.

A few years later, when I was working for *Time* magazine in New York, one of my best friends on the writing staff was Edward Cerf. Ed had been in the Marines during the war. Once when we were reminiscing about wartime experiences, it turned out that he had served in the artillery. Further, he had been on Tulagi. Still further, he had been an officer in the battery of pack howitzers that fired on a Japanese submarine one sun-drenched morning in

August 1942; the I-boat had been trying to sink a crippled Higgins boat. It made a certain bond between us.

There was another and earlier sequel. A few days after our brush with the I-boat Japanese planes made air drops to their small forces west of us. Some of the reinforced wicker baskets fell inside our lines. Among the rations and other items dropped were encouraging messages ("Banzai! Help is on the way.") and a map showing the "situation" since our landings. On the mimeographed chart the Japanese naval victory at Savo Island was sketched. The paper also showed three boats crossing from Kukum to Tulagi on August 12, explained as "high-speed boats flying the British flag and loaded with war materiel." "High-speed boats" gave us a chuckle. "British flag" puzzled us. Then it occurred to us that officers on the submarine must have seen the red signal flag our coxswain had frantically waved to tell the other boats we were in distress. Later it came out that higher Japanese headquarters had cited the incident as a desperate attempt by Americans to escape from imperial fury on Guadalcanal to the safety of Tulagi.

The prisoners we brought from Tulagi were not in danger on that crossing, at least not from us. Their reception at the dock in Kukum, however, was unusually hostile. Glowering marines gathered around, muttering "We ought to kill the sonuvabitches" (the usual Marine plural of the epithet). There was a special reason for this animosity. The Goettge patrol had met its doom the night before.

As already mentioned, marines moving toward the airfield had come upon evidence that the defenders had quickly abandoned their camps. Breakfasts were half eaten, clothing and gear strewn in disorder. Little attempt had been made to destroy valuable equipment. To where, and in what strength, had the garrison departed?

Unarmed stragglers began to come within our lines to surrender. Marines shot some of them as soon as they appeared. Surrender had no place in the Japanese military code. Throughout the war Japanese troops and seamen refused voluntarily to give themselves up. The few prisoners taken by Allied forces were usually too badly wounded to resist capture. Our influx of prisoners turned out to have come from the unarmed labor battalions that the Japanese had pressed into service, a wretched lot of skinny, ill-fed but surprisingly strong Koreans, Ryukyuans, and other subject races.

Interrogation of these "termites," as marines came to call them, and patrolling beyond our lines, gradually built up a picture of enemy strength and location. The garrison was far weaker than prelanding intelligence had led the Marine command to expect. That intelligence had depended largely on information provided by native scouts. They found it hard to count large numbers and could not distinguish between laborers and the emperor's finest. Now it seemed that termites—about 2,000 strong—made up the bulk of the garrison. Three or four hundred naval troops were the only armed forces, and they had withdrawn to the west, beyond the Matanikau River about three and a half miles west of the Lunga. Reports gleaned from the Japanese after the war show that their senior officer on the island commanded a unit of about 400, including 280 riflemen.

Marine patrols reported seeing a white flag flying near Matanikau village, just beyond the river mouth. Probably this was an ordinary infantry flag, bearing the Rising Sun. Scuttlebutt later had it that this was a false surrender signal, intended to lure marines into ambush. There is no evidence that this flag played any part in the planning of the Goettge patrol beyond being one among many indications that the Japanese defenders were in that general area. Termites had reported that there many more like themselves, up the Lunga and to the west, without food or shelter and ready to give themselves up.

First Sergeant Stephen A. Custer, chief noncom of the division intelligence section, was eager to reconnoiter the area along the Matanikau to get a more accurate estimate of Japanese strength. A captured seaman first class confirmed the laborers' stories of men ready to surrender. Lieutenant Colonel Frank B. Goettge, for his part, wanted to get word to the hungry and dispirited workers that they could safely come into our lines.

The Goettge patrol evolved from these various elements. Headed by the colonel and Sergeant Custer, the group

numbered twenty-five, including the medical officer and
Japanese-language interpreter attached to the 5th Marines.
The colonel decided to take along the captured seaman as a
possible go-between. Only six of the men had had experience or training in patrolling. The patrol of marines from
the division D-2 section and 5th Marines planned to set out
from Kukum by boat the afternoon of August 12.

The Higgins boat did not turn up at the jetty until after
dark. There is no way now to reconstruct the colloquy that
must have taken place at this turn of events. Common
sense dictated that the venture be put off until daylight, or
cancelled altogether. But the officers and men scrambled
into the landing craft and chugged the three miles to
Matanikau, their approach announced to the enemy by the
boat's noisy engine. They landed beyond the river without
incident, formed a defensive line near the beach, then
began to probe inland. Goettge was the first to be felled by
enemy fire. One by one the members of the patrol were
killed or wounded. Only three managed to escape, making
their way out of the doomed pocket by swimming or
crawling across the rough coral along the shore.

Two later patrols from the 5th Marines tried to cross the
Matanikau and reach the area where the Goettge group had
been struck down, but were turned back by heavy enemy
fire at the river's mouth. Still later, August 18 and 19,
three companies from the 5th Marines undertook a three-
pronged attack on the area, one crossing the river about a
mile from its mouth, one going by boat to land beyond
Point Cruz, the third trying, unsuccessfully, to force a
crossing of the sandbar where the Matanikau joins the sea.
About sixty-five Japanese were killed, with nineteen casualties, including four dead, among the marines.

In one of these ventures across the Matanikau the executive officer of the 5th Marines was certain he had found
the burial place of the Goettge group; arms and legs were
jutting out of the sand. But before a patrol returned to the
site a heavy storm had struck, and no trace could be found
of the bodies, then or later. Presumably they had been
washed out to sea.

The Goettge patrol was an unmitigated disaster, costing
the division's intelligence section, and that of a regiment,

some of their best men, to no purpose. Senior Marine officers have never liked to talk about it. General Vandegrift later said he had doubts about the venture, but reluctantly gave the intelligence officers their heads. Perhaps a stronger chief of staff would have forbidden it. For a small party, mostly untrained in patrolling skills, to land by night at the very spot where the small enemy garrison was assumed to be concentrated, with an ill-defined mission, was professionally embarrassing, quite apart from the unnecessary human costs.

A happier development on the intelligence front came on August 14. Captain Martin Clemens appeared in our lines with a group of his native police. Clemens was a tall, sturdy (despite the loss of forty-five pounds in six months), and handsome Scot, with straw-colored hair that was darker in the beard he wore when he joined us. He was district officer for Guadalcanal in the service of the British Solomon Islands Protectorate, which included all the islands south of Bougainville. His official base had been at Aola, about thirty-five miles down the coast eastward from Lungu Point. In 1942, as the Japanese moved into the Bismarck Archipelago and the Solomons, Clemens became part of the coastwatching service organized by the Australians in that region.

With the coming of war, Australia had taken over responsibility for defense of the area. There was little they could do except to organize a network of observers to keep an eye on, and report by radio, enemy activities. Eric Feldt, an Australian, was in charge of the coastwatcher organization, which had the code name FERDINAND. Sixty-four men took on the lonely and dangerous duty of reporting Japanese ship, plane, and troop movements. Most were men familiar with the islands—planters, traders, skippers of coastal craft, gold miners, or, like Clemens, administrative officials. At the time of our landings three were at Gold Ridge, a mining camp 4,000 feet high in the mountains south of Lunga Point. Lieutenant D. S. Macfarlan, naval intelligence officer for the area, was among them. F. A. Rhoades, manager of a coconut plantation at Lavoro, on the western end of the island, stayed on as coastwatcher there. Sending in some of their native employees to work for the Japanese in the Lunga area, these men had been among the chief sources of our intelligence about the enemy's strength and activities before the landings.

Aware of the coastwatchers' presence in the islands, the Japanese tried to track them down. Clemens had been forced to withdraw further and further into the hills behind Aola and to the west. Just before our landings he was reduced to eating arrowroot and the night of August 6 he had no dinner at all. Obviously on the run from the little men shod with Japanese *tabi* ("allsame pigpig, got'm two toes," his scouts reported), he had had increasing problems in keeping the loyalty of natives; some village chiefs were becoming restive and uncooperative. But the little band of police and other officials, hungry and dispirited as he, stuck by him. From his mountain eyrie he saw the American planes that began to swarm over the island August 7 and heard the naval bombardment. On his radio he picked up the news that marines had landed in the Tulagi area. The next day he began his trek toward our lines, walking barefoot down a mountain stream and through the grassy plains, where he found "it was quite good going for bare feet." Before hailing an outpost near the Tenaru he donned his last pair of shoes, tight-fitting and incongruously of high polish.

Clemens was attached to the D-2 section, now led by Lieutenant Colonel Edmund J. Buckley. Goettge's successor, a Reserve officer, was a sturdily built businessman from Pennsylvania, blue-eyed, with white stubbly hair and a complexion turned pink by the Guadalcanal sun. To the annoyance of some of Clemens's Australian colleagues in the coastwatching network, Clemens enjoyed a somewhat favored position at division headquarters, not only because of his winning personality but for two more sternly practical reasons: he was the representative of the legitimate government of Guadalcanal, and he commanded the services of a native constabulary that was to prove immensely valuable in scouting beyond our lines and guiding Marine patrols. I have mentioned the most famous of these—Vouza, who had retired some years before as a sergeant major of the force. Vouza was strong of body and will. Intelligence shone in his alert black eyes in a typically broad-nosed Melanesian face surmounted by a typical bush of crinkly hair. We will hear more of him.

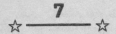

# The View from Rabaul

At dawn on August 7 the Japanese radio on Tulagi began to crackle with messages to Rabaul:

> 0435:* An enemy surface force of twenty vessels is attacking Tulagi; air attacks are going on, and they are making preparation for landing.
> 0525: Enemy started to land at Tulagi.
> 0600: The enemy is in great strength. We will defend to the last man. Pray for our success in the field of battle.

As we have already seen, the various commands in the Rabaul area reacted quickly. Naval air commanders sent two bombing raids against us on the day of the landings, and another the next day. Admiral Mikawa quickly assembled a cruiser force which struck with devastating effect off Savo the night of August 8–9. He also hustled some 350 troops of a Special Naval Landing Force aboard a transport and started them toward Guadalcanal. A U.S. submarine spotted and sank the ship soon after it left Rabaul. On August 7 Vice Admiral Nishizo Tsukahara, commanding the Eleventh Air Fleet, moved with his elite naval air units from Saipan to Rabaul, to become supreme commander of naval forces in the Southeast Area.

---

*Here and elsewhere in the Pacific war the Japanese used Tokyo time, which was two hours behind local time on Guadalcanal. Accordingly "0435" in Japanese messages and reports should be read as 0635 local time.

But the Eleventh Air Fleet's move, long planned, was aimed primarily at New Guinea, not at Guadalcanal. In our early days of nakedness to sea and air attack, Navy and Marine commands in the lower Solomons and in rear areas watched with anxiety the concentration of planes, ships, and troops at Rabaul and its neighboring bases. Loaded troop transports might at any time head thence toward Guadalcanal, two days' sail away. Fortunately for us, the Japanese had other plans for that concentration of strength.

The U.S. Joint Chiefs' directive of July 2, it will be remembered, called for a two-pronged attack on the enemy bastion at Rabaul. One would drive up the Solomons chain, beginning with Guadalcanal-Tulagi. The other would reach out from New Guinea. Both MacArthur and Imperial General Headquarters in Tokyo regarded New Guinea, and particularly Port Moresby, as the key to Australia. Partly to secure the continent against Japanese attack, partly to obtain bases for assaulting the Rabaul complex, MacArthur was racing the Japanese to get a firm grip on the New Guinea turkey's tail.

After the disaster at Midway the Army and Navy sections of IGHQ argued about what they should do next. They finally agreed to give highest priority to the capture of Port Moresby. They planned to set up bases in the Buna-Gona area on the northern shores of New Guinea opposite Port Moresby. From these an attack would be launched southward across the all-but-uncrossable Owen Stanley Mountains. When Japanese troops were ready to debouch from the mountains and descend on the port, a landing force, operating from a base to be established in Milne Bay at the tip of the turkey's tail, would move in by sea at the same time. IGHQ entrusted the unenviable task to the Seventeenth Army under Lieutenant General Haruyoshi Hyakutake. X-Day, when the combined assault on Port Moresby would take place, was tentatively set for August 7.

Meanwhile MacArthur also had his eyes on Milne Bay and the Buna-Gona area. His plan was similar to the enemy's, in reverse. Australian troops would cross the Owen Stanleys northward. When they reached the edge of the northern coastal plain other Allied combat forces and construction units would move swiftly in by sea and airlift,

seize or build airstrips, and consolidate a strong position
on the north coast of Papua. As a first step MacArthur
occupied Milne Bay in June. He originally planned for the
conjunction of forces in Buna-Gona to take place about
August 10.

The Japanese got there first. On the night of July 21–22
a big convoy arrived near Buna and unloaded troops and
construction workers. More were supposed to follow quickly.
This is not the place to describe the long and eventually
successful campaign that Allied forces under MacArthur
fought to oust the Japanese and consolidate his hold on the
northern coast of New Guinea. But we ought to keep in
mind that while the struggle raged for Guadalcanal another
bitterly fought and strategically important Allied campaign
was taking its course on the other side of the Solomon Sea.
For the first three weeks of the Guadalcanal operation the
main Japanese target was that other island, not ours. At the
time we did not know this. During the twelve days when
we had no air cover or support by surface ships the Marine
command was justifiably jittery about the formidable forces
assembled in and near Rabaul.

The day before our landings another Japanese convoy
left Rabaul for Buna. It carried 3,000 men—mostly construction units rather than combat troops, as it turned out.
After learning of our invasion of the southern Solomons
the Japanese command called it back. The ships lingered at
Rabaul until the night of the 12th, when they again set out.
Buna was still their destination.

A more threatening armada had also gathered, bearing
most of the 144th Infantry Regiment, artillery, supplies,
medical units, construction workers, and draft animals.
Those ships left Rabaul August 17. They, too, headed for
the Buna area. Another reinforced Japanese infantry regiment, the 41st, reached Rabaul from the Philippines. Most
of it also moved on to New Guinea, as the IGHQ plans
called for. By August 22 Major General Tomitaro Horii (in
command of forces in New Guinea, under Hyakutake's
Seventeenth Army) had landed 11,500 men since his advance force had arrived near Buna a month earlier. He was
ready to push south toward Port Moresby.

IGHQ's eyes, then, were still firmly fixed on New Guinea

as the target. Moreover, Japanese commanders seriously underestimated our numbers. They thought that from two to four thousand Americans had landed on Guadalcanal instead of 11,000. And they were puzzled about what the Americans had in mind. What sort of operation was this? A large-scale raid, perhaps, or reconnaissance in force? They had noted the early departure of our carriers and other ships. They saw that the airfield on Guadalcanal lay unused. "Enemy activity on Guadalcanal is not brisk" said the message air-dropped to their garrison and outposts on August 14.

Nevertheless, Americans held the airfield and something had to be done about that to protect the left flank of forces gathering to attack Port Moresby. In the early days the Japanese looked on us as a man in a hurry regards a little dog nipping at his heels—as an irritating pest that a well-placed kick can dispose of.

Hyakutake decided to divert—temporarily, he supposed—one unit that had been ordered to set up a base at the tip of New Guinea's tail before going on to Port Moresby on X-Day. It was the Kawaguchi Detachment, veterans of the Borneo campaign and drawn from the 4th Infantry Regiment. It would take some time to move Major General Kiyotaki Kawaguchi and his troops down from Palau to kick the pesky Americans out of the southern Solomons. Another unit, which was to have an earlier impact on Cactus marines, could be more quickly moved from Guam. This was the Ichiki Detachment, a crack Army unit that had earlier been given the task of assaulting and seizing Midway.

*August 15.* Our sky visitors returned at noon today. The antiaircraft opened up but I didn't hear of any hits. Everyone is getting impatient over the delay in the arrival of our aircraft. Today the Third Defense Battalion got up a letter to the Piper Cub Company, requesting "air support."

From: The Anti-Aircraft Artillery
To: Mr. Piper, Piper Cub Company, U.S.A.
Via: Division Air Officer
Subject: Piper Cub, request for
    1. Dear Mr. Piper. I hate to bring this to your attention, but we would like one of your little Piper Cub

airplanes. We forgot to bring ours. We got a pilot but no airplanes. The Jap's got both, real big ones (the airplanes, not the Japs).

2. We also got some AA guns, but they is not enough and too late.

3. If you cannot afford a plane for us marines, we compromise easy for one captive balloon, one net section for our AA, or a few more devastating raids by Mr. MacArthur's boys.*

4. If you can't help us out please bring this to the attention of Mr. S. Claus. Xmas is only four months away. The Japs is two hours away. . . .

Signed,
The A. A. Boys

P. S. Do you have any kites?

Four APDs [World War I destroyers converted into small fast transports] came in tonight, bringing aviation ground crews and equipment. [They also brought a base construction unit, which Turner had promised at Koro to send in at about this time.] The planes will follow soon—we hope! The scuttlebutt is that they will be in tomorrow.

Captain Murray and Captain Davidowitch (commanding the Military Police) took 134 Jap prisoners down to the ships to be evacuated. The commodore refused to take them aboard, saying he hadn't personnel to guard them. Murray said he would assign MPs to guard them. Then the commodore said he hadn't enough space. Murray pointed out there was plenty of room. The commodore then said any space occupied by the Japs would have to be fumigated! He didn't take them. FirstMarDiv will now request Turner to order the next ships arriving here to take away the prisoners.

*August 16.* Last night there was a report that a Jap attack may be expected. Murray ordered us [the D-1 section] to take to the coral hill behind the office tent and dig in there,

---

*A reference to bombings of Rabaul airdromes by Allied planes based in Port Moresby, the results of which were not as destructive as the communiqués led the world to suppose.

much to Banta's disgust. There we were, said the Old Marine noncom, with our backs to the wall before the attack even started instead of having the hillock to fall back on, and the office equipment was strewn on the deck instead of being piled up as a barrier. I found a coral cranny on top of the hill and managed to sleep comfortably— well, fairly comfortably, never before having slept on a coral bed. The attack didn't develop. In fact, it was a quieter night than usual.

---

"There was a report. . . ." I don't recall at exactly what point in the campaign I became aware that mysterious predictions of Japanese plans, often remarkably accurate, came from intelligence sources of a very special kind. The obvious sources were patrol reports on ground movements and enemy positions, reconnaissance of ship movements by aircraft and submarines, messages from coastwatchers up the line of islands toward Rabaul, aerial observation of enemy airfields, interrogation of prisoners, and translation of captured documents.

There was another intelligence source so ultra secret that only a few top American and British commanders and staff officers were supposed to know even that it existed. It was known as communications or radio intelligence—analysis in various ways of the enemy's radio traffic and particularly interception and decoding of his operational messages.

Even during the war a few Allied successes seemed, to canny observers, surely to involve precise knowledge of the enemy's plans; and how could this be gained except by reading his most secret radio traffic? Despite these instances the secret of "Ultra" was kept surprisingly well for three decades after the war. Then, in the middle 1970s, the dam began to leak. British participants in the arcane trade of Ultra began describing the crucial role communications intelligence played in the war with Germany. U.S. agencies remained more tight-lipped. But eventually they too began telling the story of American successes in breaking Japanese operational codes. We are here concerned only with that part of the fascinating story which affected operations on Guadalcanal.

The Japanese employed many codes in their communications—about a hundred, experts have estimated. Among the most important was the famous "Purple" code used in diplomatic channels. The U.S. Navy had long been trying to break the various naval and maritime codes used by the Japanese. When the United States entered the war, teams of cryptanalysts were already at work in Washington, Pearl Harbor, and the Philippines, trying to intercept and decode the Imperial Navy's radio traffic. By the spring of 1942 they were divining the meaning of a substantial number of encrypted groupings of letters or numbers frequently recurring in the most widely used Japanese naval code, known to our cryptologists as JN25. They had also identified many of the "additives" used by enemy communicators. These are meaningless groups of characters inserted into messages to throw off just such snoopers as were at work on the American side.

American successes in radio intelligence yielded spectacular results. Analysts detected the Japanese designs on Port Moresby in May. Informed of the two-pronged enemy naval movement into the Coral Sea, Admiral Fletcher had been able to intercept and turn back the invasion fleet headed for Port Moresby. Again, in June at Midway, only Nimitz's advance knowledge of Japanese plans had made it possible for him to counter them. He was able to place his three carriers in the right spots at the right times to take the greatly superior Japanese force by surprise and to sink four enemy carriers.

The Japanese put a new variation of JN25 into effect at the beginning of June. American radio intelligence was just beginning to make some progress toward cracking the new code when, in August, the Japanese again changed important parts of their system. Accordingly, as the Allied invasion armada was moving toward the Solomons—and, indeed, throughout most of the Guadalcanal campaign— American commanders had to do without much of the information about Japanese movements and plans that had helped so enormously, even decisively, in the Coral Sea and off Midway.

Our blindness was not complete. Naval radio intelligence experts could still make shrewd appraisals of enemy fleet movements from traffic analysis—that is, by observing, with the help of direction-finding equipment, the volume of radio messages coming from known naval units in particular locations. Heavy message traffic from destroyer squadrons moving southward, for example, might indicate that aircraft carriers or battleships, always screened by the smaller combat ships, were on the same course. In the language of this esoteric trade, radio intelligence could still estimate with considerable accuracy enemy "tendencies," but not "intentions." And some Japanese messages sent, not in JN25 but in other codes, could still be read, at least in part. The port director at Truk, for example, helpfully reported in a local code the arrivals and departures of fleet units. But it was not like the good old days in the late spring of 1942.

At midnight on August 17 the Japanese changed their call signs, the numbers or letters by which naval units or bases or commands are identified as originators or addressees of radio dispatches. Traffic analysis became more difficult. But before this further blow to U.S. radio intelligence fell, enough traffic had been readable in August to indicate major movements by the Imperial Navy and Army toward Truk, Rabaul, and the Solomons. Among the partially decipherable intercepts were some that would have been of particular interest to the Marine command on Cactus.

Naval radio intelligence intercepted and partially decrypted a message radioed, on August 14, by the headquarters of the enemy's Eighth Fleet in Rabaul to various other commands. One paragraph, with the comments and questions of the naval intelligence office shown in parentheses, read as follows:

Desdiv [Destroyer Division] 4 less second section, and Desdiv 17 are to join (?) the IKKI DETACHMENT leaving Truk at (blank) hours on 15th and accompany (?) to RXI (date of 18th is mentioned in connection latter operation but unable to determine whether this is date of arrival at RXI or some intermediate point)

The Japanese message also mentioned a convoy leaving Truk that was due to arrive at "(blank) point" at 1830—that is, at 2030 by our clocks—on the 21st.

Our sleuths at Pearl Harbor thought RXI was a new code designation for Guadalcanal, and they were correct. On the 16th, Pacific Fleet intelligence felt certain enough to send a more definite warning to U.S. naval commands in the Pacific:

Now appears that 18th is date of arrival of IKKI IKKI DETACHMENT and escorting DDs [destroyers] (about ten) off RXI

As we were soon to learn, IKKI was Colonel Kiyonao Ichiki, commanding the 28th Infantry Regiment. After the abortive effort to seize Midway, Ichiki's troops were pulled back to Guam. There they stayed until our invasion of the Solomons. Ichiki was then ordered to Truk. Thence an advance echelon—about 900 of his 1500 soldiers—came to Guadalcanal. Aboard six (not ten) destroyers they arrived as planned the night of the 18th.

This particular piece of intelligence did not, it seems, reach Vandegrift. But warnings of Japanese movements, based upon "reading the enemy's mail," did come in to Cactus throughout the campaign, delivered by one means or another from higher Navy headquarters. Intelligence derived from radio intercepts called for very special handling. The very fact that the U.S. was decrypting Japanese radio dispatches had to be kept highly secret. Transmission of the product to top commanders also had to be by most secret means. The cryptological aids and devices needed to receive such highly classified radio traffic could not be brought to a place as exposed to possible enemy capture as the Lunga perimeter. But Navy commands managed to get a great deal of "hot" intelligence to Vandegrift.

I have mentioned the captured Japanese radio station that served, for five weeks as it turned out, as our only means of communication with the outside world. Second Lieutenant Sanford B. ("Sandy") Hunt, Jr., was in charge of all communications with higher commands. His Radio NGK used the captured facilities. Not having the crypto aids necessary for highly secret traffic, he could not receive radio messages bearing intercept-derived information.

Hunt, however, became the intermediary for showing to

authorized officers in the division command—Vandegrift, his chief of staff, and sometimes his operations officer—messages delivered by other means. These might be brought in by ships equipped with the necessary crypto devices, or by special air couriers, or by visitors of the highest rank who were on the strictly limited distribution list for radio intelligence, including Turner, Nimitz, and, later, Halsey.

By the middle of September a Navy team arrived to set up its own radio station. A tunnel was dug into a northern spur of a ridge south of the airfield. Equipped with a heavy steel door, it served as headquarters for the new team, equipped with cryptological devices of a higher grade than those available earlier. Now carefully phrased "indications" of enemy movements and activities, based on radio intelligence, could be received from up the line. Sandy Hunt continued to be the link to the Marine command for "hot" traffic. Copies of the most sensitive messages were burned after the few officers authorized to read them had done so. Hunt was assigned as special assistant to the chief of staff for all communications with higher headquarters, which covered, of course, a much broader range of matters than intelligence.

Needless to say, I was wholly unaware of these arrangements while I was on Guadalcanal, although many of us in the CP were aware that, somehow, tip-offs about enemy movements and plans were coming in that could not be based on the usual sources of intelligence.

As I have mentioned, the specific information about Ichiki's movements apparently did not reach Vandegrift. But a warning of some kind did: in the evening of the 18th Vandegrift radioed Rupertus on Tulagi that "info received from CTF 62 [Turner] indicates attack on Cactus-Ringbolt [Guadalcanal-Tulagi] area possible within 48 hours."

Even if they had known that a substantial landing was imminent at "(Blank) Point," which turned out to be Taivu Point, the Marine command could have done little about it. A Marine patrol, however, soon stumbled on the new arrivals.

# The Fly and the Tortoise

Writings about Guadalcanal, official and unofficial, differ as to the reasons why Captain Charles H. Brush, Jr., was ordered to lead a strong patrol from his Company A, 1st Marines, east of the perimeter. Some accounts say that observation posts on the beach noticed waves made by ships passing silently in the night (the destroyers bearing Ichiki's troops) and another gentle plashing when they returned; Brush was sent to find out whether they had put troops ashore. Or, says another, native scouts had reported seeing fresh enemy troops, and Brush was sent out to investigate. Others say it was a routine patrol beyond our lines, of the kind that went on daily to scout out enemy strength and positions. Others give Brush a more specific mission: to destroy a Japanese observation post, equipped with a radio, at Gurabusu, some thirty-five miles to the east. Brush's personal briefing and orders confirm this last version.

In any event, the patrol set out on August 19, crossing the Tenaru and heading east. Four of Clemens's constables went with them. Near Koli Point, about five miles east of our lines, Brush's men spotted a group of Japanese officers and men, about thirty-five strong, walking toward them through the coconut palms near the beach. The patrol quietly laid an ambush, surprised the careless intruders, killed all but one, and returned to the division CP with a rich haul of documents. The enemy group were Army men, not naval troops, and were clearly the advance party for a much larger body. The 1st Marines had had their first encounter with the Ichiki Detachment. A larger and bloodier one would soon follow.

The next day was a notable one.

*August 20.* I walked over to the 5th Marines CP, the other side of the Lunga, to get Col. Whaling's account of the action at Matanikau. [Lieutenant Colonel William J. Whaling was executive officer of the 5th Marines, which had been probing beyond the Matanikau on the 19th.]

I felt pretty sick today—stomach cramps and dizziness—so I stuck close to the CP after walking back. After noon I repaired to my hilltop shelter and stretched out for a couple of hours. Was roused by the sound of planes overhead. Cheers were going up all around. Could it be that they were our own planes, the ones that have been coming in "tomorrow" for so long? They were. Grim faces brightened as the planes circled the field and came in for landings. The first hit the runway at 1607.

During the months on Guadalcanal there were a few moments of unalloyed general joy. This was one of them. Vandegrift, close to tears, was down at the strip to meet the flyers. Amid the general jubilation a staff officer at the CP wryly remarked, "The First Marine Division intends to fight to the last plane."

Nineteen Grumman Wildcat fighters and twelve Douglas Dauntless scout-bombers, in squadrons commanded by Captain John L. Smith and Major Richard C. Mangrum, comprised this first contingent of fighting aircraft to operate from our primitive landing strip. A few days earlier the general had named it Henderson Field, in honor of Marine Major Lofton R. Henderson, a dive-bomber squadron commander who was killed in the Battle of Midway.

Thus the "Cactus Air Force" was established. Robert Sherrod has traced its genesis. At the end of June, when Admiral King alerted Pacific commands to get ready for an offensive in the Solomons, Nimitz in turn alerted Colonel William Wallace and his Marine Air Group 23 (MAG-23) on Oahu. Two squadrons each, of fighters and dive-bombers, made up the group. Most of their pilots were young and green, most of their equipment old and obsolescent. They spent the month of July in intensive training.

On August 2 the first two squadrons headed south on the escort carrier *Long Island*. They picked up brand new

Wildcat fighters and improved dive-bombers just before they went aboard ship. The only other Marine combat squadron then in the South Pacific was Lieutenant Colonel Harold W. Bauer's in the New Hebrides. On August 13 (a day after McCain's aide had said Henderson Field was ready to receive light planes) the naval officer commanding the *Long Island*'s convoy radioed that the pilots needed more training in carrier flights. There were other problems; he would write a letter about them to McCain. McCain shot back a reminder that the planes were needed right now. A partial solution to the training problem was found. Some of the greener fighter pilots were traded for better-trained ones in the New Hebrides. Finally, eighteen days after the planes had started the journey from Oahu, the *Long Island* brought them within flying distance of Guadalcanal.

Almost overnight they became seasoned veterans. Wounds, rashes, or disease would soon knock most of them out of action. Some would die in combat. Out of this first contingent of bomber pilots only one would eventually be able to walk to the plane that carried him away from Henderson Field. Within ten days two more Marine squadrons came in—nineteen Wildcats (commanded by Major Robert E. Galer) and twelve dive-bombers (under Major Leo Smith)—along with the MAG commander, Colonel William J. Wallace.

Meanwhile the Army Air Forces contributed a squadron of P-400 fighters, or Airacobras. The medium-altitude fighters could not climb high enough to mix with high-flying bombers and Zeros, a limitation that led to feelings of frustration and discouragement in the AAF's 67th Fighter Squadron. But the Airacobras' nose cannons and other armament were formidable close-support weapons against Japanese ground troops. Marines came to have a special fondness for the 67th and their planes painted with shark's jaws. Three months passed before the AAF delivered to the island fighter planes of first-line quality.

With the arrival of two MAG-23 squadrons on August 20, two of the three elements needed to hold Henderson Field were tenuously in place. The third and most vital, sea power, was not yet in command of the local seas, but the Navy was doing its best to keep essential supplies moving to the island. And the fleet of carriers and attendant men-of-war was hovering in the background, waiting for its imperial counterpart to make a move.

The night of August 20–21 marked the beginning of a new phase of the campaign. Cactus now had an air weapon, able to knock down Japanese bombers, to give air support to ground operations, and to go after ships bringing in enemy reinforcements. Early that morning the Japanese made, and marines threw back, a first effort on the ground to recapture Henderson Field. A formidable enemy naval force, having gathered its strength for two weeks, was moving toward Guadalcanal, to cover the landing of more troops and to draw our carriers into battle.

The papers captured by the Brush patrol did not include information as to when and where Colonel Ichiki proposed to strike. A more prudent commander than he probably would have waited for the rest of his regiment to arrive and for our position to be carefully scouted before plunging to the attack. Knowing, after his advance party's encounter with Brush, that his presence had been detected, Ichiki perhaps thought he ought to strike immediately, however poorly informed he was about American strength around the airfield. In any event, Bushido do-or-die spirit should enable his men to overcome all obstacles. From their landing beaches at Taivu Point they moved quickly westward.

The 1st Marines manned the defenses on the eastern side of the perimeter. The line, it will be recalled, ran along the beach to the Tenaru then inland along the river for about a mile. Thinking an attack from that quarter now probable, Division had ordered the 1st Marines to extend the line farther inland.

That night Marine outposts beyond the Tenaru heard clankings and other suspicious noises to their front. They were withdrawn to the western side of the Tenaru. Then, at about three in the morning, some 200 Japanese charged out of the brush and coconuts, covered by mortar and machine-gun fire. They tried to rush the sandbar. A few got through some strings of barbed wire, salvaged by the

1st Marines from plantation fences, but heavy fire drove the rest back. Ichiki's men regrouped. An hour before dawn they charged again. This time some attackers waded out to sea and tried to come in behind the defenses at the sandspit. Again they were thrown back with heavy losses. Japanese dead sprawled on the bar and along the beach.

After daybreak the division command decided to throw in the division reserve—the 1st Battalion, 1st Marines—in an attempt to envelop whatever remained of the attacking force, which now seemed to be concentrated behind the tongue of land that reached toward the sandbar. The 1st Battalion crossed the Tenaru about a mile from its mouth and worked their way toward the beach. Cut off from escape in that direction, the Ichiki unit was now wiped out. Planes that had just arrived on the island the night before swooped down and strafed them. Tanks crossed the bar, firing cannister, like shot from huge shotgun shells. By midafternoon it was all over. Only a few escaped back to Taivu Point. Ichiki was not among them; he committed suicide on the battlefield. Ony a few wounded were taken prisoner. After the debacle Navy communications intelligencers noticed a heavy increase in radio traffic "of an urgent nature" to Rabaul from the transmitter Ichiki had left at Taivu Point.

---

*August 22.* Went up to the beach this morning to view the carnage. I'll never forget it. Jap bodies—torn, crushed, burned—lay thick near the mouth of the Tenaru. They had been neatly enveloped and didn't have a chance to escape. Already the stench was bad and the corpses were only twenty-four hours old. I ran into Col. Buckley and other D-2 officers who were looking around. They came across much interesting equipment: some intact flamethrowers [intended, presumably, for use against our planes once the attackers got through to the airfield], machine guns, mortars.

Two Jap wounded were being tended by medical corpsmen while I was there. One, hit in at least four places, was perfectly impassive as they dressed his wounds. He looked about him calmly as though nothing of particular interest was taking place. Several marines who came up remarked, "We ought to shoot the sonuvabitches." It's an attitude hard to understand. When the battle is over and a peasant kid lies helpless at your feet, why propose to shoot him through the head.

Busy getting out copy today. Didn't have a moment to write anything myself but have been pinned down clearing others' copy while they go swimming. I feel filthy, especially after the jaunt through the corpses.

---

Japanese combat troops, unlike the unfortunates they had dragooned into labor battalions, almost never surrendered, and could be taken prisoner only when they were too weak or badly wounded to resist. In the Battle of the Tenaru, several Japanese wounded had waited until an approaching American came within range, then tossed a grenade or fired a pistol at him. The ''kill-'em-in-cold-blood'' attitude, then, often was justified, and became common on both sides.

The day before Ichiki's attack, a Japanese party had captured former Sergeant Major Jacob Vouza, who had rejoined Clemens's constabulary in the summer of 1942. Vouza had gone out on a scouting mission east of the 1st Marine lines, and had run into the advancing enemy troops. They tied him to a tree, tortured him with bayonet cuts and thrusts to throat and chest, in an effort to make him talk about American defenses, and left him for dead.

Vouza managed to break loose, and crawled back to our lines to report the Japanese movement as the Battle of the Tenaru was starting. After his recovery in the field hospital, Vouza continued to be one of the most effective of the native scouts.

---

*August 23.* Bob Miller and I went over to the Lunga for a bath this morning, and to do our weekly laundry. Then we tracked down Karl Soule and went to the prison pen with some of his photographers. The prisoners are a seedy lot. They brought in five youngsters while we were there. They looked to be about thirteen or fourteen, but claimed to be eighteen or nineteen. They had been starving up in the hills ever since our landings. The prisoners seem contented and cause no trouble. I was surprised at the light guard. The MPs say, "We couldn't drive them out of the prison pen if we wanted to."

I got back to the division CP in the middle of the afternoon and found it humming. A Jap task force is on the way: two cruisers, three destroyers, and four transports. They should get in soon after midnight. Regimental and battalion commanders and air officers poured into HQ to work out defensive plans. Our dive-bombers were sent out to intercept the Japs. The weather is so soupy we're not optimistic about results. Hope the Navy will get in some good licks before the Japs arrive.

Later. The SBDs [dive-bombers] returned without finding any trace of the approaching Jap ships. Weather too thick. Thirty-odd planes from the *Saratoga* landed at dusk—a reassuring sight. All night they'll be refueling and rearming.

*August 24.* Our night of tension ended with a quiet dawn. Still no action and no report of enemy forces at noon. Can't figure out what happened to them. Perhaps they were headed somewhere else after all. Maybe they are garrisoning a nearby island. Perhaps they are lying in wait until their aircraft can soften us up a bit. No one pretends to know the true story.

At 0200 this morning something—apparently a sub—lobbed a few shells at us. I thought, "Here it is," and gathered up my gear. But the bombardment lasted just a few minutes and I soon went back to sleep.

The *Fomalhaut* [one of the freighters in our amphibious force] came in yesterday. She was to bring in some much-needed supplies and take away some little-needed and little-wanted prisoners. Late in the afternoon, however, a submarine let loose a torpedo at her. She hightailed it out of here, carrying some of our supplies and men and not carrying the prisoners, who are about to burst their confines through sheer numbers. The torpedo missed the *Fomalhaut* and skidded up on the beach at Kukum. There it now lies, the object of much curiosity exercised at a respectful distance.

*August 25.* The Jap birdmen came close today. I was crouching in my coral penthouse up on the hill and heard

(and felt) the bombs getting closer and closer. One fell
near the CP, a big one, leaving a crater about fifteen feet
deep and twenty-five across. Fragments showered the CP.
Some were found in the general's tent. Such impertinence.
The hot time seems to have encouraged plans to shift the
CP and undoubtedly we'll move soon.

Major Mangrum [commanding the dive-bomber Squad-
ron] and Lieutenant Colonel Fike [Charles L. Fike, commanding the whole Cactus Air Force at this time] came
over to D-3 this evening and gave us an account of air
activities during the day—the first coherent story we have
heard. We still don't know, however, what our carrier-
based planes have been doing. I now realize how hard it is
to get an accurate picture of what happens during an air
attack. Pilots are so concerned with finding and hitting
their target and then making a fast getaway that they can't
observe what goes on around them, and can't even be
certain of what they have done themselves. With great
patience Colonel Thomas drew out the story, bit by bit,
and it made sense when the pieces were put together.

---

What had happened in those few days after the action at
the Tenaru was a first major attempt by each side to run
the other's blockade—attempts that brought on a major
clash between their supporting naval and air arms. The
Japanese, under Rear Admiral Raizo Tanaka, were trying
to bring in the remainder of Ichiki's 28th Infantry Regiment and a thousand troops of the 5th Yokosuka Special
Naval Landing Force. The SNLF was embarked in a transport, the other troops in four converted destroyers. Tanaka,
flying his flag in the cruiser *Jintsu*, was in personal command of the convoy and its escort. The U.S. Navy, for its
part, was sending to Guadalcanal the first large supply
ships to come in since the original landings.

Each side had a double aim: to give distant support to
the supply and reinforcement runs and to engage the other's main fleet if a favorable opportunity arose. Accordingly the main striking forces of the two navies lurked
within carrier-plane range of the convoys and began moving toward each other. The Japanese came down from
Truk. The Americans were patrolling east of Guadalcanal.

Tanaka's original orders were to land his charges near Taivu Point the night of August 23. He came within 200 miles of Guadalcanal that day. But as the larger clash developed he got a series of orders from Rabaul, sometimes conflicting, that sent him northward for a time, then back toward the island.

The next day the two carrier forces found each other: two large carriers (*Zuikaku* and *Shokaku*) and a small one (*Ryujo*) on the Japanese side, two large carriers (*Enterprise* and *Saratoga*) on the American. Admiral Fletcher, unfortunately, had sent his third carrier, the *Wasp*, south to refuel. Radio intelligence—which, as earlier noted, was less reliable in this period than it had been earlier—indicated that the two big enemy carriers might still be north of Truk.

The U.S. carrier planes first found little *Ryujo* and sank her.* But while they were thus engaged, flights from the large Japanese flattops attacked Fletcher's carriers. The *Enterprise* was severely damaged by three bomb hits, had to return to Pearl Harbor for repairs, and was out of action for nearly two months. Under the threat of a nighttime attack by approaching enemy battleships Fletcher's force retired to the south. Thus ended the Battle of the Eastern Solomons.

Billowing smoke from the stricken *Enterprise* convinced the Japanese that they had disposed of at least one, and maybe two, carriers. Thus encouraged the higher commands at Rabaul, whose poorly meshed and sometimes conflicting orders exasperated Tanaka, ordered him to head toward Guadalcanal again with his convoy.

The small Cactus Air Force, just arrived at Henderson Field, had their first major brush with enemy planes on the 24th. While the flattops were duelling two or three hundred miles from the island, Marine fliers intercepted raid-

*Morison's account speaks of *Ryujo* as bait, sent ahead of the main Japanese striking force to lure American carriers away from the big ones (*The Struggle for Guadalcanal*, 82, 87–91). Japanese records throw doubt on this hypothesis. *Ryujo* had a specific and important combat mission: to guard Tanaka's convoy, and to strike at Henderson Field, to help clear the way for Tanaka's landing. (Paul S. Dull, *The Imperial Japanese Navy*)

ers from the *Ryujo* and shot down sixteen bombers and Zero fighters. They lost three of their own planes. The next day, as Tanaka bore down from the north, Mangrum's dive-bombers hit him hard. They sank the big transport carrying naval troops. Also they crippled Tanaka's flagship, the cruiser *Jintsu,* and sent it limping back toward Truk. The admiral switched his flag to one of the escorting destroyers and others tried to pick up survivors from the sinking transport. An AAF Flying Fortress from the New Hebrides bombed and sank one of the rescuing destroyers. Rabaul ordered Tanaka to take his depleted force to Shortland Island at the southern tip of Bougainville.

The American convoy was more fortunate. The first of Turner's supply ships since the exodus of August 9 reached Guadalcanal: three APDs, or destroyer transports, on the 21st and, next day, two big naval freighters, the *Alhena* and *Fomalhaut*—cargo ships that Turner pushed through from rear bases whenever he could. The *Blue,* one of the escorting destroyers that had darted ahead to contest Japanese nocturnal prowlers off our shores, fell victim to a torpedo from an enemy destroyer in the early morning hours.

From the wounded *Enterprise* a naval squadron of dive-bombers flew to Henderson Field and stayed more than a month. Cactus fliers, already battered after four days of action, welcomed the reinforcements with joy. Commanded by Navy Lieutenant Turner Caldwell, "Flight 300" won fame and warm Marine gratitude. This was the first of several instances when naval air squadrons from damaged or sinking flattops came to be based on Henderson. The unsinkable aircraft carrier—our primitive airstrip—was proving its value in more ways than one. Contingents came at one time or another from the *Enterprise, Saratoga,* and *Wasp.* Robert Sherrod has quoted the wry comment of one Marine aviation general: "What saved Guadalcanal was the loss of so many carriers."

Thus the first Japanese attempt to recapture Henderson Field had failed. The ground forces they sent to do the job were grossly inadquate. Admiral Tanaka, whose mission it was to deliver a steady stream of later reinforcements, has said of Ichiki's futile attack at the Tenaru that it was "like a housefly attacking a giant tortoise.'' The episode, he thought, ''should have taught the hopelessness of 'bamboo-spear' tactics''—sending lightly armed infantry, however much filled with spiritual zeal, against an enemy equipped with heavy modern weapons.

The convoy Tanaka unsuccessfully tried to bring through a few days after Ichiki's disaster was also inadequate, except as vanguard for a much larger force or as reinforcements for a garrison. Other units on the Seventeenth Army's roster were to follow. But many weeks would pass before IGHQ realized how large a commitment of Army troops must be made if the Americans were to be driven out. By then it was too late.

☆ ———— ☆

# Preparing for the
# Next Round

The small American air force on Henderson Field produced an entirely new situation, and it was an odd one. The two opponents were in a state of mutual siege. Each was trying to cut off supplies and reinforcements to the other. Each was trying to run the other's blockade. Japanese ships no longer dared to come in by daylight. They came by night, usually in flotillas of destroyers that landed troops on both sides of the Lunga perimeter and bombarded us in parting. Our own supply ships aimed to arrive at dawn, when they would have a friendly umbrella of Cactus planes, and departed at sunset.

In the new situation Japanese naval air commands at Rabaul now had more "lucrative targets"—in airmen's parlance—than they had earlier enjoyed: the occasional supply ships unloading in Lunga Roads and the busy airfield. Heavy bombings became our daily fare.

———————————

*August 26.* Our sky visitors returned at noon today, as usual: sixteen bombers and seventeen Zeros. They got to us with their bomb loads and peppered the airfield; killed one man and wounded ten others, mostly in the 3rd Defense Battalion [manning 90-mm. antiaircraft guns]. Then our fighters caught up with them, and knocked down seven bombers and five Zeros. One of our pilots is missing. I exchanged my hillside cranny for a better trench further down the hill. I didn't like the shower of coral fragments and thought an overhanging chunk might collapse on me up there.

A Navy lieutenant from Ghormley's staff is in today. He

brings bad news about the naval engagement of the 9th. [This was the first full and accurate report the division staff received of the Battle of Savo Island.]

The great cry from our staff officers is for more planes and supplies. They all take every opportunity to impress on Navy staff officers the great possibilities for developing auxilary airstrips here and the need for keeping up fuel and aircraft strength on the present field. The lieutenant said COMSOPAC is shouting for more planes for this area. Marine officers are critical, however, of COMSOPAC's attitude on the supply situation. The lieutenant says the Navy is afraid to send ships in while these bombing raids continue. The general pointed out this was a vicious circle: no ships, no supplies to keep our planes in the air to stop the bombings.

Tojo has taken some heavy losses here, but without replenishment of supplies we will gradually grow helpless. The general said the only way to handle the supply problem is to send in ships late in the afternoon, unload them quickly, and send them on their way during the night. Someone suggested big barges to be towed behind ships. All hands agreed they would fill the bill. The lieutenant said two have already been ordered from Pearl Harbor.

Apparently the Navy [carrier] task force is withdrawing from this area [following the Battle of the Eastern Solomons], and the Jap force too (we hope), leaving the Marines to hold the fort. Great guffaws from staff officers at this news. Everyone is withdrawing but the Marines. Now and then someone complains that the Army hasn't arrived yet, but there's no widespread discontent over the delay—thus far. But already rumors have started that the Army will soon move in and we will return to Wellington.

I saw George Goode [one of my roommates on the *Wakefield*] the other night on the airfield. He says Fox Battery has heard that we'll be out of here by Sept. 10 (overoptimistic, I'm sure). And I saw Don Dickson [regimental adjutant] at the 5th Marines this morning. He says one of their men (left aboard the *American Legion* when she pulled out) has returned from Noumea with the story that two Army divisions are embarking there, apparently heading for here, and should arrive within two weeks. My fingers are crossed. I hope we return to Wellington before taking on further ventures. D-2 isn't working up maps on any other area so apparently there are no plans for another jump from here.

------

Six weeks would pass before the first Army ground troops landed, and they would come as reinforcements, not as relieving forces. "The Book"—the Army-Navy agreement concerning the services' respective roles in landing operations—provided that when amphibiously trained forces had seized an objective, the Army would relieve them with garrison troops; the amphibians would thus be released for another operation. But much that happened during the Guadalcanal campaign was not, and could not be, according to the Book.

A Europe First strategy prevented the Army from meeting the constant and clamorous demands from other theaters—including the South and Southwest Pacific—for more and more troops and planes. Allotments to the Pacific, made in the spring of 1942, were supposed to suffice. As soon as detailed planning for WATCHTOWER got under way, Ghormley began urging Washington to send garrison troops for the lower Solomons. The Army's response, then and in the early stages of the campaign, was firm and consistent: new needs for troops and planes at advanced positions would have to be met by reducing garrisons in rear areas. Engaged in preparations for Allied landings in North Africa, scheduled for October or November, the Army could not afford significant diversions to the Pacific.

------

*August 29.* They came over on schedule today. I saw them as they came in from the South—eighteen bombers almost wing to wing. Our 90-mm.s opened up and about that time I stopped watching. Soon I heard the tat-tat-tat of machine guns up where the bombers were, and looked up to see one big silver plane crash straight to the ground, screaming, with a plume of white smoke behind.

Box score: four Jap bombers, four Zeros.

*August 30.* A new variation today—a raid in the rain. The siren blew about 1230 and we took to our shelters, I to my usual sandbagged coral trench in the hillside. Just as a formation of planes approached—enemy or friendly, I don't know—heavy clouds closed over the field. Wind rustling in the trees sounded at first like falling bombs—that distinctive sound of ripping silk. Then the rain started. A raid during rain is worst of all, I decided. Over the sound of rain you can occasionally hear the hum of airplane motors. You don't know whether they're yours or theirs, and you live through a score of raids before it is over. As it turned out, no bombs were dropped. Our fighters must have shattered them before they came over the field. There is scuttlebutt of heavy Zero losses, but no official word. We had heard that sixteen bombers were coming with heavy Zero escort, in two groups. Still don't know the story.

Later. Score: seventeen or eighteen Zeros down, and four Airacobras (one pilot saved by parachute).

Admiral McCain, COMAIRSOPAC (commander of land-based aviation in the South Pacific) flew in today in a B-17 and stayed the night. He doesn't at all fit the picture I had of him; he's a little, wizened man. No doubt he discussed weighty things with the general, though I haven't yet heard what it was all about. He cracked one joke: "Well, just send me a list of anything you want in the next month or so. I'll pass it on and that no doubt will be the end of it."

Eighteen Jap dive-bombers came out of the sky just after the all clear had sounded. They caught us unawares and sank the APD *Calhoun*. A bad loss, but few casualties.

———————————

McCain sent back a strong plea for air reinforcements. Of the nineteen Wildcat fighters that had come in ten days earlier, he reported, only five were still flyable. A squadron each of Wildcats and Dauntless dive-bombers had arrived "just in time," on the 30th. He urged that two full squadrons of P-38s (the AAF'S high-flying, long-range fighter) or Wildcats be sent at once, with replacements training in rear areas.

The situation admits of no delay whatever. No help should be expected of carrier fighters unless based ashore. With substantially the reinforcement requested Guadalcanal can be a sinkhole for enemy air power and can be consolidated, expanded, and exploited to the enemy's mortal hurt. The reverse is true if we lose Guadalcanal. If the reinforcement requested is not made available Guadalcanal cannot be supplied and hence cannot be held.

As McCain pointed out, the Wildcat fighters had suffered an attrition rate of nearly 75 percent in ten days. Then, as later, about as many planes of all types were destroyed or damaged by accidents as by enemy action. Henderson Field was a primitive base. The runway was a dust bowl on sunny days, a mire on rainy ones. To the hazards of taking off and landing through the murk or muck were added craters dug by frequent showers of Japanese missiles. Construction crews performed wonders in filling holes under bombardment and the constant threat of delayed-action bombs, but could not always fill them or smooth off the surface in time for planes to land or take off safely. They could do nothing about mud.

The field had none of the facilities for fueling, arming planes with bombs or cartridge belts, upkeep, or repairs that were taken for granted at more developed bases. Ground crews had to fill planes' gas tanks by hand-pumping from fifty-five-gallon drums. Without bomb hoists they had to lift missiles into bays by muscle. Pilots, like the rest of us, lived on or in the ground, exposed to nighttime shellings and bombings. Indeed, they and their planes were the prime target.

The managers of the little Cactus Air Force knew all too well our own losses in planes and air crews. The enemy's could be counted with much less certainty. Several of the daily entries quoted above and hereafter give the "scores." The figures for Japanese losses should be regarded as rough approximations, usually erring on the side of overestimation. I had simply repeated the raw daily reports as they reached division headquarters. Later and more careful comparing of reports from the airmen involved often led to revision. Even with these corrections there remained a wide discrepancy between our own counts of enemy losses and Japanese figures that became available after the war.

\*     \*     \*

After Tanaka's misfortunes on August 25 the Japanese did not again try to push through large troop ships for nearly eight weeks. Instead they relied mainly on what they called "Operation Rat"—movement by night in fast, troop-laden destroyers. They landed their human and material cargoes both east and west of the Lunga perimeter, usually shelling the airfield as they departed. The operating range of carrier-type fighter planes in the Cactus Air Force was roughly 200 miles. Squadrons of Japanese destroyers lurked to the north, usually in the Shortland Islands about 300 miles away, until midafternoon. Then, when bombers from Henderson Field could get in only one crack at them before nightfall, they headed southeastward at high speed and came within range. After closing on Guadalcanal and hastily unloading at night they scampered homeward, hoping to get beyond our bombers' reach soon after sunrise when Cactus planes would swarm after them.

Rat operations, under Tanaka's skillful management, became routine. Almost every night some enemy ships would dart in. Each group carried from 600 to 800 troops; on occasion, as many as 1,500. Enemy forces gradually built up on both sides of us. Late afternoon reports, from reconnaissance planes or coastwatchers, of Japanese destroyers headed down "the Slot," were normal news at the division CP. There we called the usual avenue of approach, between the two strings of islands that comprise the Solomons, the "groove" or "alley." Writers about Guadalcanal later dubbed it "the Slot," which is now the accepted name.

We called the nightly visitors the "Guadalcanal (or Cactus) Express." Again, later usage, now hallowed by time and much writing, has named them "Tokyo Express," which became a generic term used also in later operations for nocturnal Japanese shipborne reinforcements to threatened positions. Rat operations began in earnest the night of August 29 when Tanaka brought seven destroyers to Taivu Point.

On the last day of August the Allied cause suffered a severe blow at sea. Early that morning officers of a Japanese submarine saw the stately *Saratoga* through their periscope. The carrier was patrolling southeast of the Solomons.

At 0748 a torpedo slammed into her starboard side. Structural damage was not severe and by late afternoon "Sara" was able to retire under her own power. But she had to go to Pearl Harbor for repairs and was out of action for nearly three months. The explosion slightly wounded twelve men. Admiral Fletcher was among them, suffering a cut on his forehead. It was not serious enough to require more than brief attention in the sick bay.

Admiral Nimitz, however, seized the occasion to give Fletcher a rest. He returned to the United States, where he soon was given a shore-based command in Seattle. Later in the war he became commander of the North Pacific. Fletcher received the Distinguished Service Medal that King had once withheld; the citation praises him for "marked skill and resourcefulness" as commander of the carrier task force in the Coral Sea in May 1942 and again off Midway in June.

Also, on the last day of August, IGHQ in Tokyo came to a major strategic decision. They had hoped during the month to push the attack against Port Moresby while the Americans were preoccupied with their "reconnaissance in force" on Guadalcanal. Japanese Army troops had struggled across the Owen Stanleys in New Guinea to within roughly thirty miles of the prize. A landing force had occupied a position in Milne Bay (discovering that MacArthur's troops were already installed nearby). Through August IGHQ stuck to its plan to capture Moresby.

Now, on the last day of the month, the Japanese high command began to swing the turrets of its biggest guns against the lower Solomons. Ousting the Americans from Henderson Field was about to be given the highest priority. Forces in New Guinea were ordered to go on the defensive—to hold the line north of Port Moresby but not to push on. Every available weapon would be thrown against Guadalcanal. That island, thus far a sideshow for the Japanese, would become the center ring. Marines there would have been disheartened to know that so far they had had only a mild foretaste of what was coming. If IGHQ had come to its decision three weeks earlier, the outcome of the Guadalcanal campaign would probably have been quite different.

Meanwhile there was unfinished business under the old August plan. The Ichiki detachment had been sent; part had arrived and been destroyed, part had been sunk, a remnant managed to reach Taivu Point. A Special Naval Landing Force had likewise met disaster at sea. There remained, under the Seventeenth Army's original earmarking of troops for "Gadarukanaru," the brigade built around the 124th Infantry Regiment and commanded by Major General Kawaguchi. This unit began to arrive in the Shortland Islands, off the southern tip of Bougainville, at the end of August.

Admiral Tanaka had the task of getting it to Guadalcanal. Kawaguchi and Tanaka quarreled about the best method of ferrying the troops. The general wanted to send them by stages in landing craft or motor-driven barges. They would move by night along the northern shore of Santa Isabel, hole up in hidden coves by day, and finally cross to the northwestern tip of Guadalcanal. Tanaka insisted that he had been ordered to move them by destroyer. Guidance from higher Navy and Army authority in Rabaul was conflicting and confusing. The general and the admiral arrived at a compromise: both methods would be used. Tanaka would carry 2,400 of Kawaguchi's troops by destroyer to Taivu Point. The Oka Detachment of 1,100 men, commanded by a colonel of that name, would embark in barges and make their way by stages to beaches west of us.

The main body reached Taivu as planned, in Tokyo Express runs. It joined the remnants of the Ichiki Detachment—the rear guard that had stayed at the landing point while Ichiki made his rash attack at the Tenaru, and the remnants of those carried in the Tanaka convoy that had been bombed at sea on August 25. By September 4 Kawaguchi had assembled more than 3,000 troops at Tasimboko (Tadhimboko in the official gazetteer) three miles west of Taivu. There he finally got word that Oka was "approaching" the island.

But, as Tanaka had foreseen, Oka's men had run into deep trouble. Cactus fliers spotted the barges off Santa

Isabel, and bombed and strafed them for four days. Choppy seas added to the boats' woes on the last leg of their trip. Several foundered. By the end of that grim day, September 5, about 400 of the troops that had started the barge trip were dead. The shaken remainder eventually reached the northwestern end of Guadalcanal, directly or by way of Savo.

By the end of August it had become clear that the struggle for Guadalcanal was going to be long and bitter, with the outcome in considerable doubt. The press began taking more interest in us. On Admiral King's personal orders strict censorship had barred any reports of the Battle of Savo Island. Stories about the ground fighting—from Miller, Tregaskis, Hurlbut, and me—were not released until the end of the month. In those early days Sandy Hunt, the one-officer radio station, spent long and tedious hours enciphering the press reports and transmitting them to Pearl Harbor. At Pearl they were somewhat paraphrased (to safeguard the cipher system), censored, and, beginning late in August, released. Neither we, the generators of this workload for Hunt, nor a world waiting for news of Guadalcanal, realized how much was owed to Hunt's labors.

Later, in the age of television, Andy Warhol was to say that everyone could be famous for fifteen minutes. My own brief moment of glory came on Sunday, August 30, when the front pages carried stories I had written about the first days on Guadalcanal and Tulagi, with banner headlines. I knew nothing of this at the time, and was feeling superfluous and discouraged.

---

*September 2.* Till Durdin of the *New York Times* and Tom Yarbrough of the Associated Press came in last night, thinking they were the first reporters to hit the island. Ghormley and staff refused to let Till know anything was going on until the show was over, then Till got up here as fast as possible. Of course they were sick on learning that Tregaskis and Miller have been here all the time, sending out reams of copy.

I gave Till and Tom the draft of my history, to bring them up to date, and both praised it highly. Tom mentioned it so often that I think he wasn't just being kind;

said he would like to use it almost as it stands as a chronicle of the operation to date. It gave me a terrific lift to find someone who thinks I'm doing a good job.

Got a nice stack of letters from the States yesterday and today. That helps too—lots.

The bombers returned and this time dropped their loads on target. Some fell uncomfortably close. Tom Yarbrough shared my hillside trench and said that even in London he had never been through such a bombing. They fell close on both sides of the CP (I wonder if the Japs have spotted it) and I thought the whole hillside was going to collapse. We found an ugly fragment, still red hot, right at our feet.

*September 4.* General Roy S. Geiger, commanding the First Marine Air Wing, came in last night in a Douglas transport.* His plane had trouble finding the field through the clouds. 90-mm. AA guns fired some rounds to serve as a guide, but that didn't seem to help. Finally the 1st Marines sent up some white flares, which guided the plane in. The bigwigs broke out a bottle of whiskey to celebrate the general's safe arrival.

It rained hard last night. Most of us in the the D-1 tent were dampened if not soaked. It's remarkable how many leaks an apparently sound piece of canvas can spring. More rain today. I hope the Army will take over before the real rainy season sets in.

*September 5.* Raiders came over about 1230. For the first time our fighters made them drop their bombs far from the target. Some bombers attacked the *Fomalhaut* and *Burrows* [supply ships] without any success.

---

*White-thatched and rotund at the age of fifty-two, when he took command at Henderson Field, Geiger was not only a veteran combat flier but an able commander of ground troops. He had been the fifth Marine officer to qualify as an aviator, in 1917, and flown missions in World War I and later in Central American actions. After the Guadalcanal campaign he would become a corps commander of amphibious troops in four major Pacific campaigns, including Okinawa. I never came to know him except for occasional conversations, but he quickly acquired the reputation of being a hard-driving commander of the Cactus fliers.

In the middle of the afternoon the naval operating base reported that the *Fomalhaut* was burning and sinking fast. Gradually the truth came out. A smoke bomb on a destroyer on the seaward side of the freighter went off, and some jumped to the conclusion that she was afire. "Some" included the commander of the N.O.B. [Naval Operating Base]. He immediately phoned D-3 to say the ship was sinking, with all sorts of theories to offer: a delayed action bomb, a torpedo, a mine. But there had been no explosion.

*September 6.* After chow this evening Col. Webb [James W. Webb, commanding the 7th Marines] and some of his staff came to the CP. It seemed to be a great surprise to everyone although a few of the rank must have known of their coming. We all wonder if this means that the 7th Marines are going to land here. Everyone is pepped up at the prospect of their joining us. They have the reputation of being a crack outfit.

*September 7.* Labor Day, and it's raining, just as it always does at home. It rained last night, there was no sun today, and now there's a downpour this evening. A new complication developed last night. Small rats had previously made a few forays into the D-1 tent; last night they made their first large-scale raid. There were at least a dozen, chirping and scampering. The two sides of my bunk seemed to be their main thoroughfares. It's hard to sleep with their constant padding back and forth and squealings in your ears. I finally folded up in my bedding roll and managed to drop off.

Another reporter has come in—Bill Keat of the *Chicago Times*. Where can he sleep? We'll probably put him in the chow house, which Bob Miller has temporarily left to go out raiding with the Raiders at Taivu.

*September 8.* Yesterday Col. Thomas, discussing with Col. Webb the future of this division, remarked that this outfit will lose its value as a striking force if "they" don't get us out of here soon. He said they had better make up their minds whether they want us to garrison the place for the duration or continue as an attack unit. "Offensive troops should never lie behind barbed wire. They get dugout minded. I saw it happen in the last war.''

Tojo pulled an evening raid today. Just after sunset the alarm sounded. We wallowed in our trenches for an hour but no bombs fell in the area. We heard some dropped far away, but don't know where. Col. Edson, who returned from the raid at Tasimboko today, advanced the theory that the Japs have bombed that area, thinking we have a large force out there. Just as the Raiders landed this morning, from two APDs and two Yippie boats, the *Fuller* and *Bellatrix* passed through the channel behind them, with a three-destroyer escort. The Japs may well have thought the whole outfit was going to hit them.

According to Edson the Japs were prepared for an attack from the west out there, but not from the east, and the marines sneaked in their back door. Casualties were small on both sides (the two never really came to grips) but the Raiders found and destroyed much material and supplies, including some 75-mm. artllery.

-------

Native scouts told the division command that the Japanese were making landings near Taivu Point. The staff distrusted (wrongly, as it turned out) the scouts' arithmetic, discounting reports that the Japanese might total two or three thousand. On the assumption that there were only a few hundred, it was decided to send the 1st Raiders and 1st Parachutists, under Edson, to investigate. The two units, now numbering only 700, had been brought from Tulagi to Guadalcanal at the beginning of the month.

On the night of September 7 the raiders embarked at Kukum in two destroyer-transports and two Yippie boats. (Three nights earlier a group of Japanese destroyers had caught two other destroyer-transports, the *Little* and *Gregory,* off Lunga Point and sunk them.) The marines landed at dawn at Taivu Point, meeting no opposition on the beach. As Edson's report noted, an American convoy had passed through the strait behind them, fortuitously giving the false impression that a large force was about to land.

As the marines worked their way west they began to draw fire from light artillery, mortars, and machine guns. They called for air support, and Army Airacobras flew out from Henderson to bomb and strafe ahead of them. Edson began an enveloping movement, through marshy land and thick growth. Early in the afternoon marines overran Kawaguchi's rear base in the village of Tasimboko. They found the place empty of Japanese but full of booty: several artillery pieces, ammunition, clothing, rice, tinned rations, and a powerful radio transmitter. Having neither time nor means to carry much back to Kukum they destroyed most of their rich haul. Late in the afternoon the raiding party returned to the perimeter by boat.

Luckily for the marines Kawaguchi's main body had already moved farther west. And the Japanese general was under orders to keep moving. Higher headquarters had detected a major American convoy moving to Espiritu Santo (it was carrying the 7th Marines from Samoa). Kawaguchi was ordered to seize the airfield before those troops, assumed to be destined for Guadalcanal, could reinforce the American garrison.

Whenever Japanese appeared in the neighborhood the islanders abandoned their villages, and they had done so at Tasimboko. One of those who fled was a five-year-old boy named Francis Bugotu. Thirty-six years later he became the first ambassador (accredited but not in residence) to the United States and United Nations from the newly independent Solomon Islands.

In the original plans for the Solomons operation, it will be recalled, the 2nd Marines were slated to occupy Ndeni in the Santa Cruz Islands. But at Vandegrift's request Turner had released all three battalions to help seize the Tulagi group. In consequence most of the regiment was ashore when Turner had to pull out on August 9. Ndeui had to be scratched as a target—temporarily. Colonel John M. Arthur, commanding the regiment, and about 1,400 of his officers and men were still aboard the ships. They landed in Espiritu Santo where they were ordered, for the time being, to reinforce the local garrison. Most of them remained there until late September.

Admiral Turner, however, had other plans for them. He wanted more raider battalions. There were then two other Marine regiments in the South Pacific Area not committed to Guadalcanal. Turner wrote a letter to Ghormley on August 29 saying that "unless directed to the contrary" he would organize and train provisional raider battalions in all three regiments—the 2nd, 7th, and 8th Marines. He also recommended that Marine Corps Headquarters see to it that raider battalions were included in all Marine regiments sent to the South Pacific. It seemed unlikely, he added, that landing units as large as a division would be needed in future operations; how very wrong he was.

Turner's enthusiasm for raiders was shared by his superiors at Pearl Harbor and Washington. While Turner was tinkering with the 2nd Marines, Nimitz and King met in one of their periodic conferences. COMINCH noted that a third raider battalion was to be formed in the South Pacific, the nucleus of it to be taken from the 1st and 2nd Raiders. Nimitz reported that he had recently given orders to round up all marines in the Hawaiian Islands who were not doing "a man's work"; they could be used as a nucleus for an additional raider battalion. King wondered if those desk soldiers would be suitable for this particular job, to which Nimitz replied that they could at least be used to replace those who *were* suitable.

That conversation took place on September 7. The next day King sent Ghormley a dispatch telling him to put together a raider *regiment*, to be known as a fleet combat team; this could be assigned to MacArthur, who had been asking for amphibiously trained troops, along with the necessary transports and other ships. Ghormley was understandably astonished and perturbed by the opinion, apparently held in high places, that South Pacific marines could be spared from the battle then raging on and around Guadalcanal.

The admirals' fondness for raider units is puzzling. Perhaps a habit of thought survived from the days of Marine landing parties, controlled by ships' commanders, in the Caribbean and Gulf of Mexico. And in the early days of the war the Navy had few possibilities of aggressive action. Among them were hit-and-run raids on enemy bases with carrier aircraft or with landing parties, to do as much damage as possible, knock the enemy somewhat off balance, and improve morale at home and in the service. More significant militarily was the garrisoning of key Allied bases, sometimes with Marine defense battalions. Perhaps a liking for small raider and defense units lingered on from those restricted days. In the Solomons the Navy was having its first experience with the larger-scaled combined operations that would be necessary for the drive across the Pacific.

And we must suppose it was not entirely absent from admirals' minds that lieutenant colonels commanding battalions are more easily manageable than generals commanding divisions and corps. From the first days at Guadalcanal, as I have mentioned, Admiral Turner wanted detachments of marines dispersed at various points along the northern coast of Guadalcanal to prevent Japanese landings. At a time when the airfield itself, the cause and prize of the struggle, was threatened from all sides, such dispersal of meager forces seemed the utmost folly. If we had been able to win control of the local seas—a mission appropriate for someone in Turner's line of work—a stronger case could have been made for weakening the perimeter and setting up isolated detachments elsewhere. Control of the local seas was one of the things we did not have. Nevertheless Turner repeatedly urged, and Vandegrift as often resisted, a dispersal of ground forces. If Turner had had direct control of small units, such as raider battalions, he could have sent them where he wanted to, without arguing with the general.

The creation of raider battalions was a controversial matter within the Marine Corps itself. Commanders of standard infantry battalions resented what were touted as elite units that did nothing—as they saw it—that any properly trained and equipped Marine battalion would not be equally capable of doing. Commanders of divisions saw their best officers and men skimmed off to create raider units. The special battalions were undoubtedly very good, but they achieved their quality at the expense of others.

Let us leave the matter there, without pursuing the pros and cons of the debate within the Corps and between the Corps and Navy. The main point for present purposes is that the establishment of raider battalions was essentially an internal organizational problem of the Corps—to be worked out, certainly, in consultation with the Fleet, for whose larger operations Marine units had to be effectively designed. It was the business of the Marine Corps to organize, train, and equip units that would then be placed under Fleet command. It could be argued that admirals were within their legal rights, once Marine units were assigned to them, to reorganize them in ways that seemed most useful for naval operations. Whatever the legal "rights" of the matter—and they are questionable—it was atrocious military manners for Turner to meddle as he did without even discussing the matter with Vandegrift.

Ghormley, for one, saw the point. He sent Turner's proposal up the chain of command with the comment that the commandant of the Marine Corps should be consulted before there was any reorganization in the South Pacific. Nimitz seemed to agree, commenting that "extemporized organization of Marine Forces should be made only in case of dire necessity." General Thomas Holcomb, Marine Corps commandant, replied that CINCPAC'S comment seemed to take care of the matter. He also noted "with regret" that Turner had not talked things over with Vandegrift.

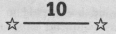

# The Ridge

The division command post, as I have mentioned, had been set up on the southern, or landward, side of a low coral outcropping between the western end of the airstrip and the sea. Accordingly the site was somewhat protected from Japanese naval bombardment. But when those silver, stretched-out Vs of enemy bomber formations passed high overhead to pound the airfield, the CP area often caught a few bombs. I have mentioned several such occasions. We sometimes wondered whether the enemy had located the Marine nerve center and was aiming specifically at us. Colonel Twining dubbed the site "Impact Center." After a month of nerve-wracking indignities, General Vandegrift decided that we ought to move.

About a mile south of the runway the ground slopes up to a grass-covered coral ridge. It runs south for more than half a mile, roughly parallel to the Lunga River, which flows west of it. On either side, in the ravines and flatlands, the rain forest encroaches. Three steep, stubby grass-covered spurs jut into the tangled growth on either side, meeting in three distinct knobs or rises along the spine of the ridge. The Japanese code name for this terrain feature was *Mugabe,* or Centipede.

For its new CP the Marine command chose the L-shaped spur nearest to the airfield, at the northeastern end of the ridge. Close to where the spur joins the main body of the ridge a jeep park was established, from which a short trail led into the headquarters area, masked by towering trees. On either side the spur drops off into deep ravines, forested and brush-covered. Most of the CP tents were put atop the spur. Toward the airfield to the north the 11th Marines, the artillery regiment, set up its own CP. On the southern slope of the spur, away from the airfield, D-1 officers put up tents that served as sleeping quarters. One was for civilian correspondents. Being on the landward side of the spur we were somewhat sheltered from naval gunfire. The location had little else to commend it, as we soon learned.

We set about digging foxholes under the towering trees. Many of these were what the natives call "Tawa," reaching heights up to 120 feet and girths of ten. Often the tree is clear of branches for forty to fifty feet. At the top, boughs and leaves form a thick canopy. At their bases the trunks flare out in buttresses—huge membranes of living wood. The spaces between the buttresses could be even better than slit trenches as shelters, depending on the direction a shell burst or bomb explosion came from.

---

*September 9.* The only good thing about the rain is that it keeps Tojo out of the skies. No, there are two good things: it also keeps the rats down. My sleep has not been disturbed the past two nights. But the rain has kept us from moving the CP and we are living in a quagmire. Perhaps we'll move today. The sun is out but the roads are still terribly muddy.

Later. We did move the CP. In D-1 [personnel section] we never got any official word on it; we just sensed it in the air and started packing. The NCOs were growling because no one told them to move, but they knew they had better start preparing for the exodus before the orders came to strike the office tent. I have learned *something* in the Marine Corps, enough to know that I must take care of myself at such a time. So I requisitioned the press jeep, piled my gear into it, and got moved over to the new CP before the old timers did. Then an afternoon of hard work getting our new tent shipshape. Murray, Banta, Cox [a lieutenant in D-1], and I share a tent. We are a strange foursome. Another tent has been put up nearby for the press.

*September 10.* Just when I am beginning to feel no one gives a damn about what I am doing, and get upset that busy officers duck when I come around to ask questions, someone peps me up by inquiring how I'm getting along. This evening after chow I wandered past the D-3 tent. Colonal Thomas, sitting alone out in front, asked how the history was coming. I told him I was trying to keep it up to date and would appreciate his help some time when the Japs give him a moment's rest. He said he would go over it with me; that he had trouble keeping a diary himself but knew he would remember all important details. And I'm sure he will. He strikes me as the most capable of the staff officers, perhaps the ablest officer in the division. I look forward to the day when he reviews my account of the goings-on here.

I am having trouble keeping up with events. The days seem far too short, and are usually interrupted by one or more air raid alarms. I went around to the Raiders today to get the story of their encounter at Tasimboko—with my charges in tow. There is a split in the Press's ranks. Yarbrough (A.P.), Durdin (*NY Times*) and Kent (*Chicago Times*) are vastly annoyed that Miller and Tregaskis have been here from the start, and never lose a chance to take a dig at them.

There's something in the air tonight. Several (perhaps five) thousand Japs were spotted by native scouts six or eight miles east of here. They may attack tonight.

---

Much more than division headquarters was moving to or toward the Ridge. Kawaguchi's four battalions, for one thing, were approaching. After leaving Tasimboko they had hacked their way inland, at first close to the coast, then up river valleys across terrain that grew progressively rougher as they worked into the network of coral ridges. Kawaguchi was planning a three-pronged attack, aiming at weak points in the southern part of the perimeter. One battalion would peel off and strike across the Tenaru some two and a half miles above its mouth. Three battalions would continue through the rugged ridge country until they were in position to attack along the Centipede. Oka's battered troops in the west would hit at the point where the 5th Marines' organized defenses ended and a more lightly held series of outposts began, southwest of Kukum. Kawaguchi planned, of course, that all three pushes be made at the same time.

From conflicting postwar accounts of those primarily involved, this much seems clear: that Edson was the first to see the narrow north-south ridge, to whose northeastern spur the division CP was moving, as a finger pointing to the airfield and the likely avenue of Kawaguchi's drive; that Vandergrift only slowly and reluctantly accepted this possibility and ordered the raiders and parachutists under Edson's command to the sector south of his new CP. There they were to set up defensive points and patrol to their front for a few days before being relieved by the division's reserve battalion. This was the 2nd Battalion, 5th Marines, which had moved over from Tulagi after the action at the Tenaru on August 21. The Pioneer and Engineer Battalions continued doing what they had done for five weeks—manning little defensive perimeters at night, one across the Lunga from the Ridge, the other at the edge of the airfield just northeast of the new CP, working through the days at hauling supplies, building bridges and roads, preparing beaches for the landing of supplies, and working on the airfield.

A battalion of 105-mm. howitzers moved into positions just south of the airfield to back up the tenuous defenses. Marine and native patrols reported Kawaguchi was getting closer, but no one knew just when or where, or in what numbers, he would try to break through to the airfield. As an effort to get the CP out of the regular Japanese bombing pattern, the move to the ridge was a failure. For when the CP shifted so, as it turned out, did the pattern; enemy airmen began aiming at the Centipede, not the airfield, to soften defenses against the impending attack.

———————————

*September 11.* The bombs fell close today. Tom Yarbrough, Corporal McSwiggin, and I were hugging the roots of a big tree by the D-1 tent. I have never felt them fall so terrifyingly close. Each seemed nearer than the one before, and I thought "the next one will hit us." Then it stopped. Banta is in a fine rage because a correspondent took over a foxhole a D-1 man laboriously dug today. Banta had a point all right. But he does rave on.

*September 12.* The bombing is beginning to get on my nerves. Yesterday, for the first time after a raid, I noticed I was trembling. Am I going to be one of those cases of war neurosis that long exposure to bombardment is supposed to produce? It's annoying to react in this way but I don't know what can be done about it.

I spent the day going through the dispatch file and D-2 journal, catching up on events of the past week. Admiral Turner is up at the general's "palace." He and McCain [who was visiting Geiger] got in last night. Colonal James groaned when I handed him the day's stack of press stories, and said he was "getting damned tired of reading this crap." [We did not yet know what arrangements had been made up the line of Navy commands in the Pacific for censoring and forwarding press stories written on the island. Meanwhile I and then the chief of staff read them to guard against release of information that might be useful to the enemy.]

Last night, further down in the ravine below our tent, a sentry's challenge was not answered and he fired a shot. Major Murray [he had been on a promotion list at the end of August] promptly routed the entire D-1 section out of their sacks and ordered them up the hill. There we sat, feeling rather foolish in the dark while the rest of HQ apparently slept. Banta, in dudgeon as usual, said that if the location of D-1 was so dangerous it ought never to have been put there. Besides, was D-1 expected to act as security for the whole CP? Murray explained to the men that several thousand Japs are working around to our rear and we have a vulnerable position. He warned that they might be called out again soon.

*September 13.* Last night the trouble started. I expect the next few nights will be even worse.

We had just turned in, and not yet fallen asleep, when we heard Louie the Louse overhead (about 2115). He dropped a flare, brilliantly illuminating the whole area, and we knew the show had begun. We took to the hillside and hit the ground. At about 2200 guns boomed out at sea. After half an hour of bombardment the fire fight that had been sporadically going on south of us grew heavier.

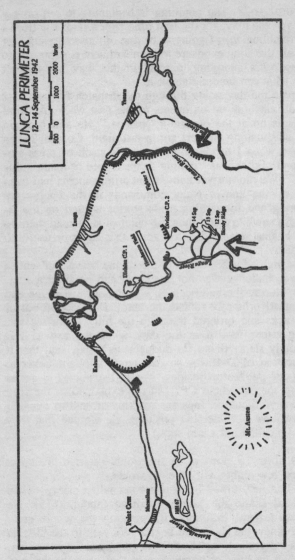

The perimeter during the Battle of Bloody Ridge, with location of division command post before and during the battle

There was the usual front-line medley of rifles, machine guns, mortars, and grenades. From the top of the spur it seemed some of the firing came from the ravine below us, beyond our tents.

Thus until midnight. Then the shelling from the sea started again, so we moved to the southern side of the spur. When the naval guns stopped, the fire fight grew heavy again to the south, so back to the top we went. Brilliant searchlights from Jap ships lighted the shore line. Flares from Jap lines to the south seemed to signal the end of each bombardment and the beginning of each ground attack.

The Jap ships didn't pull away until after 0300, and the damned floatplanes continued droning overhead the rest of the night. Expecting an early morning air raid (the siren sounded about 0530) we took to our foxholes, but the planes never came over.

Admiral Turner left this morning. As our men stretched out on top of the spur last night, straining eyes and ears for Japanese infiltrators, with a naval bombardment coming from the sea, he talked in a loud voice that could be heard through the camp—chitchat, jokes, hearty laughter. Once, when the shelling from the sea started up again, he bellowed: "What are they doing to my boats? That's what worries me!"

The correspondents had a chat with the admiral after dinner last night. They seemed to get the same impression our officers have of him: stubborn, ship-minded, unsympathetic to marines. They gathered from Turner that marines will garrison this place for a long time; no news could be more bitter to the locals. Turner added, "And things will get worse before they get better."

The major called me "Herb" this morning. I could scarcely believe my ears, and felt warmer toward him.

Enemy ships and planes stayed uncommonly late that morning because they expected at any moment to have a signal from Kawaguchi that his troops had overrun the airstrip. According to instructions from Rabaul, once they had come into "complete possession" of the field they were to show two signals on the runway, fifty meters apart, for ten minutes beginning each hour after one o'clock in the morning until sunrise.

Since August 17, on a powerful transmitter somewhere on Guadalcanal (probably the one captured months later at Tassafaronga), the Japanese had been sending out radio messages which our Fleet radio intelligence had been reading. According to this traffic Rabaul, by September 11, was showing great interest in the condition of Henderson Field, asking that the Guadalcanal station make periodic reports. On September 13 Rabaul asked repeatedly if the airstrip had yet been captured. Kawaguchi flashed no signals from the field in the early morning hours of September 13. The flight of planes that swept down from the northwest at dawn (our "false" alert), hoping to land, turned back confused and disappointed.

Kawaguchi's first effort, then, had failed. Of the three attacks he had ambitiously planned, only one had come off on schedule—a hastily organized assault on the hastily formed Raider-Parachutist positions. After the first naval bombardment the night of the 12th—a poor approximation of artillery preparation—the Japanese charged out of the rain forest, two battalions strong, between the Lunga and the ridge. They broke through the raiders' lines, cut off one platoon, and forced the marines to fall back on to the second knob, there joining Edson's reserve company. Kawaguchi began hitting the knoll with mortar fire. Marine artillery was pounding the attackers.

One enemy thrust hit the parachutists. They too were pushed back to the knob. Infiltrators worked through the jungly ravines on their left. But as the night sky brightened, Kawaguchi's men pulled back. By daylight Edson's men tried, without success, to clear the enemy out of ground they had taken between the ridge and the river. Samuel Griffith, who was there (as Edson's No. 2), has described the scene at the Raider CP the next morning. "Red Mike" called his company commanders together and, as he munched on a canful of cold hash, told them: "They were testing, just testing. They'll be back. But maybe not so many of them. Or maybe more. I want all positions improved, all wire lines paralleled, a hot meal for the men. Today, dig, wire up tight, get some sleep. We'll all need it.''

Actually, Kawaguchi had meant to put all he had into the attack the night of September 12–13. "But," he later explained, "because of the devilish jungle, the brigade was scattered all over and completely beyond control. In my life I have never felt so helpless.'' He was out of radio contact with Rabaul, which had ordered him to attack that night; he could not urge a one-night postponement.

Edson's men dug in on the slopes of the second knob. The division's reserve battalion (2–5) moved across the airfield to the northern end of the ridge. A depleted Cactus Air Force got some badly needed accretions during the day. On the 11th Ghormley had released two dozen Wildcats from the stricken *Saratoga* to reinforce the fighters on Henderson. On the 13th eighteen more *Saratoga* pilots and planes flew up to Cactus: twelve dive-bombers and eight torpedo planes. And Navy pilots ferried in eighteen more Wildcats from the *Hornet* and *Wasp*. A sixty-plane reinforcement within three days was a huge improvement, by Cactus standards. But in the same period a whole new air flotilla of 140 planes had arrived in Rabaul.

---

*September 14.* The night of the 12th–13th was mild compared to last night, when the main Jap attack hit. I had turned in early and dozed off, despite occasional bursts of firing from a distance to the south. Then I half awoke to hear the major ordering the men to the top of the ridge. He came in the tent and I asked him what was up. He said that he was moving the men up as a precaution; no details. Banta asked if he should notify the reporters in their tent. Murray said to tell them "the situation" and they could move up if they wanted to.

I heard them all scrambling up the hill, and lay alone in the tent wondering what "the situation" was. I called out to a sentry: "McSwiggin, what's up?" He came over to the tent and said, in surprise, "Didn't you get the word, Mr. Merillat? Colonel Edson says quite a few Japs are filtering through his lines, and everyone has gone up to the top of the ridge.'' I chose to join the others.

The fire fight to the south grew heavier and closer. But I

was so tired that I dozed off for about an hour, stretched out near the D-4 tent. Then, about 2100, a terrific blast woke me up. Shells were screaming overhead. From the front, now about a quarter of a mile away, came the sound of rifles, automatic arms, machine guns, mortars, and hand grenades, and the jabbering of Japs—and maybe of marines too. (Some in the CP claimed they could hear Edson exhorting his men.)

Then I realized that the heavy stuff, the shells, were coming from our own artillery, emplaced down the hill north of us. The bombardment was terrific; it lasted all night. At times the shouting, small-arms fire, thunk-thunk of machine guns, and explosions sounded very close. After 0200 they seemed to recede, the artillery barrage following.

We were close to the batteries of 105-mm. howitzers on the one side, and close to their target, the Japanese, on the other. The shells ripped through the air right over our heads. We could hear artillery officers shout their firing orders. Two shells, falling short, hit the CP, and fragments wounded several men. The offending gun was taken out of action for the rest of the night. I sat by the D-3 tent, listening to reports on the fighting and to plans for pursuing the Japs who, in the early morning hours, seemed to be withdrawing into the jungle whence they had erupted.

But the artillery barrage grew closer again. This time, a bit wary of short bursts, I hit the deck by the message-center shelter. Soon I was glad I had. Tracers started coming into the CP. Firing seemed to come from all sides [a common impression, I am told, on such occasions]. We could make out the distinctive ping of a Jap .25-caliber rifle close by. At least one seemed to be right on the spur where the CP stood, firing at random. Now and then bullets kicked up the dirt nearby. I could have sworn the Jap was right in front of the general's house. (Later I found out he was further along the spur toward the main ridge, near the jeep park.) I slipped further down into the ravine to the north and crawled under a log that stuck up at an angle from the ground. I watched the time closely, praying for dawn.

Then, as it began to grow light, it became clear that my refuge was in full view of snipers on the west side of the

ravine. Others nearby had already begun to find better
cover. I dashed up the slope into the D-2 tent and hit the
deck. Two others closely followed. Just as they got inside
a bullet clanged against a steal plate propped near the
entrance. Ducking around behind the D-2 tent I saw Colonel Buckley, also looking for cover, and asked him where
everyone was (no one else was in sight). He said I could
hop into one of the D-2 shelters, which I did with alacrity,
to find I shared it with Martin Clemens (who didn't recognize me in the dark and was inclined to dispute my right of
entry), a wounded raider, two British missionaries, and a
couple of D-2 marines. By now it was about 0500. I
stayed until the sky was bright.

Sniping continued all day. I got out of the CP early in
the morning with the gentlemen of the press, trying to find
a relatively quiet place to sleep for a while. We went down
to Kukum near the Lunga. Two of the correspondents,
thoroughly shaken, lit out from the CP with only their
typewriters and mess gear, and took the Yippie boat to
Tulagi, there to embark on a transport that was leaving the
area. I decided to try to spend a quiet night outside the CP,
found that Bob Barnes had an extra cot in the Quartermaster's area down in the palms near the beach, and moved in.

---

Such, then, was the experience of a supernumerary staff
officer at the division CP; it was a harrowing night. For
those on the firing line, two or three hundred yards away,
it was a hellish one. From about ten o'clock until daybreak
two of Kawaguchi's battalions made a series of charges
against the Marine lines (twelve distinct attacks, according
to some accounts, but reports of this battle vary greatly in
detail). The Japanese surged out of the jungle shouting
*"Totsugeki."** The attackers bent the defenders in a semi-
circle around the knob where they were making their
stand. In the melee Edson and his officers somehow man-

---

*Aparently this was the shout that has passed into Guadalcanal lore as
"Gas attack! Gas attack!" I regard with skepticism attributions of English phrases to Japanese infantrymen, although I am guilty of having
perpetrated some myself (including this particular one) in wartime writings. *Totsugeki* means "Charge!"

aged to keep their men well enough organized to hold in
the face of mortar barrages followed by determined charges.
We had a weapon the Japanese did not have, one that was
probably decisive in this otherwise unequal battle: the battalion of 105-mm. howitzers. Del Valle's artillery began
pounding the attackers as soon as they had withdrawn to
regroup after their first unsuccessful attempt to break through
Edson's lines. And, as my diary entry indicates, the barrages continued through the night, often churning up the
ground only one or two hundred yards ahead of our own
troops. Once, when Edson called urgently for a concentration, he reported back to the artillery commanders: "Perfect. Now march it back and forth." And march it they
did.

Together the mixed units under Edson's command and
the artillery saved the day—rather, the night. By about
two-thirty in the monning the assaults were petering out.
Edson informed Division, "We can hold." The 2nd Battalion, 5th Marines—the division reserve—was fed into
the lines, to strengthen the left flank. On that side a small
enemy group had broken through just east of the division
CP and got into an unsuccessful fight with a company of
engineers. Before dawn two more efforts, feebler than the
earlier ones, were made to break through on what became
known as "Bloody Ridge," or simply, "the Ridge." They
were thrown back. As soon as the sun was up Airacobras
added to Japanese misery, swooping low to strafe as the
remnants of Kawaguchi's force gathered beneath the canopy of rain forest.

That night Kawaguchi had launched another battalion-
sized attack more than a mile east of the Ridge, where the
lst Marines had thrown a defensive line, including barbed
wire, along the west side of a grassy field bordering the
Tenaru. The Japanese, trying to break through at night,
were thrown back across the field. By daylight six Marine
light tanks, trying to sweep any lurking Japanese out of the
grass and attack the opposite side, lost half their number.
Sporadic fighting continued into the night. The third and
weakest prong called for by Kawaguchi's plan was formed
by Oka's shrunken force in the west. Balatedly, early in
the morning of the 14th, when the issue had already been

decided on the Ridge, Oka struck at a hill in the 5th Marines' sector, southwest of Kukum, but was thrown back.

Kawaguchi had started his ill-omened venture with more than 6,000 of the emperor's finest—five infantry battalions and supporting troops. Of these some 400 had been lost off Santa Isabel and Savo as they were being barged to Guadalcanal. In addition 800 had been killed, wounded, or missing in the Battle of the Ridge. In Japanese doctrine any unit taking more than one-third casualties was considered *zenmetsu*—annihilated, and the two battalions attacking the Ridge had suffered far worse than that. But so had the 1st Raiders and 1st Parachutists, since their first landings in the Tulagi area. Both were ripe for relief and evacuation.

The defenders of Henderson Field were too shorthanded to pursue the enemy although our casualties were not heavy compared to those of the Japanese. In the three actions—at the Ridge, the grassy field by the Tenaru, and the other ridge beyond Kukum—we lost fifty-nine dead and 204 wounded. But the division reserve had already been committed to the southern defense sector, relieving raiders and parachutists. Edson, for one, thought there were still some two thousand Japanese lurking in the rain forest to the south. In this he was wrong. Kawaguchi's shattered brigade was withdrawing. It faced enemies as deadly as marines—exhaustion, heat, hunger, starvation, and malaria.

One battalion made its way back to Koli Point. The main body headed west. Abandoning weapons and many of their wounded, scrabbling for nourishment from forest plants as rice supplies ran out, they straggled in little groups over steep ridges and through tangled ravines. Painfully they made their way south of Mount Austen and across the upper reaches of the Matanikau. The leading elements gained the beach at Point Cruz three days after the defeat at the Ridge, which four decades later was still known on maps of Guadalcanal as "Bloody Ridge."

It had been a close call at the Ridge. Some 2,000 Japanese, backed by another thousand who never got into the battle, had almost broken through Edson's 400 men.

We can only speculate about what would have happened if several hundred soldiers of Nippon had overrun the airfield. Their primary targets were the planes and artillery. They would have overrun the division CP, putting the Marine nerve center out of action at a crucial time. Japanese skips and naval air force units were poised to surge in quickly if the field were captured. Marines outnumbered the attackers by three or four to one, but were spread throughout the perimeter. Presumably they would have had a reasonable chance to retake the field, depending on how quickly the Japanese had run in reinforcements by air and sea, unopposed this time by Cactus planes.

In any event the Marine command, and Navy commands up the line, had solid reasons for thanksgiving that there had been no substantial breakthrough. Even so, they knew that grim times lay ahead. Turner had arrived at the CP with a disheartening appraisal of the situation, put together by Ghormley's staff. It pointed to the massing of Japanese naval and air forces and troops at Bougainville, Rabaul, and Truk. Naval intelligence expected this concentration to move on us within two or three weeks (this was before the Battle of the Ridge). Ghormley then listed the meager naval and air assets he had to counter the enemy's, and concluded that the Navy could no longer undertake to support Guadalcanal effectively.

Only a few—probably only Vandegrift, Geiger, Thomas, and Twining—knew of this pessimistic appraisal, which Turner handed to the general on a standard message form. Thomas carried it in his shirt pocket through the rest of the campaign. On his instructions Twining secretly drew up an undated operation order for continued resistance from the hills, if it should come to that, and filed it in his safe.

In later years Vandegrift was pressed, by a writer who was helping him to record his memoirs, to speak of the times when he might have doubted the outcome on Guadalcanal. The general diplomatically insisted that, however rough things became at times, he was confident that commanders up the line would come through with the ships, planes, and supplies necessary for him to hold on. But he did regard the Battle of the Ridge as the most crucial moment he faced on the island: "Had it been a successful

assault we would have been in a pretty bad condition.''
Indeed we would have been.

Major General Suichi Miyazaki, chief of staff of the
17th Army, would later say: ''The view that the Battle of
Guadalcanal was the decisive battle of the Pacific War
was, I believe, strongly recognized and accepted, not only
by the Army and Navy in the area but also by the IGHQ in
Tokyo, from around the time it was decided that the 2nd
Division should be sent into Guadalcanal''—that is, after
Kawaguchi was thrown back at the Ridge.

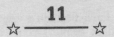
# After the Ridge

Kawaguchi had been ordered to seize the airfield before its defenders' reinforcements arrived. He failed. The Navy would bring in the 7th Marines. The arrival of the First Marine Division's third organic infantry regiment would turn a toehold into solid footing. The Japanese on the island were temporarily in disarray. More than 3,000 fresh and well-trained troops would make it possible for the Marine command not only to strengthen the cordon around the airfield but also to expand it and to pursue more vigorously the enfeebled enemy to the west.

General Vandegrift and his staff decided to move the CP back to its original site in the northwest corner of Henderson Field. The shift meant that Major Snedeker and his hard-worked signals people, who had just finished laying telephone wires to the spur of the Ridge, must now re-lay the network. For a week or two after the mid-September battle the Lunga perimeter was bustling as units were shifted, supplies brought in by the 7th Marines moved to dumps, and the division nerve center reestablished at Impact Center.

---

*September 18.* At 1415 I'm having a moment of peace and quiet in the guest tent at Sniper's Roost. We are getting ready to move again. D-1 will be in the 5th Marines' area near Kukum, in a warehouse with a concrete floor. Such high living! From where I'm sitting on top of the ridge I can see the thicket down in the ravine where my foxhole is—the one I so laboriously dug the day the Japs began their attack, the one which I never used, but which may have given shelter to some Jap.

The 7th Marines arrived today; a very good sight to see. Lunga Roads is full of ships. I counted six transports or cargo ships and at least seven escort vessels, including some cruisers. We expected Tojo to be over early today but there has not yet been an air raid. It is ominously quiet.

We saw a heartbreaking incident on the beach where the 7th is unloading. A Douglas dive-bomber was circling low overhead, presumably on anti-submarine patrol. Suddenly anti-aircraft guns on one of the ships opened fire on it. At least one other ship joined in, and the bomber began trailing smoke. The pilot headed toward the beach to crash-land, running into more fire. The stars on the plane's wings were plainly visible, but the newcomers refused to believe the plane was ours. When the poor devil crashed in the water a great cheer went up from the apes on the beach, who seconds before had stampeded into the palms. Those of us who knew our own planes couldn't believe our eyes and ears. We shouted: "Don't shoot, goddammit, it's *our* plane, *our* plane." But there was no stopping it. A Higgins boat brought in one of the crew, badly shot up. The other, I suppose, is dead.

Bob Miller is leaving today. Frank McCarthy came in to relieve him for the United Press, with Jack Dowling of the *Chicago Sun*. Our correspondents now number four. I'm sorry in a way to see Bob go. He's a good reporter and a cheery, pleasant chap. But he was beginning to get on our nerves, and his brassiness and lectures on strategy infuriated some of the staff.

---

When the 7th Marines left Samoa their destination, after a pause at Espiritu Santo, had not been decided. Earlier Ghormley and Turner had wanted to send them to Ndeni in the Santa Cruz Islands. All along that had been one of the targets in the Joint Chiefs' directive for Task One. At the beginning of September the Joint Chiefs left it to Ghormley's discretion to decide when to occupy Ndeni. The top Navy commanders still favored developing a base on the island as a backup for Guadalcanal or a fallback position if Guadalcanal were lost. Vandegrift strongly opposed sending the 7th Marines to another island in the rear when it was badly needed to bolster the defenses of Henderson Field. Even after Turner came to the view that the regiment was needed on Guadalcanal, he wanted to land it, not within the Lunga perimeter, but at Koli Point.

During his visit to Guadalcanal September 12 and 13 Turner personally saw what the defenders of Henderson Field were up against. Vandegrift later said he thought that noisy sojourn had "given him religion." Before he left Guadalcanal Turner promised to send the 7th Marines wherever the general wanted them, and that, of course, was to the Lunga perimeter. Ghormley still hesitated to send the regiment to Cactus; the island might be indefensible with the South Pacific's meager assets. But Ghormley finally consented.

The move got under way. A strong naval task force built around two aircraft carriers—*Wasp* and *Hornet*—provided distant cover for Turner's convoy. Strong forces of the Imperial Navy, including carriers and battleships, had gathered north of the Santa Cruz Islands and in the upper Solomons, and submarines had been deployed across the Americans' likely avenue of approach. The Japanese were prepared to move in quickly once Kawaguchi had captured Henderson Field, and they were also looking for the very convoy that was trying to run their blockade.

The 7th Marines were safely delivered, but at heavy cost to the Navy. In the afternoon of September 15 Japanese submarines torpedoed and sank the *Wasp* and the destroyer *O'Brien*, and tore a big hole in the battleship *North Carolina*. The *Hornet* recovered most of her sister stinger's planes, some of which later flew in to reinforce the Cactus Air Force. For the time being the *Hornet* was the only operational American aircraft carrier in the South Pacific. We did not know of this sad toll at the time and were full of undiluted delight to see Turner's ships bearing the 7th Marines on the morning of the 18th.

Although he had landed the regiment inside the perimeter Admiral Turner had not lost his liking for dispersal of troops and for amateur generalship. A few days later, reporting to his superiors on the successful delivery of the 7th Marines, he reverted to his favorite thesis: the only way to stop enemy landings ("pending a decided strengthening of local air and naval defense forces'') was to establish "one or two additional outlying strong positions with intermediate minor posts." Those units, he thought, should be able to defeat "minor" landings. His "personal reconnaissance" at Cactus as the Battle of the Ridge was starting had convinced him that, while "wide deployment of a force along north Guadalcanal was essential to ultimate security," the immediate threat to the Lunga perimeter had called for reinforcement there.

Having landed the 7th Marines where Vandegrift wanted them, Turner had ideas as to how the general should use his newfound strength. He sent the Marine commander a list of "items" on which "now would seem to be the time to push as hard as possible." One, on which the division command hardly needed prodding, was to push westward. Turner put the idea in terms bound to raise Marine hackles: "I believe you are in a position to take some chances and go after them hard." Another item: Rupertus, from Tulagi, should "establish detachments" in and around Florida Island.

One item was to be a venture of Turner's very own. He was going to send two companies of the 2nd Raider Battalion to knock out Japanese observation posts at the southern tips of Malaita and Guadalcanal, and perhaps leave them there until they could be relieved "with other line troops." "We want to coordinate these operations with you and get your approval of the plan," he graciously added.

Vandegrift promptly replied that the Japanese, after further reinforcement, could be expected to attack the perimeter again soon. Reserves within the perimeter were still so few that the Japanese threat could be serious. As for the 2nd Raiders, they were needed in the Lunga position to relieve the 1st Raiders, now depleted and fatigued by their long series of engagements—on Tulagi, on Florida, at Tasimboko, and on the Ridge.

During the weeks when Turner had been prodding the Marine command to diversify its landholdings, as if the one major investment were wholly secure, the Japanese navy had had, and would have for many weeks to come, virtually uncontested nighttime control of the waters around Guadalcanal. Four five-inch coastal guns, emplaced on both sides of Lunga Point on September 10, could keep Japanese destroyers at a respectful distance. On bright nights, when the moon was near the full, Cactus planes sometimes tried to bomb Tanaka's ships as they unloaded to the west or east. Results were dishearteningly meager, hardly justifying the frequent crackups that resulted from nighttime operations. For sixty-three nights, however, no American surface force tried to block the Tokyo Express.

---

*September 20.* I "slept" at Sniper's Roost again last night. A battalion of the 7th Marines had just moved into position south of the CP. Still being green troops they were trigger happy. They blasted away all night with rifles, machine guns, and hand grenades.

The CP is still in process of being moved back to the old location. This has gone on for nearly a week now. The Press has to find places to lay their heads and get some chow as best they can. I try to do what I can to get them permanent quarters in the new (that is, the old) CP, but they must depend almost entirely on the whims of the new HQ Commandant [a colonel transferred from a line command], who is no whiz.

Tonight the correspondents and I will stay at Impact Center, if we can get a tent up in time. It will be pleasant to be away from Banta's perpetual growling. But there will be problems in being detached from an organized section, such as getting water, toilet paper, etc. The new chief of staff may take things in hand and see that the boys are taken care of.

Which reminds me—changes impend in high places. Colonel James is returning to Wellington to take command of the rear echelon. Thomas, who has just been elevated to a full colonelcy, will be chief of staff. Edson will command the 5th Marines.

My four charges are out in the boondocks today, accompanying Edson on a patrol. Those raiders are really rugged. Less than a week after taking 50 percent casualties [actually 30 percent] on the Ridge they are back on the job—at the colonel's own request. I saw them marching across the airfield last evening, on their way to take up positions to the west. I felt my throat tighten as they filed past, but saw no gloom in those faces. What an outfit.

---

The latest promotion list had resulted in a surfeit of full colonels—seven more than the division table of organization called for. General Vandegrift had the unpleasant duty of deciding which ones to send home for reassignment to other units where they were needed. The departure of the chief of staff was no surprise. It had been obvious from the outset that Jerry Thomas was the guiding mind and driving force of the First Marine Division. Clearly he was the staff officer on whom the general leaned most heavily. He was given a field promotion to full colonel and made chief of staff. Twining succeeded him as D-3.

"The air," Thomas later told a friend, "was thick with bitterness." Making the change all the more personally difficult, James's wife was a cousin of Thomas's, and the regular officer corps was a tight little group, if not exactly a family.

A couple of weeks before the change I found Colonel James sitting glumly on a little rise within the CP at Impact Center. My dealings with him had been almost entirely concerned with the review of reporters' news copy before it was flown out to Pearl Harbor. That day he said, "Why do they write so much about Colonel Thomas?" I could not give the reply that came to mind: Thomas is forceful, clearheaded, and obviously on top of the situation.

Vandegrift and Thomas had been unhappy with the performance of the 5th Marines from the day of the original landing, and thought the regiment and its battalions were poorly led. Colonel Hunt, the regiment's commanding officer, was among those who departed at this time. As I have already mentioned, "Red Mike" Edson was given command of the 5th. There was ironic justice in this transfer. When Edson had been appointed to lead the 1st Raiders, early in 1942, he had skimmed off the cream of officers and noncoms in the 5th Marines to fill his own ranks. If the regiment had not measured up thus far on Guadalcanal, it was due in part to the 1st Raiders' raid on its best men. Now Edson would have the job of bringing up to the mark units he had earlier depleted. There were those who thought Red Mike overzealous in leading his men into battle, too indifferent to casualties. But he did lead.

_____

*September 21.* Still no tent for the Press. They get comfortable quarters and good chow elsewhere in the division; only at the CP do they have to sleep on the ground and live as though it was the day of a landing. The whole CP is unsettled but I notice that everyone else is taken care of.

The 7th Marines were at it again last night. From the noise you would have supposed a major battle was going on. I understand they found two Japs at dawn—one naked, another in Marine clothes. It seems inevitable that troops never before under fire will shoot all night at nothing. It's easy to talk, of course, when you are not in the firing line yourself.

*September 22.* No air raids for eight days now. The Japs on the island have withdrawn to lick their wounds and reorganize. They seem to have given up trying to land to the east but have made more landings to the west. All day today our planes worked them over out toward Cape Esperance. The last plane over that area this evening reported several fires and one terrific explosion among the buildings the Japs have put up back of the coconut groves at Visale. They must be short of food and badly demoralized. We hope so; we also recognize the threat in these continuing landings.

I succeeded in rounding up three cots for the Press and one for myself. Still no tent for them. The HQ Commandant has done nothing but give them a corner of his own pyramidal tent, pending the erection of another. I finally mentioned the Press's bunkless state to the general and chief of staff, and cots promptly appeared.

Major General Harmon of the Army [Millard F. Harmon, commanding general of U.S. Army Forces in the South Pacific] was at the CP tonight. The three major generals—Vandegrift, Geiger, and Harmon—were chatting by the latter's jeep. I don't know what that constellation of six stars portends, but like to think that Harmon's visit means the Army is preparing to take over.

Till Durdin of the *New York Times* left this morning by plane. I'm sorry to see him go; he is one of the most intelligent and thoughtful of the newsmen who have descended on us.

*September 23.* Last night was a shoes-off night. ["Shoes-on nights" followed sightings of approaching Tokyo Express runs, when we could expect to be shelled.] Bright moon, bad flying weather to the north, no reports of slant-eyed warships approaching. I even went so far as to take my socks off. For the first time I have a cot I can call my own, with a mosquito bar properly rigged. I slept deeply. On these quiet nights, with a brilliant tropical moon in the skies, it is hard to realize there's a war on and that we are in the front lines.

Had a bull session near the D-2 tent, sitting in the moonlight with Pappy Moran, Martin Clemens, Jim Whitehead, and Karl Soule [all in the intelligence section]. Lt. Col. Griffith, who now commands the 1st Raiders, stopped by and joined us. Pappy [a Japanese language expert and our chief interrogator of prisoners and translator of captured documents] is a delightful man, full of bounce and verve at God knows what age. He annoys a lot of marines by praising the good qualities of the Japs and contrasting their behavior with that of our rougher types—to the latter's disadvantage. But he thinks clearly and sees better than most do the moral issues of this set-to.

————————————

"Pappy," whose real name was Sherwood F. Moran, had spent much of his life as a Christian missionary in Japan. Just before the war he was a YMCA secretary there. Bald, blue-eyed, wearing thick-rimmed spectacles (which often rested halfway down his nose as he peered at the person he was talking to), he had a penetrating voice, crackling with energy. He admired the subtleties of the Japanese language. His own mastery of it and his sympathetic manner seemed to put at ease the prisoners he interrogated.

Occasionally Pappy interrupted a colloquy with a captured soldier to remark: "How well he said that," or "What a nice phrase he just used." Pappy seemed to endure with patience the monotonous stream of obscenities common in Marine as in all military talk, including the favorite adjective. But one day he turned on a man just back from patrol and barked at the startled marine:"Yes, I know, you saw the fucking Jap coming up the fucking hill and raised your fucking rifle and shot him between the fucking eyes."

One of Pappy's duties was to decide what passwords should be used. D-2 notified all units of the words that would distinguish friend from foe on occasions, especially nocturnal, when there might be doubt. These countersigns were passed to units in batches covering periods of two weeks. Pappy chose words containing the letter "L," which Japanese cannot pronounce in a convincingly American way. "Honolulu" and "lollipop" turned up early in Pappy's lists. "Sullenly" and "surlily" came later. "Guadalcanal" would have served well, but I do not recall that it was ever used.

---

*September 23* (continued). There has been a shameful amount of looting in this lash-up. Measures taken against it are half-hearted. When the parachutists were leaving, their gear was broken into—even locks were sawed off. When rations are landed a lot of food is always pilfered. The dead are robbed of their belongings by their own buddies. We hear tough talk of shooting a few looters as an object lesson, but I haven't heard of its being done.

---

The prim little note about looting shows that the press officer was still naive. Larceny and soldiers, of whatever uniform, seem to go together. There were, of course, none of the opportunities for large-scale "liberating" that Europe offered. What could be worthwhile to steal on an isolated battleground, apart from obvious items such as food? Wristwatches, cameras, flashlights, rings, and Japanese swords, flags, and similar souvenirs were substantial treasures in that setting. Even such things as a clean shirt or pair of socks had scarcity value.

I did not hear of one of the most spectacular—and

somehow gratifying—pieces of thievery until long after the war. General Vandegrift mentioned it in his memoirs. He offered to swap a case of Scotch with General Geiger for a case of bourbon, the division commander's preferred drink. The whiskey was duly delivered to Geiger's shack, and he later offered Vandegrift a drink. In a cursory, then frantic search of his modest quarters the air general found no Scotch. Someone had made off with it. Mere second lieutenants like myself envied the brass's evening nips.

The move back to Impact Center involved personal changes for me beyond those connected with housekeeping arrangements and getting a press center set up. Nothing was said about it, but it became clear that now I was to be more directly under the wing of the chief of staff than of D-1, which had moved to another site. The staff had got used to my being around. Clippings about the early days on Guadalcanal from Stateside papers had begun to trickle back and apparently it was decided that the public relations types were not doing badly.

I moved more freely in and out of the operations section, the division's cerebrum. To keep up the daily Record of Events I had to read the message files, and D-2 and D-3 journals, and to note all other major developments. I was at the same time writing a running account of the campaign, which turned out eventually to be the first rough draft of a campaign history.

The CP now had a much more substantial look than earlier ones had had. We now had tents with wooden decks, connected by all-weather walks. Everyone had cots with mosquito bars. Engineers built new dugouts, sturdier than old ones and covered with palm logs and sand bags. The general got a shower bath, fed by a pipeline from the Lunga. The new comforts were welcome; the air of permanence was not.

---

*September 24.* I had a long talk with Martin Clemens, who told me of the British administrative system for the Solomons, the wartime coastwatching system, and native organization. He gave me an acount of events he saw and reported from his mountain hideout while the Japs were in the Lunga area. [Nothing could be published about the coastwatching network during the war. The Japanese were well aware of the system, and were constantly trying to hunt down individual watchers, but published stories might give them useful tips about organization and locations.]

Felt miserable today—a touch of diarrhea, stomach cramps after evening chow, and a degree and a half of fever. I feel better now that I've washed off the day's accumulation of dust. Colonel Thomas told me today to get the Record of Events ready for use in a report on our mission. Of all times, I would be so sick that I had to lie in my sack all afternoon and didn't even get a start on the job.

Still quiet on land, at sea, and in the air. The lull is bound to end soon. Colonel Edson thinks the Japs will hit again when they have built up a force of about five thousand, with air and sea support. He doesn't look for an attack until the dark of the moon, after October 1.

At last the press tent is up and we are squared away in relative comfort. Just as we began to feel settled two more correspondents arrived: Douglas Gardner of the *Sydney Herald* and Sherman Montrose of Acme Newspictures. They will have to sleep on the deck tonight, until I can round up two more cots. Glad to see them in a way, particularly an energetic news photographer. But I am lazy and dislike having life further complicated.

*September 26.* I practically finished the Record of Events today and gave it to the chief of staff. It seems to be what he wants. But there are big gaps in it. Getting an account of operations from D-3 is like snatching a bone from a hungry dog. Much that happens is not committed to written reports. How in hell am I ever going to get a complete record of what goes on?

Feeling better today. I got down to the river for a swim, which always helps lift the spirits. This evening it is raining, for the first time in many weeks.

*September 27.* This afternoon we had our first air raid in two weeks. They came over about 1400. I took to a slit trench on the hill behind the CP. Lying there I could see vapor trails left by fighters, twisting and turning. Then suddenly I saw the bombers—seventeen of them in a shallow, uneven V. They were coming right overhead. If they were aiming at the CP they did a good job. One "daisy-cutter" slashed the D-2 tents, levelling the officers' tent and setting much of their personal gear on fire. Another hit about ten feet from the D-3 tent and their new dugout. The interior of their tent is a mess. Another bomb landed about fifty feet from me. This one must have been armor-piercing. It dug a hole about twenty feet deep but only a yard wide. Never saw a bomb crater quite like it. There were many other hits close by. I wonder if those devils *were* aiming at the CP.

The press missed the show. They have gone down to the Matanikau. Three battalions are out there, attacking the familiar Jap position, trying once again to envelop and destroy them. Our folks think they have caught 500 Japs out there. 2-5 [2nd Battalion, 5th Marines] is this side of the river, the Raiders are coming in from the south, and 1-7 is coming in from the west. Edson is directing the show. Maybe he can accomplish what no one else yet has. I haven't yet heard any reports on the action. We laid down a short artillery barrage about 1300—Zero hour. Our planes have been heckling the Japs. I hope the noose is pulled tight this time. Matanikau has been a thorn in the flesh ever since we got here.

*September 28.* Yesterday down at the Matanikau they ran into more trouble than they expected. There turns out to be a Jap force of about 3000, not just 500, in that neck of the woods. The Raiders couldn't get across the river. Major Bailey was killed, Colonel Griffith wounded. Murray told me today that we have suffered about 300 casualties in three days. Our battalions were pulled back from the river. Something new is cooking; the Japs will be hit unless they hit us first. A prisoner brought disturbing news. He says his people plan to land a whole division to attack us. It wouldn't be so bad if our strength wasn't scattered around the whole damned perimeter.

We had another air raid today, but no bombs fell near us at the CP. It was a great day for our side. Twenty-three out of twenty-five Jap bombers were shot down, which should give Tojo pause. Apparently the Zeros stayed clear of the fight. We didn't lose a single plane. Twenty-three of them! It certainly lifted our spirits. Last night everyone was glum over the news from the Matanikau. Scarcely a word was said in the officers' mess. Today everyone was laughing and chattering. What will be the mood two or three days from now?

[The action at the Matanikau, and others near that ill-omened river, are reported in the following chapter.]

*September 29.* Waiting for an air raid. Condition Yellow was just flashed.

Last night Fred Kidde [an assistant D-2] remarked: "Herb, you seem to be one of the few people around here who has stayed on an even keel." This surprised me, for there have been times when I have definitely wobbled. I told him that I have my bad moments. Fred, saying that we all have them, launched into a discussion of personal clashes—how men in the field get on each other's nerves, quarrel needlessly, blame each other for things that go wrong. I sometimes think these intramural squabbles are as nerve-wracking as enemy bombs and gunfire. There is too much of everyone-for-himself, growling about little things, criticism of others, bitter recriminations. Perhaps it is unavoidable and characteristic of all forces in the field.

*September 30.* [Admiral Nimitz was about to arrive, and would award some medals.]

I worked until ten o'clock last night, by the light of an electric flashlight in the chief of staff's tent, writing up citations for the men to be decorated today. People would be amazed at the behind-the-scenes activity in hero-making: quarrels over which cases are most deserving; seeing that all ranks and units are properly represented; dressing up weak cases to make them appear stronger; last-minute switches from one class of decoration to another.

While writing up one citation I happened to mention that it didn't seem to make a case for a Navy Cross [next to the Medal of Honor the highest decoration for exceptional bravery]. Thereupon it was summarily decided that the man in question wouldn't get one. I was taken aback, feeling that my remark had robbed a brave man of his reward. It so happens that in this case the man is sure to get a high decoration later. The number of decorations is determined, not by the number of deserving cases, but by the number and types of medals the admiral totes along. I wouldn't like to have to pick who gets what; there are so many real heroes here.

Admiral Nimitz was due to arrive at three o'clock in the afternoon, but it rained violently and his plane was delayed. He finally got in about four.

*October 1.* The admiral decorated our heroes this morning. About 0630 they gathered in front of the general's shack. Nimitz came out and everyone snapped to attention. He read a statement praising the Marines for their performance here, saying he was "inordinately" proud of them. Then he read the citations and pinned the medals on the recipients. Fortunately the rain had stopped and the sun was bright but not yet scorching. The clearing in front of the general's quarters was full of onlookers. Most of the field officers on the island were here. Someone up on the hill shouted "Chow!" and someone else started to sing loudly until he was told to "knock it off up there." The general, whose Navy Cross came as a surprise arranged by Nimitz personally, smiled at the singing.

*October 2.* The Japs staged a couple of surprise air raids last night—nothing big, but annoying. One plane came over about 2100, another (perhaps several) about 0400. They dropped some light stuff. I didn't have time to get into my shoes before the bombs fell early this morning, and hit the deck right outside the tent. Everyone is cussing the radar this morning for not giving the alarm.

This morning I took the press jeep and drove over to the new fighter strip near Kukum. It is a beautiful spot, with a steep coral ridge on one side, a coconut grove on the other. [The new airstrip, known as Fighter No. 2, would come into operation in December. Fighter No. 1 was a grassy field, about a mile east of the original airstrip, that Seabees had leveled early in September.]

*October 4.* White women in the Lunga perimeter! They didn't stay long. In fact, they never got ashore, but their presence is no less astonishing for that. Seven sisters from the Visale Mission at the northwestern tip of the island were finally evacuated from that hot spot by Captain Clemens's schooner. They came into Kukum and there transferred to the cargo ship *Fomalhaut*, to be taken away from this pest-hole. Seven sisters and seven priests. It caused, of course, a great stir.

I doubt if the distinctive condition of nuns has ever been so menaced—in words—by so many at one time. It is well that their chaste ears did not hear the obscenities that travelled from Kukum to the Tenaru—all in good clean Marine fun, of course. I had heard that they were coming in by air, and speculated on the agitation it would cause in sisterly bosoms to see the open heads [latrines], the all-but-naked marines in all directions, and the thoroughly naked marines in the Lunga. I supposed the MPs would be dispatched to chase bathers and launderers from the river, to clear a path fit for virgins across this thoroughly male area. But it never became necessary. The bishop came ashore and visited the CP, but bishops are not so interesting.

*October 5.* John Hersey of *Time-Life* came round to the CP this morning. It turns out he was a classmate of Jim Murray's at Yale. Hersey gave me, for clearance, a story such as I had not seen before. It was a gloomy article, highly critical of the planning of this campaign, of the naval command, equipment, morale—scarcely a cheerful or commendatory word in it. Murray read it, and seemed to think it okay except for some inaccuracies. I still felt certain the chief of staff would go through the roof if he read it. So I urged Hersey not to submit it, and it is on hold for the time being. [Hersey was gathering material for a *Time* magazine cover story on Vandegrift, which appeared in the November 2 number. The Stateside press, after initial euphoria over the first Allied offensive in the Pacific, was becoming increasingly critical of the naval commands in the area.]

Here's a tidbit that turned up today from one of Whaling's Scout-Sniper detachment—a jolly bunch! "We found a Jap sleeping under a tree. I gave him three vertical butt strokes with my rifle. The Jap was still breathing when the last man in the column passed, so he put his bayonet through the Jap's throat. He didn't mean to stick it all the way through—just a little bit—but it went in so easy it pushed right through. I guess the Jap had been wounded. He had only one hand. Guess it was from mortar fire. Looked pretty messy." All this was told calmly and dispassionately, by one who was obviously a connoisseur in the art of killing Japs.

Among the new full colonels whom Vandegrift decided to keep on Guadalcanal was William J. Whaling, who was executive officer, or No. 2, of the 5th Marines when we landed. A solidly built, ruggedly handsome Minnesotan, aged forty-eight, Whaling had served with the Marines in France in World War I and later in Nicaragua and Haiti. He was known throughout the Corps as a crack marksman with pistol and rifle. He was also a keen woodsman.

From the outset of the Guadalcanal operation patrols probing beyond the perimeter had had trouble finding their way and keeping in touch during their forays into the rain forest. The Marine command yearned for bushwhackers of the kind who had learned to get around on similar terrain on various Caribbean islands, and thought Whaling was just the man to produce them.

Whaling was given the job of training promising candidates; men who were hunters and hunters' guides were favored. He taught his expert marksmen to move quickly and silently through the jungle, to lie in wait patiently to set an ambush, leaving no traces. They learned every track and possible track in key areas outside the perimeter, such as the upper Lunga. Then they could quickly guide their own or other battalions to any spot where they might be needed. Operating in small groups of ten to fifteen, they became experts at patrolling and laying ambushes. Whaling himself often led patrols and was sometimes put in command of battalions guided by men of his Scout-Snipers Detachment.

As executive officer of the 5th Marines, Whaling had been among the earliest to venture beyond the Matanikau. Now, after the Battle of Bloody Ridge, he would again be involved in the frustrating effort to eliminate the enemy's main position, west of that river. The main burden in that attempt would fall, initially, on the 7th Marines, who had just landed.

I have referred several times to actions beyond the Matanikau, setting some aside for the time being. Now I turn to that region, the crucial batleground of the long campaign, reviewing what had happened there earlier as background for an account of the new push.

# 12

✩ —————— ✩

# Matanikau—
# Sinister River

Late in 1566 Alvaro de Mendana, nephew of the Spanish
governor of Peru, sailed west from Callao. His two ships
were in search of gold and also, according to his chief
pilot, of infidels whom Spanish missionaries could guide
"into the vineyards of the Lord." On February 7, 1567,
the little expedition sighted an island. Mendana named it
Santa Isabel del Estrella—"of the star" because Venus
was visible in the morning sky that day. A local chieftain
sent Mendana a well-intended but unwelcome present: a
quarter of a boy, including arm and hand, together with
some edible roots. The Spaniards buried the grisly re-
mains, to make clear that they were not cannibals.*

On Santa Isabel the Spaniards built a little brigantine in
which they set out to explore nearby islands. After a visit
to the one they named Florida they proceeded to the bigger
island to the south. This one they named Guadalcanal,
after the home town of Pedro de Ortega Valencia, the
expedition's commander of troops. At the mouth of a
river—probably the one we called the Metapona—"Indians"
in canoes gave the visitors a rope and began to haul the
brigantine toward the beach. But their intentions were not
friendly. Locals on the shore began throwing stones and

---

*Cannibals and headhunters were then to be found in some of the
Solomons. Their practices, it seems, had more to do with appropriating
the spirit or "mana" of the deceased than with a desire for food,
although we may suppose that a taste for human flesh, which is said to be
delicious, also played a part. Some anthropologists have reported that,
contrary to wartime stories, the Guadalcanalese were never cannibals.
New Georgia Island was the main center of headhunting in the Solomons.

shouting "Maté, maté"—or, "Kill, kill." The Spanish party did not improve relations when they fired shots, felling two islanders, and later landed to seize provisions—roots, ginger, and a hog.

A month later Mendana brought his two ships to Guadalcanal. They anchored in the shelter of a spit of land and planted the cross. They named the spot Puerto de la Cruz, Port of the Cross. In modern times the little peninsular appendage has been called Point Cruz. Shaped like a lopsided arrow head, it juts into the sea about three-quarters of a mile west of the Matanikau River. Four miles west of Point Cruz, early in 1942, stood the collection of huts known as Kokumbona (in the official gazetteer, Kakambona).

Matanikau, Point Cruz, Kokumbona: the three place-names became most disagreeably familiar to Americans during the autumn of 1942. The five-mile stretch of coast and inland ridges between the river and Kokumbona village was the scene of the campaign's most protracted ground fighting, which seesawed back and forth across the Matanikau and the tangle of grassy heights and jungly ravines to its west.

The river itself races down from the mountains, fed by many tributaries, through a volcanic fissure, emerging placidly in its lower reaches. Except when the stream is in spate, during monsoon rains or heavy storms, its mouth is blocked from the sea by a sandbar through which a little water trickles into the sound. The Japanese connection with the river and five-mile stretch beyond was even more bloodily intimate than ours. The area was their main permanent base during the campaign and their last major redoubt.

The Japanese first drew blood themselves on that front when the Goettge patrol landed just west of the river's mouth. When three survivors of the doomed reconnaissance party made their way back to the perimeter two companies of the 5th Marines crossed the river (one of them landing from boats west of Point Cruz) to look for survivors or to bring back the dead. After putting up a brief fight at the river's edge the Japanese melted into the forested ravines. As we earlier saw, if this patrol found

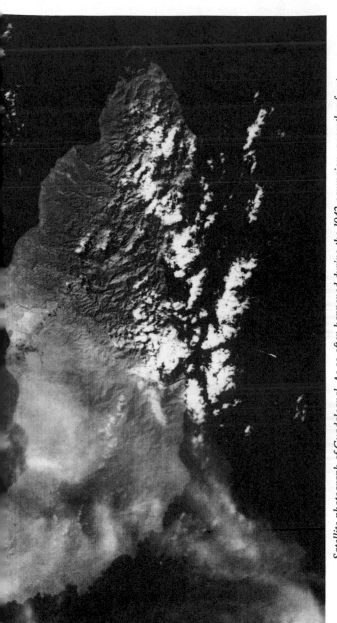

*Satellite photograph of Guadalcanal. As so often happened during the 1942 campaign, a weather front is moving in from the northwest.* U.S. GEOLOGICAL SURVEY

*Marines starting out on a patrol, near the mouth of the Lunga River.*
U.S. MARINE CORPS

COMMAND
POST NO. 1

COMMA▸
POST NO

*Sites of the division command posts are indicated on this photograph
of Henderson Field. CP No. 1 ("Impact Center") was on the landward side of the low ridge in the left foreground; No. 2, at the ex-
treme right, at the beginning of Bloody Ridge.* U.S. MARINE CORPS

*Major General Alexander Archer Vandegrift, USMC, commanding general of the First Marine Division, Reinforced.*
U.S. MARINE CORPS

*Vice Admiral Robert L. Ghormely, USN, Commander, South Pacific (COM-SOPAC).*
NATIONAL ARCHIVES

Vice Admiral Frank Jack Fletcher, USN, commander of the Expeditionary Force and aircraft-carrier groups.
NATIONAL ARCHIVES

Rear Admiral Richmond Kelly Turner, USN, commander of the Amphibious Force—convoy, naval screen, and embarked troops. U.S. NAVY

Colonel Kiyanao Ichiki, commanding officer of the Japanese troops who were destroyed in the first counterattack against the Lunga perimeter.
U.S. MARINE CORPS

Lieutenant General Masao Maruyama, commanding the Second ("Sendai") Division, which attacked the American perimeter around Henderson Field in October. U.S. MARINE CORPS

Lieutenant General Harukichi Hyakutake, commanding general of the Seventeenth Army, assigned the mission recapturing Guadalcanal. U.S. MARINE CORPS

*After the Battle of the Tenaru. A tide has washed over the bodies of Ichiki's men killed in their attack at the mouth of the Tenaru on August 21.* U.S. MARINE CORPS

*Bloody Ridge. The knobs in the background at left center were Colonel Edson's final defensive position. The airfield lies just beyond the trees in the background.* U.S. MARINE CORPS

*Vice Admiral William F. Halsey, USN, and Colonel Gerald C. Thomas, USMC, in the Division CP at Guadalcanal. Halsey became Commander, South Pacific, in the middle of October. Thomas was Vandegrift's operations officer at the time of the landings and later his chief of staff.* U.S. MARINE CORPS

*Japanese tanks knocked out at the mouth of the Matanikau River on the night of October 23-24. Point Cruz appears in the background at the left.* U.S. MARINE CORPS

*Defensive line south of Henderson Field. A double-apron of barbed wire is being installed in a corridor hacked out of the jungle. The Sendai Division tried to break through a line of this kind late in October.* U.S. MARINE CORPS

*Lieutenant Colonel Merrill B. Twining in the operations dugout at Vandegrift's CP. Twining succeeded Thomas as operations officer in September.* U.S. MARINE CORPS

the buried bodies of Goettge's group along the shore—and Whaling was sure they had—they had been washed away in a storm before marines next ventured across the river.

On August 18 and 19 the 5th Marines launched a three-company effort. One company was to traverse the sandbar, another to cross about half a mile upstream and work its way back toward the sea across the ridges, and the third was to be boated to Kokumbona to cut off a possible enemy withdrawal to the west. The company at the river's outlet was pinned down by fire from the other bank. The inland unit made its way to Matanikau village and got into a brisk fight before the Japanese withdrew into the hills. The landing party at Kokumbona ran into fire as they came ashore, but again the Japanese pulled back. They were not ready to make a determined stand west of the Matanikau—not just yet.

For a few days after these indecisive encounters the Marine command was preoccupied with the stronger threat posed by Ichiki on the other side of the perimeter. Having disposed of that at the Tenaru, they decided on a more ambitious venture west of the Matanikau. A large combat patrol—the 1st Battalion, 5th Marines—landed early in the morning of August 27 near Kokumbona, with orders to move east along the coast to Matanikau village at the river's mouth. There it was to reembark in landing craft in time to be back within the perimeter by nightfall. Giving highest priority to protection of the airfield, and fearing a Japanese assault across the beaches, Division then and for many weeks later ordered that all large patrols return to the perimeter at the end of the day.

The battalion near Kokumbona, beyond the range of artillery support, found the Japanese vigorously defending positions dug into one of the ravines that debouch into the coastal strip. The attack bogged down. At two-thirty in the afternoon the battalion commander called for boats to carry his men back to Kukum. Reaction at the division CP to that request was sharp and angry. Vandegrift and his operations section were convinced that the battalion commander was not pushing his men hard enough, and he was asking for boats to pick them up two hours before sundown. They ordered him to turn over command to his No. 2 and directed Colonel Hunt, the regimental commander, to go to Kokumbona under orders to continue the attack.

The battalion dug in for the night and resumed the attack shortly before dawn the next morning. By that time the Japanese had again withdrawn into the bush. The marines made their way with little opposition to Matanikau village, whence they returned by boat to the Lunga perimeter. The trans-Matanikau region was well on its way to acquiring its sinister reputation. Several careers were ended or badly frayed in that fruitless encounter. And there were predictably some harsh recriminations against division HQ for expecting too much of commanders whose troops were operating in terrain division staff officers had never seen. Some officers in the regiment thought the division command had a prejudice against the 5th Marines. Certainly Vandegrift and his staff were unhappy with their performance, beginning with the first day of the landings. In any event, there was soon a complete shake-up in the regimental and battalion commands.

A month passed before there was further action beyond the Matanikau. By then Kawaguchi's effort, coming mainly from the east, had been thrown back. And by then the 7th Marines had come in. With a fresh, well-trained, well-led regiment on the island Vandegrift again decided to turn to the west. He now had enough troops both to defend the airfield and to launch an offensive across the Matanikau.

He quickly put the newly arrived 7th Marines to work. Most of the regiment was assigned to strengthen the weak southern sector of the cordon. There they hacked a corridor through the rain forest and strung barbed wire along it. The narrow clearing was hardly a "field of fire" but at least attackers would have to come somewhat out in the open and cut through double aprons of prickly steel before they could get at defenders.

One battalion of the 7th was immediately used more aggressively. It was to head inland across the seaward slopes of Mount Austen, gain the opposite bank of the Matanikau about a mile and a half from its mouth, and push across a network of ridges toward Kokumbona, now thought to be a key Japanese base. This was to be a four-day patrol by the 1st Battalion, commanded by Lieu-

tenant Colonel Lewis B. Puller. As his troops approached
Kokumbona the 1st Raiders, now commanded by Lieutenant Colonel Griffith, were to strike across the Matanikau at
its mouth and also head for Kokumbona.

"Chesty" Puller, a veteran of World War I and various United States ventures in Central America, had a
short, sturdy body with a head that seemed mostly forehead. Beneath that impressive dome was the face of a
tenacious bulldog. Like Whaling, he liked to strike
out on his own without much control from higher headquarters—one of those who preferred to be out of touch
with Division, unless he was in trouble. He was one of
the most colorful and effective troop leaders in the
Corps.

Puller and 1–7 set out from the perimeter on September
23 and soon ran into enemy groups on Mount Austen.
The battalion suffered casualties. The evacuation of
wounded over rough terrain drained away more of his
numbers; it took four able-bodied men to carry a wounded
one in a litter. This was one of the occasions when Puller
was glad to be in touch with the CP; he called for
reinforcements.

The 2nd Battalion, 5th Marines, was sent to join him.
But the combined force, on approaching the Matanikau,
found their crossing barred by heavy machine-gun and
mortar fire. Puller probed northward along the river gorge,
drawing fire from the opposite bank all the way. He
headed for the river's mouth. Again the two battalions ran
into heavy fire and, as the four days allotted for the patrol
ended, gave up hope of gaining the other side.

If the results were disappointing the Puller expedition
had at least demonstrated that the Japanese were in considerable strength all along the Matanikau, and were determined to prevent a crossing. Headquarters decided on a
larger and more complicated effort to dislodge the defenders. Colonel Edson, now in command of the 5th Marines,
was put in charge.

Griffith's understrength 1st Raiders were ordered to do,
on September 27, what Puller had been unable to do a few
days earlier—force a crossing upriver. The raiders were to

make their attempt near the "Jap Bridge."* At the same time the 2nd Battalion, 5th Marines, was to cross the river near its mouth. Puller was named Edson's second in command for this operation. If the battle developed favorably, his own battalion, temporarily commanded by Major Otho Rogers, was to land from boats west of Point Cruz and hit the Japanese from the rear.

Nothing worked out as planned. The battalion of 5th Marines could not force a crossing at the river's mouth. Inland, the 1st Raiders were blocked in the river gorge by an enemy unit that had come over the river at night. Colonel Griffith was wounded in this encounter and his executive officer killed. The 1st Battalion, 7th Marines, was sent out by boat to land beyond Point Cruz under the mistaken impression that the raiders had successfully gained the other bank. The troops of 1–7, boated from Kukum, got ashore without opposition, but as they moved inland Japanese troops almost surrounded them. Major Rogers was killed.

Meanwhile an air raid against Henderson Field had knocked out communications at the division CP. There was no way for headquarters to give coordinated orders. The new commander of 1–7 could not inform others of his plight. A Marine dive-bomber pilot saw a plea for "Help" spelled out in T-shirts on the hillside where 1–7 was beleaguered. Puller quickly came to the rescue of his boys. He rounded up landing craft, boarded a destroyer-minesweeper which had earlier supported his battalion's landing, and headed for the beach beyond Point Cruz.

Fire from the destroyer's guns, from machine guns on the landing craft, and from the entrapped marines' own weapons formed a protective circle around the men as they pulled back to the beach and clambered aboard the T-boats. They made their way back to Kukum by nightfall. The dismal day's work cost the marines sixty-six dead and 100

---

*The "Ippon" ("Log") Bridge, as it was called on captured Japanese maps, was what the name implies: forest logs thrown across a narrow point in the gorge. But "Nippon" was a more familiar word than "Ippon." The crude span became known in operations orders and reports, and later in Guadalcanal lore, as the "Nip" or "Jap" bridge.

wounded, with no benefit to the cause beyond a clear demonstration that the Japanese now occupied the territory from the Matanikau westward for at least a mile and were determined to defend their turf. This was not just the tattered remnant of Kawaguchi's brigade. Fresh troops had moved in, in unknown numbers. No longer would they fade into the bush as they had done in August.

I have already mentioned the gloom at the CP that night. Among senior officers in the division some had special reason for glumness. For Edson the operation was the first in which he had commanded the equivalent of a regiment. For Twining it was his first major performance as D-3. Vandegrift's Final Report on the Guadalcanal campaign, written many months later, speaks of the errors in the action at the Matanikau: trying with insufficient force to cross the river when it was known resistance would be stiff, committing forces piecemeal, "sketchy arrangements" for supporting 1–7's landing. Perhaps for Twining, who wrote the report, the passage had an element of *mea culpa*.

Postbellum recollections, by three of the officers most intimately involved in that day's painful events, vary considerably. As Twining recalled, energetic and aggressive troop commanders, angered by their earlier repulse along the lower Matanikau, prodded him into authorizing a new attack. On the other hand, Puller and Griffith viewed the plan, according to their later writings, as one too hastily devised and ordered by the division command, without adequate knowledge of the terrain or of enemy strength, and with an ambiguous and improvised command structure. In any event, it was a bad day for our side.

Although division headquarters did not know it, the Japanese were gathering their strength for a drive of their own across the Matanikau, to dislodge marines from the east bank. In the next clash along that detested stream each side would consider itself on the attack.

Vandegrift scheduled his offensive for October 8. So did Lieutenant General Masao Maruyama, the newly arrived commander of the Second Division, also called the Sendai Division after the district in Japan where it had been recruited. The Marine plan of attack was much like that of late September except that troops were to be landed from the sea behind enemy lines, beyond Point Cruz, only if it should prove profitable to do so as the battle developed. This time the U.S. attack would involve the equivalent of two regiments. Two battalions of the 7th Marines were to cross the Matanikau about a mile and a half inland and drive down two roughly parallel ridges, half a mile apart, toward Point Cruz.

At the same time a battalion of the 2nd Marines and the scout-sniper unit, all under Whaling's command, were to move along a ridge line, also beyond the Matanikau but closer to the river than the other two prongs, headed for the stream's mouth. Meanwhile the 5th Marines, plus the remnant of the 1st Raiders, were to push across the river near its mouth. The common objective was to clear the trans-Matanikau area of Japanese, open the road to Kokumbona (where Division planned to set up a forward patrol base) and to keep Japanese artillery from moving east.

The Japanese planned almost a mirror image of this operation, but on a more modest scale with more limited objectives. They expected to put troops on the east (our) side of the Matanikau, both at its mouth and also further upstream, trapping whatever Americans could be caught in between the two prongs and clearing the way for artillery to move to the right bank. The task was to fall mainly on the newly arrived 4th Infantry Regiment, commanded by Colonel Tadamasu Nakaguma.

On October 7 marines began moving into bivouac areas near their jump-off lines. Approaching the Matanikau's mouth, the combined 5th Marines—1st Raiders found Japanese troops in stubborn possession of the right bank. They were still there as night fell, compressed within a bridgehead extending a quarter of a mile from the sandbar. That night the rains came, in torrents. The jump-off had to be delayed a day.

---

*October 8.* At 1515 it seems things are not going too well at the front. Dowling just got back with the story that the 5th Marines, or at least a good part of them, have not yet got up to the Matanikau. Jap machine guns are still raising hell this side of the river. Edson told his boys that if they didn't clean them out before dark they would be in trouble. They didn't, and they were. Japs hit them with knives and bayonets and Company I was badly cut up. The Raiders were called into the battle. I suppose Edson thinks they are the only troops he can rely on. A half-track is up there now blasting at a Jap machine gun at short range with its 75-mm. gun. It rained steadily and hard all morning.

Apparently Whaling's boys got across the Matanikau but I hear the 7th are not yet in action. No one here is quite sure what is going on. The 3rd Battalion, 2nd Marines has gone out in boats, apparently to make a feint in back of the Japs. Some confusion, here again, as to just what they will do. And night fast approaches.

Some good news. Scuttlebutt says a regiment of Army is due to arrive the 10th. By itself the rumor would be worthless, but NOB [Naval Operating Base, at Kukum] seems to confirm it, and they are often right. Also, the general, at the front, was heard to tell Edson some "very good news" which the colonel agreed was "the best news I have heard on this island." Of such odd pieces a beautiful rumor is built. I'll believe the Army is coming when I see them cross the beach.

Later. I found out the rumor is true. An Army regiment is due to arrive on the 13th. It's supposed to be very secret; everyone on the island knows about it except that most are off on the date and few know the identity of the regiment—the 164th Infantry [commanded by Colonel Bryant E. Moore].

———————————

As the entry indicates, there had been a fierce battle, often hand to hand, as Japanese soldiers in the right-bank pocket tried to break out and regain the left bank by crossing the sandbar. Some got across. By daybreak the awkward bridgehead had been eliminated. Marines occupied the right bank and this time Division meant to hold it.

On the 9th the three battalions upstream crossed the river, swung to the west, and then hooked to the north. Only Puller, in the left most column of the three, met serious opposition. Chesty's men came across a battalion-sized Japanese bivouac area in a ravine just south of Point

Cruz. Puller called for artillery concentrations. A down-pour of shells and mortar fire against the far side of the bowl-shaped ravine drove enemy troops up the nearer side, where the battalion's automatic rifles, machine guns, and grenades cut them down. Caught between the two walls of fire some 700 troops of the 4th Infantry perished; the figure was confirmed by a diary found later.

Meanwhile Division had received warnings from Turner that the menacing concentration of enemy ships, planes, and troops in Rabaul and the northern Solomons was about to move toward the island in the biggest offensive the Japanese had yet mounted. As always, when a major threat to Henderson Field impended, the Marine command re-called troops to the perimeter. Battalions west of the Matanikau recrossed the river the evening of the 9th, without attempting to reach Kokumbona.

---

*October 9.* The gentlemen of the press are again out near the Matanikau. They were badly out of sorts yesterday—growling at each other, complaining about everything, after an unpleasant day at the front in a driving rain. They take it out on each other and everyone else within earshot. Seeing men die around you, watching the stretchers bring out the wounded, with artillery and mortar fire blasting your ears and machine-gun bullets pinging all about does not promote good spirits and bonhomie.

I was in the D-3 tent this morning when they decided to order the withdrawal of units from the other side of the Matanikau. The order had just been issued when the general, who has been conspicuous at the front the past two days, called in to order a drop to a unit he had spotted across the river (which in his eyes was doing nothing), instructing them to secure the point west of the river mouth. He also ordered the 5th Marines to stay in position and MPs to bring up Jap prisoners to bury their dead.

It seemed, said D-3, that the CP was now out there on that sand spit. There was much tearing of hair over the general's interference with operations plans, but also a conclusion that he is a fine old man, "the best we have had."

---

John Hersey (who stayed with a navy-flier friend on the airfield instead of at the CP) wrote a vivid vignette of the battle for the Matanikau. *Into the Valley* tells of one company's troubles during the three-day clash. It was a weapons company, ordered to put its machine guns and mortars on the banks of the Matanikau a mile or so from its mouth. The Japanese, already installed on the opposite side of the gorge, brought the marines under heavy fire and forced them to pull back, taking their wounded with them over slippery and precipitous ridges. No account of the Guadalcanal campaign better gives the flavor of the fighting there—the struggle against weather and terrain as hostile as the enemy, the confusion of battle, the difficulty of keeping contact with other units, along with the terror and frustrations of coming under mortar and machine-gun fire with no effective way of fighting back.

In Hersey's book the captain commanding the weapons company is apologetic to the visiting reporter when his men have to withdraw without seeming to have accomplished anything. Hersey is a bit apologetic, too. But if this segment of the larger encounter was going badly the whole operation was a distinct success. The Japanese had lost most of a battalion to Puller in the ravine behind Point Cruz, a battalion of Nakaguma's 4th Infantry that now would be out of the larger battle for Henderson Field that was about to start. Even more important, Hyakutake's troops had been driven from the east bank of the river, from its mouth to a point more than a mile inland. That key terrain would stay in American hands for the rest of the campaign.

On October 9 General Hyakutake, commanding the Seventeenth Army, came ashore near Tassafaronga. He took personal charge of the ground troops for the drive that the Imperial Navy and Army were about to launch. He was greeted with bitter news: one infantry battalion had just been annihilated and his troops had lost their bridgehead at the mouth of the Matanikau. It would no longer be easy to put artillery and tanks across the sandbar. But he readjusted his plans.

☆ ─────── ☆

# October Crisis:
# First Phase

The Tokyo Express chugged on. Some nights as many as a thousand fresh troops came ashore west of us. General Hyakutake had a plan for capturing the airfield. Before he launched his ground attack, however, he must have more troops than could be carried by Rat. They must be brought in by large transports. But planes from Henderson Field would surely sink slow troop carriers before they reached the island. Therefore the Cactus Air Force must be knocked out of action long enough for a convoy to come in. Accordingly the first phase of Japanese attack plans for October called for heavy bombardment by air and sea to destroy American planes and make their field temporarily unusable.

An important Express run was scheduled for October 11. It was bringing in long-range artillery and eighteen-ton tanks, among other items. To carry the heavy stuff, two seaplane tenders came along with six Japanese destroyers. A separate force of cruisers and destroyers under Rear Admiral Aritomo Goto came behind the troop carriers and supply ships. Its mission was to start a series of naval bombardments of Henderson Field. The softening up had begun during the day when the largest flock of aerial raiders yet to be sent against us came down from the Rabaul complex: seventy-seven planes, bombers and Zero fighters, in four waves. Fortunately for the defenders heavy clouds hid Henderson Field and the raids did little damage.

By skillful timing and maneuvering fast Japanese Rat destroyers had managed for weeks to dodge most of the Cactus dive-bombers that usually attacked them in one presunset strike. And for two months the Express had made its runs without interference from American surface ships. The U.S. Navy planned an unpleasant surprise for the night of October 11.

Rear Admiral Norman Scott, with two heavy and two light cruisers and five destroyers, was covering the movement of important reinforcements for the American garrison. At last a U.S. Army regiment was coming in. It was the 164th Infantry (minus one battalion), built around National Guardsmen from North Dakota. Scott had been drilling his ships in tactics of night combat, a Japanese speciality, and was looking for an opportunity to avenge the defeat at Savo Island. After sundown on the 11th Scott's ships sped toward the northwest tip of Guadalcanal to intercept the Tokyo Express.

Shortly before midnight the battle was joined. As he had hoped to do, Scott took the Japanese by surprise. His column was somewhat in disarray at the crucial moment because it was engaged in reversing course just as Goto's ships emerged from the Slot. Nevertheless he managed to bring his column across the bows of Goto's, in a classic crossing of the T. American fire, beginning at the short range of three miles, devastated the leading Japanese cruiser (killing Goto, whose flagship it was), and sank the second cruiser in line. One of the flanking destroyers was also sent to the bottom. But the Japanese quickly recovered from their initial surprise. They heavily damaged the cruiser *Boise*. The American destroyer *Duncan*, mauled by both friend and foe, was sunk.

Meanwhile, as the sea battle raged, the eight Japanese ships in the reinforcement run were busily unloading on the northwestern coast of Guadalcanal. Cactus dive-bombers pursued them in the morning, sank one destroyer and crippled another. Altogether, in the Battle of Cape Esperance, the Japanese lost one heavy cruiser (with heavy damage to another) and three destroyers. And Henderson Field had been spared a bombardment. It was an impressive enough victory to give Washington an opportunity to announce good news from the Solomons. Along with it some bad news was also finally released—our losses in the Battle of Savo Island two months earlier.

More than incidentally, Scott's force had run distant

interference for the convoy bringing the Army's 164th Infantry Regiment to Cactus. Turner successfully shepherded the North Dakotans to our shores early in the morning of October 13. Their arrival substantially improved the American position for the coming battle. But COMSOPAC's decision to dispatch them to Guadalcanal had been a close thing.

The Santa Cruz Islands, it will be recalled, were among the original targets in Task One under the Joint Chiefs' directive of July 2. To Navy planners that island group, 350 miles east of Guadalcanal, looked like an important backup base for the new acquisitions in the Solomons and an added protection for the line of communications with Australia. The debacle at Savo Island and landing of the 2nd Marines on Tulagi had forced temporary deferment of the occupation of Ndeni, the Santa Cruz island chosen as the most promising base.

Turner, Ghormley, and their superiors still wanted to occupy and develop Ndeni, although to do so would drain off men, arms, and construction equipment needed at Guadalcanal. From time to time the South Pacific admirals would propose landing a Marine or Army unit at the Santa Cruz site. As the American hold on Guadalcanal came to seem more tenuous, the attractions of Ndeni seemed to grow; it could be a fallback position. On October 1 Turner again offered a plan to occupy Ndeni: in two convoys he would take in two Army battalions, Seabees, and other units. Ghormley tentatively agreed.

Then Major General Millard F. Harmon stepped in. Like Vandegrift, he was alarmed at the admirals' tendency to disperse ground forces instead of concentrating them to win the battle then raging at Guadalcanal. Harmon, an Army Air Force officer, was the commander of all Army forces in the South Pacific. His was an administrative command, for all operations in the area were directed by the Navy. But he was consulted and listened to when operational plans involved Army ground and air units.

On October 6 Harmon wrote a letter to Ghormley, strongly urging that any available Army troops be sent to Guadalcanal, not Ndeni. If Guadalcanal were lost—and it might well be if Americans there were not immediately reinforced—Ndeni would also be lost. Its occupation would be "a diversion from the main effort and dispersion of force." "It is my personal conviction," he wrote, "that the Jap is capable of retaking Cactus-Ringbolt [Guadalcanal-Tulagi] and that he will do so in the near future unless it is materially strengthened." The loss of Guadalcanal would be a major gain for the Japanese—a threat to the New Hebrides, protection for operations against New Guinea, and denial to us of a jumping-off place against Rabaul.

Ghormley stuck to his decision to occupy Ndeni but agreed to defer action once again. The Army troops he had planned to use—the 164th Infantry—would be used instead to reinforce Guadalcanal.

When the 164th Infantry came across the beaches on October 13, they got a warm reception from thankful marines and a hot one from the Japanese. In their first twenty-four hours ashore, the Lunga perimeter was pounded as it had never been pounded before, and never again would be. When it was over, I felt as if I should seek out a newly arrived North Dakotan and tell him, "Look, it's really not always this bad."

The proceedings started with an air raid, shortly before noon. Twenty-four twin-engined bombers escorted by Zeros whined high over the field. For once our fighters were not warned in time; they rose too late to break up the attack. The full bomb loads fell on Henderson Field and its environs. Two hours later another formation—fifteen bombers—again bombed the runway. And again, our fighters did not get enough advance notice to climb to the attackers' altitude. The two raids blasted holes in the main runway and in the grass fighter strip. Worse, about 5,000 gallons of precious aviation gasoline went up in flames.

At dusk we heard what we had long expected and feared to hear—Japanese artillery registering near the airfield. The first rounds fell short of the runway. Firing stopped after about fifteen minutes. When the first shell whistled and crashed on the western end of the main runway, near the CP, we supposed it was an unannounced air raid and headed for our dugouts. Technical Sergeant "Butch" Morgan, the general's cook, grabbed up his helmet and joined in the scramble. I was standing near the entrance to a dugout, near the general's "house," when another shell screeched through the air nearby. Vandegrift listened thoughtfully and said, "Why, that isn't a bomb. It's artillery." Butch Morgan, who had been through the massed fires of World War I, took off his helmet in disgust. "Hell," he said, "only artillery! I thought it was a bomb."

The Japanese had succeeded in landing not only fresh troops and supplies but 150-mm. (about 6-inch) howitzers. We then had nothing bigger than 105-mm. howitzers, too short-ranged to fire effective counterbattery. Like each new menace the Japanese long-range guns quickly got a nickname. They were called collectively Pistol Pete.

The general's cook could shrug off the personal danger from a familiar weapon. The general had much more than personal danger to think of. Long-range howitzers, firing from Japanese-held territory well west of the Matanikau beyond the reach of our own artillery, were a serious threat to Cactus Air Force operations, and therefore to the American hold on Guadalcanal. One essential of mutual air-sea-ground defense was that ground troops keep enemy artillery beyond range of the airfield. It was an awkward situation for the Marine command.

The night of October 13–14 was the purplest of what Colonel Thomas called our "purple nights." Japanese planes were over from time to time through the hours of darkness. Soon after a steady blast from the sirens signaled "Condition Green" (all clear), they would wail a warning that more bombers were coming in. Pistol Pete fired intermittently at the airfield. We stumbled in and out of our shelters as the planes came and went. There was some respite after midnight. At about one-thirty sirens again sounded "Condition Red" (enemy planes overhead).

———————————

I grumbled and stumbled out of bed, thinking at first it was a false alarm. How little I knew. About 0215 Louie the Louse came over and dropped a flare. I watched with interest from the mouth of a dugout. Then a star shell burst like a 4th of July display right smack over the airfield, followed by the heaviest blasts I have ever heard. It didn't take me long to get underground. There I huddled with about a dozen others, at the bottom of a quaking heap, while we went through the worst bombardment we have yet had. The shelter shook as if it was set in jelly. Bombs, artillery, big naval shells made it sheer hell.

At the height of the bombardment I was certain the field would be a shambles. We no sooner got back to our tents than relays of planes again started to come over. The first bomber-load caught me on the way to the dugout. I dived into an open hole and thought my end had come. They hit close. We finally got out of the shelter as the sky began to lighten about 0430. Jap artillery opened up again at about 0530, trying to hit the runway. But some planes got off in the midst of the shelling, so apparently it was still falling short. I haven't heard it open up since the planes got off, but we must now expect it at any moment of the day or night.

----

Two battleships—the *Haruna* and *Kongo*—had stood about ten miles out, near Savo Island, and shelled us for eighty minutes. For the occasion the Japanese were using a new kind of special bombardment missile, thin-skinned with a tremendous surface burst, instead of the armor-piercing shells that would be used against ships. In the morning marines and soldiers, awed and wide-eyed, picked up 14-inch (360-mm.) base plates and huge chunks of casing.

Admiral Tanaka had been one of those watching the bombardment out at sea. The scene, he later wrote,

> baffled description as the fires and explosions from the 36-cm. shell hits on the airfield set off enemy planes, fuel dumps, and ammunition storage places . . . The night's pitch dark was transformed by fire into the brightness of day. Spontaneous cries and shouts of excitement ran throughout our ships.

"A most unenviable experience," said Henry Keys of the *London Daily Express,* who, with six other correspondents, had just arrived on the island. Within thirty hours after "The Night" six of the eight pressmen then on Guadalcanal departed. I would have been happy to join them. Only Keys and Robert Cromie of the *Chicago Tribune* remained. Those who decamped wrote of their experience with a last dateline, for the time being, from Guadalcanal. One perfervid report had this to say: "It is almost beyond belief that we are still here, still alive, still waiting and still ready. We cannot write in this madness but we keep notes with shaking hands. . . . The worst experience I've ever been through in my life. . . . It goes on hour after hour. I begin trembling."

The most serious damage, as the Japanese intended, was to Cactus Air Force and its field. On the morning of October 13 thirty-nine dive-bombers had been in condition to fly. After the Night only four were operable. A dive-bomber squadron from Marine Air Group 14 had flown in on the 13th. In the bombardment that night its commanding officer, executive officer, flight officer, and two pilots were killed. Fortunately there was less damage to the fighter planes and pilots, dispersed on the grassy field that served as Fighter No. 1.

The Japanese kept the pressure high. Again on the 14th we had two air raids. Throughout the day Pistol Pete fired intermittently at the main runway, gradually increasing his range. Cactus Air Force had to abandon the main runway temporarily. A few undamaged B-17s, which had been staging through the island, managed to get away to Espiritu Santo. The heavies did not return for several weeks. Our lighter planes—Marine and Navy dive-bombers and fighters and Army fighters still in condition to fly—switched their operations to the grass surface of Fighter No. 1.

Meanwhile the Japanese convoy for which the assorted bombardments had been meant to clear the way started to move toward the island. In the afternoon of the 14th our search planes spotted six big transports, escorted by eight destroyers, north of Santa Isabel. A supporting force—a battleship, three cruisers, and four destroyers—was in the Slot. Ground crews at Henderson Field worked feverishly to get more dive-bombers into flyable condition.

By late afternoon, when the convoy was rounding the southern end of Santa Isabel, the Cactus air command managed to send out two small strikes. They reported they had sunk one transport but they had not. The transports pressed on in the gathering dusk. They were safe from any more air strikes that day. Again, that night, the emperor's ships shelled us, but this time only with 8-inch missiles from cruisers—small potatoes compared with the 14-inch variety.

---

*October 15.* Glum faces today. Five [actually, six] transports were brazenly unloading this morning within sight of Kukum. Our aviation gas is exhausted. Some of our planes miraculously survived the pounding they got the past two nights, but they are helpless without fuel. They are flying some avgas [aviation gasoline] in, and have found a dump of drums that had been forgotten. The Japs have the run of the waters around Guadalcanal. They have landed unknown thousands of troops in the past two nights. They have made determined attempts to knock out the airfield, and have come close to succeeding, what with bombings, artillery shelling, and naval gunfire.

Where is our Navy, everyone wants to know. I still have confidence in them, and feel sure they are doing something to counter this threat. If not, we are lost. We have no idea, of course, what is happening elsewhere.

---

It was profoundly disheartening for the defenders of Henderson Field to see ships bearing thousands of fresh enemy troops unload a few miles to the west, beyond Point Cruz. As some marines said, "They are landin' 'em faster than we can kill 'em." After two days and nights of bombing and shelling only three Cactus dive-bombers were in condition to take off as the eastern sky began to lighten that day. Two of the three fell into bomb or shell craters before they could get off the ground.

Again ground crews feverishly patched up patchable planes. Within an hour of sunrise four dive-bombers attacked the transports through heavy antiaircraft fire and a screen of Zeros. Later, small groups were able to continue the pounding. By the end of the day three transports were beached and burning. Three were able to pull away. All six had unloaded their troops and most of their cargoes. Three of the gallant Douglas Dauntlesses were shot down that day.

My diary entries for this period mention several times a shortage or complete lack of aviation gasoline. "Complete" lack is too strong; there was always a little. But there was a chilling message from Geiger's air command the morning of October 15, when Japanese transports were unloading to the west: "We have no more avgas." When the few planes then flyable were fueled, they said, the supply would be exhausted.

Marines started a desperate search for caches that might have been forgotten. As a precaution against air raids and naval shellings, dumps of avgas had been widely scattered. Drums were partly buried and covered with earth. Lieutenant Colonel John D. Macklin—a Reserve officer from Ohio, where he had been superintendent of schools, who was now the division ammunition officer—told me of his own search. He had supervised the movement of avgas to dumps in the early days.

Taking with him another officer, so that if anything happened to one the other would know where the precious fuel was hidden, Macklin found about a hundred drums. Pioneers found about 200 more in their area. An additional hundred turned up near Kukum, where a new fighter strip was being built. Macklin spotted another lot of forty drums, then twenty-five more. By the end of the day more than 400 drums had been found. The night of October 15 two Yippie boats slipped over from Tulagi with about 200 drums.

---

*October 16.* More shelling last night [the fourth night in a row] by cruisers and destroyers. The day has been a quiet one—two or three air-raid alerts but nothing came over.

Later. We had a raid after all. In the evening eight Jap dive-bombers hit a big barge that had brought in avgas. Fortunately all the drums had been taken off. The barge was unloading bulk gas at the time. It's a bad loss, but not as grave a development as some other things that have been happening.

It's interesting how men's spirits rise and fall in times like these. After the Japs had blasted us from the sea and landed thousands of troops, and our planes were grounded through lack of gas, everyone was profoundly depressed. Many were about at the breaking point. The reporters were most unhappy and eager to get out, except for Cromie and Keys.

A flight of our fighters came in tonight [nineteen Wildcats, led by Lieutenant Colonel Harold W. Bauer]. It was a welcome sight when we realized what they were. But men's nerves are so on edge that we watched the formation uneasily while it circled high above, with our helmets in hand and an eye on the nearest shelter. What a blessed let-up of tension when we made certain they were ours.

———————

At sundown on the 13th, before the Night, General Geigar had had ninety planes of various types able to take the air. Before the reinforcement by Bauer's squadron, Cactus was down to thirty-four planes after three days and nights of bombings and shellings. Only nine of them were fighters. The last of the "originals," pilots and crews from Marine and Navy squadrons that had carried an almost intolerable burden through September, had left by now. Mangrum, leader of the first dive-bomber squadron to arrive, was the last of his group to be evacuated. Seven of his pilots had been killed, four wounded, and the rest taken out for hospitalization. Mangrum alone was able to walk to his evacuation plane.

Through the early part of October, the Eleventh Air Fleet at Rabaul had been able to keep its operational strength up to roughly 180 by drawing reinforcements from rear bases and carriers. Geiger had only about a third that number early in the month. Strength on both sides fluctuated violently. Even a new tactic adopted by the Japanese at Rabaul after heavy bomber losses at the end of September did not staunch a steady hemorrhaging. For several days they sent only a few bombers, as lures and as guides for swarms of Zeros. The bombers would turn back short of Guadalcanal, leaving the Zeros to whittle down American fighter strength in dog fights. Though faster and more maneuverable than the sturdy Wildcats, Zeros had two telling handicaps: their fuel tanks and cockpits were far more vulnerable than the Grummans' and they had to carry belly tanks, even in combat, for the long return haul to Rabaul or other bases. In the first two weeks of October the Eleventh Air Fleet lost twenty-five Bettys (their twin-engined Mitsubishi bombers) and about eighty Zero fighters.

During the critical mid-October days our Navy had only one aircraft carrier still able to operate in the South Pacific. The *Hornet* task force came up from the neighborhood of New Caledonia as the crisis mounted and patrolled south of Guadalcanal. A day too late to intercept the Japanese convoy, her planes helped to bomb the beached enemy ships and supply dumps beyond Point Cruz. A Japanese carrier, the *Zuikaku*, was on a similar patrol north of Malaita, in distant support of the ships that were pasting us nightly and landing reinforcements.

Our "little" Navy—of destroyers, minelayers, submarines, tugs, and barges—was deeply and heroically (a word not to be used lightly in that setting) involved in the dangerous game of blockade-running. They were trying by every available means to keep a trickle of aviation gas and munitions flowing to the beleaguered island. And the effort cost them dearly.

Two destroyers and an ocean-going tug, each pulling a barge laden with 2,000 drums of avgas and 500 quarter-ton bombs, were part of a major supply convoy. *Zuikaku*'s planes hit them when they were seventy-five miles from Guadalcanal, sank the destroyer *Meredith*, whose skipper had ordered the tug *Vireo* abandoned and was just beginning to take off its crew. Survivors of the two vessels—many of them horribly burned, wounded, and repeatedly attacked by sharks—went through three days and nights of hell before a remnant was rescued. The tug and barges were salvaged.

Seaplane-tender *McFarland* came in on the 16th, bearing precious gifts—40,000 gallons of aviation gas, some in tanks below, some in drums on the deck. The drums were safely offloaded, but while the *McFarland* was still pumping gas from the tanks into a fuel barge, Japanese dive-bombers swooped down. The tender was badly hurt but managed to crawl to the relative safety of Tulagi.

The submarine *Amberjack* brought in 9,000 gallons of gas and ten tons of bombs. Douglas Skymasters of the Air

Transport Command shuttled between Guadalcanal and the New Hebrides, bringing in drums of gasoline, taking out sick and wounded. Each planeload was enough to keep twelve fighters in the air for an hour. By such improvisations, orchestrated by Kelly Turner and Rear Admiral Aubrey W. Fitch (who had succeeded McCain as commander of land-based aviation in the South Pacific), the fuel crisis was resolved.

———————————

*October 17.* A quiet night last night: no naval gunfire, no Jap artillery, no bombs. We had a plane up to wait for Louie the Louse but he never came over. Some fine night he will be shot down and that will do more to boost morale than the arrival of a regiment.

A couple of our destroyers came in this morning to give the Japs up the line a taste of naval gunfire. [We had learned a lesson from the vulnerable stacks of supplies piled on Beach Red in our original landings; now our destroyers were pounding dumps of ammunition, rations, and other supplies that the Japanese had just landed west of us.] At 0730 Jap dive-bombers and some Zeros came over to attack the destroyers. Our antiaircraft opened up, and fighters were high in the sky waiting for the Japs. We saw at least four bombers burst into flames—a great tonic for drooping spirits. (Later. I just heard that sixteen dive-bombers and two Zeros were shot down.)

We had another bombing today. Three "eggs" crashed near us in the CP, lifted the roof of the shelter, and riddled our tent. How long, oh God? I hope by some miracle to get out of this mess, to live through the hard days that will be coming. Suddenly I find there is much to live for, and yearn to get back to tell the story.

*October 19.* Last night I lay on a poncho outside the tent, looking up at a brilliant half moon, chatting with Cromie and Keys and our two British officers (Martin Clemens and Major Mathers). Listening to the Britishers' descriptions of Guadalcanal in peacetime, of its marvelous fertility and pleasant places, I could hardly remember there is a war on, that the Japs are making a determined effort to annihilate us.

The general asked me how the history was coming along. He said it was an extremely important project, that the Marine Corps has always been handicapped by lack of good records of events, that the history will mean much to marines after the war. [Neither of us foresaw the floods of printers' ink this campaign would cause to flow.] All this was a great fillip to my spirits. Colonel Thomas directed me, "when this show is over," to get up a history of the First Marine Air Wing. That is a project I really warm to. Our flyers have been our salvation—if we are saved.

It's interesting to see how people react to the pounding we have been taking lately. There are some boys—some officers, too—who never venture far from their shelters, jump at every noise, shout out when they hear a plane in the sky, lie sleepless all night, waiting tensely to hear an enemy plane or naval bombardment. Others bounce back easily and go about their business as if nothing extraordinary is happening. I seem to fall somewhere in between; certainly I am upset, but I haven't yet got that stony stare, anxious expression, and jumpiness that have sent so many officers and men, many of them old veterans, out of here as nervous wrecks.

*October 22.* Lieutenant General Thomas Holcomb, Commandant of the Marine Corps, and a party of seven came in last night. Louie the Louse welcomed them with a fifteen-bomb salute. Today the Commandant has been making a tour of the area. There are rumors, of course, of imminent reinforcements. I haven't been able to make out anything definite.

After chow tonight the Commandant received the Press. I didn't get the word and missed meeting him. But he told Bob Cromie that he would like to see me. He seems a genial, solid, and trust-inspiring man. Said he had heard a "big newspaperman" say that my stories of the fighting here were "perfect reporting." That, of course, gave me a lift. He also said that Navy and Marine Corps are clamoring for more and more from the combat reporters.

I had not, so far, heard anything from Denig or Van der Hoef or anyone else in the Public Relations Divison in

Washington. Presumably they were going on the sound principle that the man in the field should be left to do his job without interference from the home office. But I needed guidance. I had left Washington just as the plans for combat reporters were getting under way. Nothing had been said about the desire for a steady flow of Joe Blow stories about individual marines of all ranks, intended for their hometown papers. When I left the name "combat correspondent" had not yet been invented.

Sergeant Ned Burman had arrived, with orders to report to the 2nd Marines. He told me two more combat correspondents were on their way, to join the 7th Marines. Absorbed in keeping a running record of the campaign, and knowing what a flood of copy civilian correspondents kept flowing to American papers, I was not sure what the new arrivals were supposed to do.

Fortunately Hurlbut, the first in the field, was an enterprising and hardworking reporter who needed no guidance from me. But even he seemed superfluous, and I did not know what was expected of three or four additional sergeants, assigned to regiments. A more imaginative and experienced PRO presumably would have hit upon the Joe Blow idea on his own without instructions from headquarters. At the time it seemed foolish to be sending into combat zones other Marine reporters who would be risking their lives to little purpose. But such personal concerns were not at the forefront of my mind during the days after the Japanese brought in six transports.

In the first half of October the Japanese had put ashore, west of us, about 13,500 fresh troops. These supplemented other recent arrivals and survivors of the Ichiki and Kawaguchi detachments. The Second Infantry Division (also known as the Sendai, after the prefecture from which it was recruited) was the biggest infantry element. Lieutenant General Masao Maruyama was its commander. The division was reinforced by two battalions of the Thirty-eighth (or Hiroshima) Division, which had also been assigned to Hyakutake's Seventeenth Army; most of that division was still in the northern Solomons. Major General Tadashi Sumiyoshi was in command of the Seventeenth Army's artillery on Guadalcanal: the 4th Heavy Field Artillery Regiment (the 6-inch Pistol Petes) and several batteries of lighter artillery. Under Sumiyoshi also came at least one company of 18-ton tanks and five battalions of infantry, mostly from the 4th Regiment.

All in all, there were about 22,000 enemy combat and service troops on the island. Some estimates place the number closer to 26,000. To oppose them we mustered some 23,000 officers and men of all services, mostly Marine and Army, with another 4,500 on Tulagi. The numbers are deceptive. Except for fresh arrivals on both sides, troops were in bad physical condition. Malaria was beginning to strike down large numbers, already weakened by other tropical diseases, malnutrition, and fatigue— physical and mental.

As I mentioned earlier, Hyakutake arrived at Tassafaronga the night of October 9 to take personal command in the forthcoming ground attack. He had devised a plan to "capture the enemy positions, especially the airfield and artillery positions, in one blow." When the airfield had been seized, more troops would move in by sea. General Vandegrift would be ordered to come on foot to the mouth of the Matanikau, accompanied by an aide, and there he would surrender. Once the Japanese had the Lunga area they expected it would be simple matter to recapture Tulagi and seize other places in the lower Solomons. With their right flank thus secured the Seventeenth Army would again bestow its full attentions on New Guinea, from which they had been diverted since early September.

Hyakutake's plans underwent several changes but the central idea remained the same: put tanks, troops, and artillery across the Matanikau and strike up the coast to Kukum; support that drive with a flanking movement inland, hooking behind whatever American defenses might be met in the ridges east of the Matanikau; at the same time, deliver the heaviest infantry blow against the American line south of the airfield, near Bloody Ridge. Maruyama was to be in command of the southern effort. Before a concerted assault could be launched, he must get his troops into position. And that would take a little time—longer than optimistic Japanese generals had reckoned.

*     *     *

On October 15, after the Japanese had landed a fresh division, Admiral Nimitz and his staff made an estimate of the situation, known to only a few: "It now appears that we are unable to control the sea in the Guadalcanal area. Thus our supply of the position will only be done at great expense to us. The situation is not hopeless, but it is certainly critical."

That same day Fitch, commander of land-based aviation in the South Pacific, passed on to Ghormley a message from Vandegrift or someone speaking in his name. Apparently Vandegrift had not wanted to send it out by radio from Cactus and had given it to a visitor from Fitch's staff to be relayed from Espiritu Santo. The message: tell Ghormley "that the Jap has moved in and emplaced artillery of longer range than his [Vandegrift's] which is shelling his positions and airfield at will; that enemy surface craft move at will in surrounding waters and shell his positions destructively both day and night; and that he will be unable indefinitely to hold these positions if this continues." Fitch's emissary added: "Geiger states that he can use no more aircraft until avgas situation improves and until destructive enemy fire on airfield from both land and sea is halted."

These somber appraisals were, of course, not known to any but a few on Guadalcanal. But makers of public opinion in the United States did not need top-secret briefings to realize that Guadalcanal might well be lost. Headlines warned: "Japs Believed to Rule Sea in Solomons," "Japanese Fleet Massing North of Guadalcanal as Decisive Battle Rages," "Fate of U.S. Airfield on Island in Doubt." An editorial in the *New York Times* of October 16 reads like an epitaph: "We know that these American young men will do all that humanly can be done to stand their ground and advance . . . Guadalcanal. The name will not die out of the memories of this generation. It will endure in honor."

Echoes of the worried chorus came to us over the airwaves, including the words of Secretary of the Navy Knox. On October 19, asked if he thought we could hold the island, Knox said in a press conference: "I certainly hope so. I expect so. I don't want to make any predictions, but every man out there, ashore or afloat, will give a good account of himself.''

On October 18 Admiral Nimitz came to a personally painful decision. In a letter to his wife he said that he had reached it only after "hours of anguished consideration." Finally he had concluded that Ghormley must be relieved because he had been "too immersed in detail and not sufficiently bold and aggressive at the right time."

Before returning to a carrier command (or so he hoped) after a long bout of illness, Vice Admiral William F. Halsey made a swing through the South Pacific. Arriving by seaplane in Noumea on October 18, he was handed a sealed envelope marked "Secret." Halsey tore it open and read the message within: "You will take command of the South Pacific Area and South Pacific Forces immediately." One of his staff has reported the admiral's reaction: "Jesus Christ and General Jackson! This is the hottest potato they ever handed me!" Halsey proceeded to COMSOPAC's headquarters aboard the *Argonne* in Noumea harbor. There he took over command from an old friend.*

Among those few who knew the reputations of senior admirals the news of Halsey's appointment was a boost to morale. He was known as an aggressive, risk-taking leader. Vandegrift, for one, welcomed the change. Within five days he was summoned to Noumea for a conference with the new COMSOPAC. He flew to New Caledonia with the Marine Corps Commandant on October 23.

On the American side, the arrival of the North Dakotan Army regiment had greatly improved the odds in the next clash of ground forces. For the first time the Marine command had enough men to set up strong defenses on the eastern bank of the Matanikau. There a horseshoe strongpoint was established, a roughly U-shaped line commanding the river from the sandbar to about a mile inland (Hill 67),

---

*According to later reports, Ghormley had been suffering from abscessed teeth, and all his teeth were removed when he arrived back in Washington. In February 1943 he was made Commandant, 14th Naval District, and Commander, Hawaiian Sea Frontier.

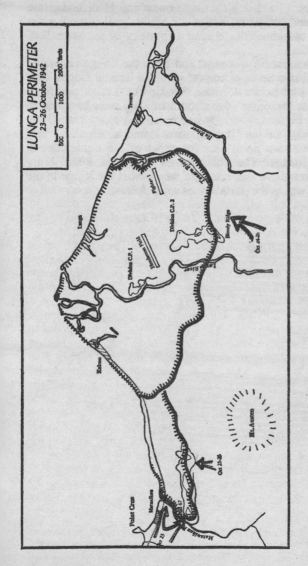

*The perimeter and extension to the Matanikau during the October fighting*

bent back at either end. One arm of the U defended the beach for 1000 yards east of the Matanikau. The other ran along a ridgeline overlooking a tributary of the Matanikau to the south.

The horseshoe was separated from the Lunga perimeter by about two miles of coastal strip and interior ridges—the Kukum-Matanikau corridor. Within the Lunga perimeter the North Dakotans of the 164th Infantry were assigned to the eastern sector—a long line extending along part of the beach west of the Tenaru, then inland along that river, then west to a point near the snout of the Centipede, or Bloody Ridge. The 7th Marines' line joined the Army regiment's there and extended west across the Ridge to the Lunga, where the 1st Marines took over.

☆ ──────── ☆

# October Crisis:
# Second Phase

To execute Hyakutake's plan for the recapture of Henderson Field, General Maruyama's three regiments had to move inland across dismayingly rugged terrain. And, to achieve surprise, they had to move as secretly as possible, hidden by the rain forest from prying American planes. Their starting point was Kokumbona.

The "trail" along which they struggled, through jungle-choked ravines and across precipitous ridges to their jumping-off points, was nothing more than an indistinct track hacked through dense undergrowth. Later, when U.S. Army troops controlled Mount Austen, they could never locate the so-called Maruyama Trail leading across the Matanikau and south of Austen; it had been quickly swallowed up by the rain forest. And after the war, when interrogated by Americans, Japanese generals could not trace the track on maps.

On October 16 Maruyama's men set forth. The general optimistically tried to take along light artillery pieces, which had to be manhandled. Each soldier was to carry, in addition to his usual combat gear, one artillery shell. Both guns and ammunition had to be abandoned along the track. Weary footsoldiers, on short rations of rice, struggled slowly through the rain-sodden jungle and over steep ridges.

Maruyama had to tell Hyakutake that he would not be ready to attack until the 22nd. Again, he had to postpone X-Day to the 23rd, and again, still not in position south of Bloody Ridge, to the 24th. It is not clear that Hyakutake and Sumiyoshi (in charge on the Matanikau front) ever got Maruyama's message about the last postponement.

In any event, Sumiyoshi did not wait. On the night of
October 23 he began his attack across the Matanikau.
During the day there was the usual air raid, but the bombers unloaded on the shoreline far from the airfield. Pistol
Pete fired intermittently through the day, hitting the new
naval operating base at Lunga Lagoon (it had been driven
out of Kukum) and far into the runway at Henderson
Field. As night fell the big howitzers' firing grew steadier
and more purposeful. Joined by lighter artillery and mortars the Pistol Petes shelled deep into Marine positions,
then drew their fire back to concentrate on the east bank of
the Matanikau. It was the closest thing to an artillery
preparation the Japanese ever managed to achieve on Guadalcanal. As reports came in from the Matanikau, D-3
concluded that "This is the night." And it was.

Four Japanese 18-ton tanks rumbled up the coast road from
Point Cruz and started across the sandbar. Marine antitank
guns knocked out three of them. The fourth managed to get
across the river. A marine put a hand grenade in its tracks
when it paused. Disabled, it fell victim to a half-track—a
tank destroyer mounting a 75-mm. gun. Five more tanks wad-
dled onto the bar. Point-blank fire stopped them.

While this one-sided encounter was taking place 11th
Marines artillery began laying down the heaviest concentrations that they had ever been called upon to deliver.
Their target was the area between the sandbar and Point
Cruz; it was assumed that enemy infantry was gathered
there to exploit the breach in our lines they hoped the tanks
would make. And indeed much of the 4th Infantry Regiment of the Japanese Army was massed there. They were
all but destroyed. When marines were able to patrol west
of the river a few days later they found the blasted bodies
of five to six hundred Japanese and three more wrecked
tanks. Captured diaries confirmed that it had been a devastating blow. Sumiyoshi's attack had failed. He could not
again effectively support the main attack from the south,
which began the following night.

On October 24 Maruyama decided to attack, ready or
not. At least most of his weary troops were east of the
upper Lunga. One regiment (the 29th Infantry) was more
or less in position on the western end of his chosen front,

just east of the Ridge. The other had not yet reached its jump-off positions further east. It was commanded by the unfortunate Kawaguchi, who had been on this bloody ground before. But he might, with a little luck and a bright moon, be ready that night.

Maruyama's troops had slipped across the Lunga undetected. The dense canopy of jungle treetops had concealed their tortured and tortuous movement south of Mount Austen. The Marine command's attention, as Hyakutake had hoped, was fixed on the Matanikau front. Marine patrols had gone daily into the ridges and rain forest to the south, finding nothing but stragglers. Native scouts had gone far up the Lunga. The Japanese had eluded even Whaling's vaunted scout-snipers, on a special three-day patrol to the south.

Division headquarters decided that the upper Lunga was clear of the enemy. But they were worried about the long gap between the Lunga perimeter and the horseshoe at the Matanikau. They pulled the 2nd battalion, 7th Marines (commanded by Lieutenant Colonel Herman H. Hanneken) out of the line east of the Lunga leaving only one battalion (Puller's) to defend that segment. His line now ran east of the Lunga, across the southern knob of Bloody Ridge to a point about half a mile farther east—a little more than a mile and a half in all. There it joined the Army sector, which held, as earlier noted, roughly the line of the Tenaru. The 1st Battalion, 164th Infantry, was Puller's immediate neighbor.

The first signs that trouble might be brewing south of Henderson Field came in the afternoon. An observer in front of Puller's thin line reported seeing a Japanese officer scrutinizing Bloody Ridge through field glasses. One of Whaling's men saw smoke, which he thought came from rice fires, rising a mile or so up the Lunga. It was too late to do much about improving defenses in the south beyond alerting Puller and the artillery.

The moon was full that night. Maruyama had hoped its light would help his assault units sort themselves out in the rain forest. But about 1730 it began to rain in torrents. The downpour continued through the night. Maruyama's attack, which he had optimistically scheduled to begin at 1900, soon after sunset, was delayed.

On regimental orders, Puller had staked out forty-six men as a listening post, nearly a mile to the south of his lines, connected to his CP by a telephone wire. About nine-thirty the men in the outpost thought they heard sounds other than the pelting rain. Indeed they had. Puller's phone rang. The outpost reported that hundreds of Japanese were swarming around them, headed Puller's way. The colonel told his men in the outpost to head east, and then for the 164th Infantry lines.

For a time Puller delayed calling for artillery fire, to give the forty-six men a chance to escape. But soon the Japanese began cutting his barbed wire, and soon thereafter they made the first of many charges that continued through the night. Some of the 29th Infantry, including their commander, Colonel Masajiro Furumiya, broke through Marine defenses, but no one followed them. Perhaps it was a report of this minor success that prompted Maruyama, somewhat prematurely, to radio a code word to Hyakutake: "Banzai!" It meant that the airfield had been captured.

In the confusion of that sodden night the Japanese did not exploit Furumiya's penetration. Only his own regiment ever took part in the night-long battle. Kawaguchi's force, which was to attack farther east, never got into action. Before the battle had even started, Kawaguchi himself had been relieved of command, apparently because he had questioned the wisdom of an assault in that place. Colonel Toshinaro Shoji replaced him. By now del Valle's artillery was hitting the Japanese hard.

The division command ordered Lieutenant Colonel Robert K. Hall's 3rd Battalion of the 164th Infantry, in regimental reserve, to help Puller. Coming up to the front through driving rain, Army troops filtered into Marine lines. Puller and Hall did not attempt to keep them organized as separate units. By three-thirty in the morning the Japanese charges were petering out. As dawn approached Maruyama pulled back his men to reorganize for another night of fighting.

On the 25th Puller and Hall reorganized their own lines. The Army battalion took over east of Bloody Ridge, the

Marine unit shortening its segment to the stretch between the Ridge and the Lunga. Soldiers and marines spent the day feverishly improving their positions. Colonel Furumiya and his handful were among the victims of this reorganization. They found new machine-gun emplacements and many more riflemen blocking their attempts to get back to the Japanese lines.

Those who were there and those who have read about the Guadalcanal campaign will remember October 25 as "Dugout Sunday." I am not sure how it got its name. Presumably it is because Japanese planes, mostly Zeros, were over the island most of the day and the sirens repeatedly wailed "Condition Red." But few men spent much time in their shelters. There was too much to do within the perimeter, getting ready for a continuation of the battle, and too much to watch in the sky, including some spectacular dogfights.

It was an unusual day in several respects. Early in the morning Japanese naval and air commands at Rabaul and at sea thought that their Army brethren had swept onto Henderson Field. Their ships and planes did some things they would not ordinarily have done. Zero fighters came in early to see if Hyakutake's men actually held the field. Disappointed to find us still in possession they continued to come, taking advantage of the fact that most of our planes were grounded by the torrential rains of the previous night.

At midmorning three Japanese destroyers made a rare sunlit foray into the waters off Lunga. They gave chase to a pair of old U.S. destroyer-minelayers that had been landing supplies at Tulagi. Driven off by a few Wildcats they sank, in departing, two smaller vessels—a tug and a Yippie boat—that had just brought a battery of the 10th Marines from Tulagi. A hundred or so miles to the north lurked the light cruiser *Yura* and five destroyers which were ready to support Hyakutake with shellings and landings.

I give below the notes I took in the D-3 section beginning late in the morning. They are varied and disjointed, but so are the matters D-3 had to deal with. My explanatory remarks are in brackets.

1100: Puller reports large Jap concentration on ridge south of fighter strip. Calls for artillery.

1115: Decision by D-3 to move the 3rd battalion, 2nd Marines [then the division's motorized reserve, under Lt. Col. Robert G. Hunt, bivouacked in the coconut grove north of Henderson Field].

1115: Wildcats have strafed destroyers [the ones that had sunk the tug *Seminole* and the Yippie boat]. One SBD can take the air. All planes are landing on the metal strip [main runway of Henderson Field, covered with perforated steel Marston mats] despite Pistol Pete.

1120: Zeros coming in; one shot down.

1120: *Seminole* and Yippie reported lost. Battery I and personnel safely landed; one life lost.

1130: The SBD got off [this was the first dive-bomber able to get into the air that day]. Hunt ordered to move into the 7th Marines sector; relieve Engineers, who are needed on the beach.

1135: Two Zeros shot down, two smoking. Base Defense says "There's one Zero up there with his tail shot off. That poor son of a bitch." Wildcats into them. Three Zeros down. Two Wildcats chasing another Zero. Finally got him; wing fell off; Jap pilot bailed out. Two more Zeros over; one shot down.

1145: Edson [whose 5th Marines were in the western defense sector, just beyond Kukum] reports a patrol, sent out this morning, contacted Japs. He sent out four men to tell them not to get too heavily involved. Got word to one patrol, then the four men were fired on by about thirty Japs. Japs are on the northeast end of ridge 1200 yards south of Edson's left battalion.

1145: Unidentified flight going out, at 63 miles. Tulagi is told *not* to embark rifle company on *Trevor* [one of the destroyer-minelayers chased by the Japanese destroyers an hour earlier] for Aola mission.

1145: Unidentified flight going out.

1147: Three Jap planes (probably Zeros) coming in. Two SBDs about to take off, with bombs.

1200: Condition Green. All flights going out.

1200: Whaling, after visit to lines, reports troops of 1–7 [more likely 2–7, on a ridge a mile east of the Matanikau] "jitterbugging," firing at nothing. Suggested word be passed to Frisbie [executive officer of the 7th Marines] that troops be warned *not* to fire—safest course is to lie low in daytime. Whaling thinks there may be "quite a few Japs" up there. He advises that most of troops be put in the line now, to guard against having to move at night. Trails are knee-high in mud. Whaling thinks Jap attack in that sector likely tonight. [This was to be the third prong of Hyakutake's attack, against the Kukum-Matanikau corridor.] They have probably pulled out of mortar range for daytime.

Puller says two Army companies are to left of ridge, one on right. Twenty or thirty Japs broke through; are being cleaned up now. [This, we later found out, was the group led by Colonel Furumiya, commanding the crack 29th Regiment; he later destroyed the regimental colors and committed suicide.]

Question whether to put all troops in the line, or hold a battalion back. Division decides to put two battalions in line (2300 yards) since troops movement almost impossible in the jungle at night. Best plan is to try to hold the line. Decided not to put the reserve [Hunt's battalion] in 7th's line; to occupy Engineers' bivouac area. Thomas warns Frisbie artillery ammo should be conserved; battalion not to call for support unless it has definite targets.

1225: Unidentified flight coming in, 46 miles out to NW. Not more than ten planes, coming in fast.

1237: Six Zeros overhead. Dogfights until 1310. Four Zeros, one Wildcat down.

1312: Two Zeros chased four SBDs across airfield.

1317: Three more Zeros high overhead. Jap guns [Pistol Pete] hitting on northeast end of main runway.

1330: Report of SBD strike against Jap task force. Found one heavy cruiser, one light cruiser, two destroyers 120 miles out, headed for Guadalcanal. [These were actually the light cruiser *Yura* and five destroyers.] One direct hit with a thousand-pound bomb on forecastle of the heavy cruiser; also one very near miss and possible hit; cruiser dead in water. One damaging near miss on light cruiser. Did not see any transports [which an earlier search, at 0800, had reported].

1345: Report of one heavy cruiser, one light, three destroyers [again, the *Yura* group] 40 miles out at 1300, speed 20; correction of earlier report [*not* 120 miles].

1350: Report [from a coastwatcher] of 17 large, 13 small planes over New Georgia at 1320.

1410: Six ships, course 310, distance 60, bearing 60 [that is, 60 miles to the northeast, beyond Florida Island, moving northwest; again, the *Yura* group]. Three destroyers to northwest, off Russell Island, moving northeast.

1412: Large flight of *friendly* planes, 60 miles out.

1418: Five Zeros south of field; another flight 37 miles out.

1419: Friendly planes coming in [returning from attack on *Yura* group].

1423: Condition Red. 16 bombers 5 miles out, at 20,000 feet.

1424: Splitting into two groups, flying in straight line.

1430: Bombs dropped along beach near Kukum.

1434: One bomber coming down.

1435: One bomber with motor shot out. Fighters wheeling and diving overhead. Bombers at seven miles, going out.

1436: Two Zeros coming down on field; another bomber coming down.

1442: Unidentified planes 52 miles out, coming in.

1450: Dogfights overhead.

1451: One Zero down.

1452: Another flight, unidentified, coming in, range 10 miles (maybe surface craft—they are very low).

1456: Zeros strafed field.

1457: Three Zeros coming in; 5 miles out.

1500: Six dive-bombers over field; three bombs dropped.

1501: Eight Zeros to southwest. More dive-bombers reported near.

Two transports seen northwest of Rekata Bay [on Santa Isabel]; evidently the ones sighted this morning at 0800; probably landed troops on Santa Isabel, to be ferried over.

1503: Two more groups of planes going out; 57 and 62 miles away. A few Zeros still prowling around.

1507: Six Zeros or dive-bombers, at 4000 feet, coming in.

1508: Three groups of planes going out. Dive-bombers dropped bombs on the main field, near wrecked planes [in what General Geiger called his "boneyard"].

1516: Condition Green.

Receive report that Japs have been told to "expedite" their ground operations; suggest possible landing at "enemy base." [This must have come from Fleet radio intelligence.] Attempted landings tonight? One D-3 officer says "It looks like this is the night." Discussion of beach defenses; they seem solid. Del Valle thinks landings will be accompanied by pressure from all sides.

We now have 7 PT boats.

Apparently Jap transports aren't coming in. They probably have landed all they mean to for the present.

1526: Report from aviation. Enemy force previously bombed off Florida [the *Yura* group] is going out, on course 330 [to northwest], at speed of 10 knots; sighted at 1400; the heavy cruiser has been damaged.

1535: Condition Red. Small group, apparently Zeros, coming in. Two planes to north apparently in dogfight.

1545: Condition Green.

Puller reports he found more than 100 dead Japs in front of one company position, 37 in front of another's. D-3 says, "That's one outfit that won't have much fight in it."

1645: Condition Red. Five to 8 Zeros over the field. Small group going out, at 70 miles. Zeros circling the field, 5 to 6 miles out.

1647: Zeros now at 12,000 feet; have belly tanks. Report from second strike by our SBDs against force north of Florida; found heavy cruiser, light cruiser, and destroyer 30 miles north of Florida, headed north; possible hits on both cruisers; heavy cruiser trailing oil and smoking badly. Third strike is now out.

1709: Small flight, probably the Zeros, going out. Report on third strike: Two SBDs got two misses on the light cruiser; Army planes [B-17s from Espiritu Santo] made 500-pound bomb hit or very near miss on bow of light cruiser; Jap ships are now 80 miles to the north, proceeding slowly.

Warning received that Japs may try to land east of us [apparently based on radio intelligence]. Our Navy has a striking force in the area. PT boats are patrolling.

1930: Firing heard from 1–7 [Puller's] area—mortars, artillery, and machine guns.

2000: Jap artillery opens up, replying to ours.

Action both at the Matanikau and on the 1–7 ridge [Bloody Ridge]. Taxis [3rd Defense Battalion] thinks Japs are firing a battery of five to six-inch guns.

2005: Sims [commanding the 7th Marines, then on ridges between the Matanikau and the perimeter] reports receiving pretty heavy artillery fire; no attack yet.

Thus began another night of fighting on the perimeter. The Japanese struck again in the jungle between Bloody Ridge and the Lunga and against the ridge east of the Matanikau that another battalion of the 7th Marines had occupied on the 24th. Colonel Oka was supposed—according to Japanese plans—to have hit the latter line with about a battalion, in concert with the major drive from the south. He was a day late. Hyakutake had planned that all three assaults—across the Matanikau, near Bloody Ridge, and between the Matanikau and the perimeter—were to be concerted. If they had succeeded in coordinating the attacks, the outcome might well have been quite different. Even an artillery regiment as fast-moving as del Valle's would have found it hard to lay down adequate concentrations in all three sectors at the same time.

Both of the assaults the night of October 25–26 were thrown back with dreadful Japanese losses. At dawn on the 26th it looked as though some might break through in the south. D-3 sent a precautionary message to the air command: "Japs are driving hard toward fighter strip. We'll probably stop them but take security measures around planes." He sent the much-moved-about Engineers to act as security guards at the strip.

Colonel Furumiya, trapped behind our lines, wrote in his diary on the 26th: "With the condition of the division as it is at present, it is best to attack to Centipede [Bloody Ridge] at dusk." General Maruyama apparently came to the same conclusion. The Sendai Division hit Puller again about quarter past seven that night—the third successive night—trying to work along the east slope of Bloody Ridge. But the American line was no longer the tenuous, hastily improvised one it had been in September. "Same old place," said Twining when the report came in. "It's a good sign. Looks like they didn't like what they got into last night. But it's now a better position than the one they hit last night. It's been developed a lot—lots of wire out there."

The Sendai Division was also trying to work its way down both sides of the Lunga, west of the Ridge. And to the east the Japanese struck repeatedly in the area where Hall's battalion joined its brethren North Dakotans of the 2nd battalion. They threw back the Japanese effort to break through to the airfield from the southeast.

"Oh, for another battalion," said Twining at the division CP. A lack of reserves had plagued the Marine command throughout the campaign. At this point it consisted of one understrength battalion. But Army and Marine lines south of the airfield, breached in a few places, were restored and held. And so was the ridge Colonel Oka had attacked a couple of miles east of the Matanikau.

The Sendai Division's back had been broken.

\*    \*    \*

Japanese ships that ventured into the waters off Guadalcanal on Dugout Sunday were on the far fringes of a much mightier concentration of imperial naval power. The Japanese Army had promised to take Henderson Field by October 25. As the day began a naval liaison officer with the Seventeenth Army on Guadalcanal had triumphantly gotten off a radio message to his Navy superiors up the line, repeating Maruyama's Army signal: "Banzai! Occupied airfield at 2300 [0100 Guadalcanal time]."

Admiral Yamamoto was ready to exploit such a breakthrough. He was certain it would draw out the U.S. Pacific Fleet, which he intended to destroy. His Combined Fleet had sortied from Truk, ready to fight the ever elusive "decisive battle," and to help eliminate American remnants on Guadalcanal. Frustrated and impatient when he learned that the report of Henderson's fall was false, Yamamoto was still determined to decide the issue, which it now seemed must be done purely by naval means.

Yamamoto threw four aircraft carriers, four battleships, ten cruisers, and thirty destroyers into the scales, in addition to the two light forces he had dispatched to Guadalcanal to help mop up on Dugout Sunday. He himself stayed in Truk aboard his flagship, the giant battleship *Yamato*. As usual he divided his formidable fleet into several task forces, steaming southeast from Truk in roughly parallel paths. A Vanguard Force, under Vice Admiral Nobutake Kondo, was built around two battleships, one aircraft carrier, and four cruisers. It led the way, about sixty miles ahead and somewhat to the east of the main carrier striking force, commanded by Vice Admiral Chuichi Nagumo.

Nagumo's three flattops—two heavies and one light—were guarded by the two battleships that had bombarded Henderson Field in the middle of the month and other attendant fighting ships. Farther west was another light carrier. Yamamoto intended to hurl 427 planes against the Americans: 207 from the carriers would be helped by 220 land-based naval aircraft flying from the Rabaul-Northern Solomons complex.

During the night of October 25–26 U.S. carriers and their satellites headed northwest toward the Combined Fleet.

Halsey, the new COMSOPAC, had a surprise for his foe. He had not just one but two big carriers. The *Enterprise*, back in action after healing her wounds of a month earlier, had joined the *Hornet*. The flattops could muster 171 Wildcat fighters, Dauntless dive-bombers, and Avenger torpedo bombers.

At dawn on October 26 the opposing carrier groups were only 220 miles apart, just north of the Santa Cruz Islands. As in all carrier engagements each side suffered through an anxious period of searching and probing, seeking the advantage of the first strike. Catalina flying boats, searching by moonlight, had found one of the big Japanese carriers. From his headquarters at Noumea Halsey sent a bold order to his outnumbered ships: "Attack Repeat Attack."

Early in the morning dive-bombers from the "Big E" found the light carrier *Zuiho*, cratered her flight deck, and sent her back to Truk for repairs. But *Zuiho* had already launched her strike. Having spotted the U.S. flattops a few minutes before they found his, Nagumo had flights from all four of his carriers on the way to attack them. At the same time the Americans had half as many planes speeding northwestward to return the favor. The foes passed each other in the South Pacific skies. Some broke out of formation to dogfight.

The Japanese reached their targets first. Concentrating on the *Hornet* they blasted her with bombs, torpedoes, and crashing planes. The stricken carrier managed to put out fires, but had to be taken in tow. Val dive-bombers and Betty torpedo planes turned their fury on the *Enterprise*, and hit her twice. Among her other injuries the forward airraft elevator was knocked out of action and a big hole was put in the flight deck. Four more Japanese flights went after the helpless *Hornet*. She had to be abandoned at nightfall and was later sunk by Japanese destroyers.

Meanwhile the *Hornet*'s morning strike had planted four bombs on the *Shokaku*. Of Nagumo's floating airstrips a small one and a big one had been so damaged that they had to retire for extensive repairs. Another small and another big one were almost unscathed. As Yamamoto had hoped, his Vanguard Force had drawn some of the American fire that might otherwise have reached his flattops.

The United States had lost one of its two remaining large carriers and the other, as a result of her injuries, could swing only one arm. She wisely withdrew. The new battleship *South Dakota* and antiaircraft cruiser *San Juan* had also been hit, but not badly.

More than a hundred of the emperor's "sea eagles" had been knocked out in one way or another. Probably it was this loss more than any other factor that persuaded Yamamoto not to pursue his crippled enemy even though he had a clear advantage in firepower. But he was also fearful of getting close to U.S. land-based aviation on Espiritu Santo. His vanguard of battleships and lighter vessels swept the "battlefield" north of Ndeni, sank the blazing *Hornet,* and retired toward Truk.

The Battle of the Santa Cruz Islands was the last chance Yamamoto's carriers ever had to avenge their defeat at Midway and finish off the existing U.S. carrier force. It was also the last encounter between opposing flattops for twenty months. The next clash came in the Philippine Sea in June 1944. By then the United States could throw into the fray 956 carrier-borne planes, of improved types, with superbly trained crews. The Japanese could then muster only 473 with poorly trained crews. They had long since lost their best pilots, mostly in the Solomons, and were never able to replace them.

In the long October seesaw first one side then the other seemed to hold the advantage. Marines had ousted the Japanese from their important bridgehead across the Matanikau. But the Japanese, having temporarily whittled down the Cactus Air Force by aerial bombardment, long-range artillery fire, and heavy naval shelling, had succeeded in bringing in a fresh division; then they had squandered their ground strength in uncoordinated attacks. At sea Admiral Scott had beaten back one surface bombardment force, but the Imperial Navy battered the island in four successive night shellings, including the Night. After the final clash of big navies in the area the U.S. Pacific Fleet was left with only one aircraft carrier—a

damaged one at that—but the Imperial Combined Fleet
had withdrawn after heavy losses in planes and pilots. As
the month closed Japanese IGHQ was as determined as
ever to recapture Henderson Field. With diminished assets
at sea an aggressive new U.S. Navy area commander was
determined to hold on. Neither side had yet succeeded in
imposing an effective blockade. The struggle could still go
either way.

General Vandegrift had missed the October battle for
Henderson Field. As noted earlier, he flew to Noumea on
the 23rd for a conference with the new COMSOPAC. In his
absence, General Geiger, who had closely followed ground-
force dispositions and operations during his tour of duty on
the island, took command of all U.S. forces on Guadalcanal. During the four days of Japanese ground attacks he
called at the division CP each morning to confer with
Thomas and Twining, and, having decided on a general
plan of action, left it to them to make the moment-to-
moment decisions.

However disappointed Vandegrift may have been to be
absent at such a time, his visit to Noumea was gratifying.
After hearing his principal subordinates' reports, including
Turner's and Vandegrift's, Halsey turned to the general
and asked, "Can you hold?" Vandegrift said he could, but
he would have to have more active support than he had
been getting. Halsey promised "everything I've got." One
of his first decisions was to cancel the long-debated occupation of Ndeni. He would concentrate available forces on
holding Guadalcanal.

At the same time, new support was coming from even
higher quarters. The Allies were then gathering their forces
for their first combined confrontation of Hitler's war machine in North Africa. The buildup for that operation—
TORCH—was one of the main reasons so little reinforcement,
particularly in the air, was reaching the South Pacific. But
on October 24 President Roosevelt sent a handwritten note
to the Joint Chiefs of Staff:

My anxiety about the S.W. Pac. is to make sure that
every possible weapon gets into that area to hold Gua-

dalcanal. And that having held it in this crisis that munitions and planes and crews are on the way to take advantage of our success. We will soon find ourselves engaged in two active fronts and we must have adequate air support in both places even tho it means delay in our other commitments, particularly to England.

The emphasis on air support was significant. General Henry H. ("Hap") Arnold of the Army Air Forces had been, of all the Joint Chiefs of Staff, the firmest in holding to Europe First priorities. He had consistently refused to yield to King's repeated pleas—more and more strident as the Guadalcanal campaign wore on—for some of the AAF's best fighter planes, particularly P-38s (Lockheed Lightnings). It was one of the most acrimonious disputes among the Joint Chiefs of Staff during the war. Arnold yielded a bit as the Japanese carried out their October offensive. After the JCS had arrived at tentative figures on the 22nd he agreed, on the 27th, to maintain somewhat higher levels of AAF strength in the South Pacific, including 150 fighters in addition to those needed on minor islands. P-38s would be among them.

# Two Fronts

The shattered Sendai Division reeled back into the rain forest south of Bloody Ridge late in October. One remnant, under Colonel Shoji, made its way toward the shore near Koli Point, east of the Lunga perimeter. The bulk of Maruyama's battered troops crawled back along the jungle trails by which they had so painfully advanced, back toward Mount Austen and the Japanese beachhead west of the Matanikau. They were now desperately short of food, reduced to eating jungle plants. Many of their sick and wounded had to be abandoned along the way. Malaria was beginning to take a heavy toll.

The Sendai was no longer a threat to the airfield. With U.S. Army reinforcements now ashore, and more in the offing, the Marine command decided to make an immediate counterattack across the Matanikau. This is the way the situation looked to D-3 at the end of October: a Japanese regiment and some mixed forces had been almost entirely destroyed in the southern sector, east and west of Bloody Ridge. Another regiment had been nearly destroyed at the Matanikau. The bulk of Japanese supplies must be near Tassafaronga.

"By attacking now," said Twining, "we stand a good chance of pushing the Japs beyond the Poha River, securing the airfield from artillery fire. The Jap will probably make his most determined stand west of the Poha, where the terrain is more favorable to him. Our division is not in good moral or physical position to attack, and we are also short of ammunition. But the need to secure the airfield makes it necessary to accept the risks involved and make a limited attack now."

By the last day of October, Division had made its plans. Twining outlined them. "The west bank of the Matanikau is outposted tonight by a detachment of the 1st Marines [from the 3rd Battalion]. We will throw four assault bridges across the river tonight, at intervals of 1200 yards. The attack will start at 0630. Two regiments, the 5th Marines and 2nd Marines, will attack in columns, the 5th ahead. If the 5th meets heavy resistance, the 2nd will launch an attack in depth and make a penetration. The attack will be supported by artillery, dive-bombers, attack planes, and B-17s. The Navy will not be able to give immediate support but we hope for it by the second day. The Whaling Group [Scout-Snipers and 3rd Battalion, 7th Marines] is to swing south and operate semi-independently [through the ridge-ribbed terrain behind the line Point Cruz-Matanikau] with the mission of protecting our left flank."

Colonel Thomas summed up one aim of this effort: "Our object is to give them a sense of futility, especially that concentration up at Buin," at the south end of Bougainville, where the Japanese had been massing fighting ships, troop transports, and planes. One cheering bit of news was that new U.S. submarines had arrived in the South Pacific and fourteen were to be maintained on station at all times in the lower Solomons and northward.

---

*November 1.* Our counterattack in the west started this morning at 0630. The advance has been slow although there has not been much opposition [too optimistic an appraisal, as it turned out]. I went down to the front with Hurlbut and Keys. We walked out toward the mouth of the Matanikau and found a machine-gun emplacement on the beach where the boys said a Jap machine gun had been peppering them all morning. Hurlbut stayed with them, while Keys and I started out to look for the assault bridges. We had just reached the road along the river when a Jap machine gun opened up and bullets zipped over our heads. We hit the deck, and quickly. We decided not to go on up the road, and to go back to the CP. I started back toward the river mouth to get Hurlbut when a machine gun began to kick up the sand and water around the log on the beach where I had taken shelter. In a lull I hightailed toward the rear. Harry and I hitched a ride back.

At 1030 Edson reported that the 5th Marines were still east of Point Cruz. Vandegrift, Thomas, and Twining discussed whether they should order the 5th Marines to move on as far as possible and dig in for the night or order the 2nd Marines to move through them at 1300. The decision had to be made by noon. D-3 said he didn't want anyone in front of the 5th to protect them from night raiders: "They've had too much of that." An hour later Edson reported that his left battalion is moving forward. [The main problem, it later became known, was along the beach where Edson's right battalion had run into a strong enemy position at the base of Point Cruz; this was not yet known at the CP.] Tentative decision: the 5th should push on beyond Point Cruz in the afternoon and dig in there for the night; the 5th or 2nd to jump off from there tomorrow at dawn.

---

About noon a new and disturbing development called for a more difficult decision. A warning based on radio intelligence reached the CP. Five Japanese destroyers were to arrive near Koli Point, east of us, shortly after midnight the next night. The decoders were not sure whether their mission was to land fresh troops or to carry out a bombardment. Should a party be sent out to greet them?

---

*November 1* (continued). At 1245 it was decided to move Hanneken's 2nd Battalion, 7th Marines, to Koli Point by boats this afternoon, to intercept the expected landing. But Dexter [commanding the naval operating base] reported that only eighteen landing craft are available. All tank lighters are in use on the Matanikau front. It was then decided to move Hanneken's battalion to the Ilu River by trucks this afternoon, then to Koli Point (about five miles farther east) by foot tomorrow.

At 1530 a report came in that the 5th Marines are closing up to 0–2 [second objective line, half a mile beyond Point Cruz]. But in the evening it was learned that 1–5 has not yet even passed 0–1. Much disgust at headquarters. 1–5 will never get anywhere, D-3 officers say, and 3–5 wouldn't do any better. Decision to direct the 2nd Marines to pass through the 5th and attack along the coast road.

---

Impatience at the CP with the performance of the 5th Marines shows the gulf that often divides a division staff from officers and men fighting on the front line. The 1st Battalion of the 5th had run into a stubbornly defended Japanese strongpoint at the base of Point Cruz and somewhat to the west. It took two more days, and a convergence of two battalions, to clean up that nasty pocket. There 350 Japanese were killed and many heavy weapons captured—three field artillery pieces, twelve 37-mm. guns, and thirty machine guns.

One Marine casualty in this nasty set-to was Second Lieutenant Paul Moore, Jr.; twenty-two years later he would become Episcopalian Suffragan Bishop of Washington, D.C., and then Bishop of New York. He was badly wounded while leading his platoon in charges that pushed the Japanese to the beach. Forced to lie on his back Moore continued to give orders until he lost consciousness. A few hundred yards away his longtime friend (and my new friend, from the Pacific crossing), George Mead, had been killed on August 18. During the 5th Marines' first foray across the Matanikau after the Goettge patrol had met disaster, Mead tracked down a sniper who was holding up his platoon. He killed the sniper, but was himself mortally wounded.

---

*November 2*. 155-mm. howitzers were landed this morning. At 1545 they were already in position and beginning to register. Although they are set up a quarter of a mile away the blast is terrific all the way over here at the CP.

We have the makings of a grand mix-up. Japs are expected to try a landing at Koli Point tonight. We have a battalion out there to greet them. We expect to land troops at Aola tomorrow [more on this later], and reinforcements here in the perimeter. Japs, Americans, Japs, Americans, all along the coast. We have a task force approaching [bringing in the 8th Marines]. Jap ships have left the Buin area, undoubtedly on the way down here.

*November 3.* I woke up about 0500 to hear distant detonations, like naval gunfire, to the east. Heard them for about an hour. Now, at 0730, the firing has resumed. No one knows where our ships are or where the Jap ships are. So we sit and wait, wondering what is happening and praying that our reinforcements aren't at the bottom.

At 0700 Pistol Pete opened up and fired eight or nine rounds at the airfield. Thank God we now have seven 155s; once Pistol Pete is spotted, he's a goner.

Plans for the future: as soon as the 8th Marines have landed the transports will return to bring up another contingent of the Americal Division [a name combining "America" with "New Caledonia," where it had been on garrison duty]. The Army's 25th or 43rd Infantry Division is on the way south from Pearl Harbor and may be routed directly here.

Later. It turns out Japs landed east of Koli Point last night. They attacked Hanneken, who is now on the Nalimbiu River (so far as we know). Hanneken's message wasn't received until 1445. Puller's battalion, along with 7th Marines HQ, is being sent by Higgins boat to reinforce Hanneken; also a company each of pioneers and engineers. At 1700 Hanneken says that our planes, sent out to support him, have been bombing and strafing his troops.

The 5th Marines have captured a document indicating Jap plans to land another division (the 38th) east of us. Last night's landing apparently was the forerunner. Two Army battalions are to move up to the Nalimbiu River to join the 7th Marines. General Rupertus is to be in command in that sector. Whaling's scouts are to patrol inland from the mouth of the Nalimbiu. Tomorrow the 8th Marines land—*Deo volente.*

---

Herman H. Hanneken was famous as a capable, combatwise "Old" Marine long before he came to Guadalcanal. He had enlisted as a private in 1914. Commissioned as a second lieutenant five years later, he was assigned to duty in Haiti, where he tracked down and killed Charlemagne Peralte in the *caco* leader's hideout. He repeated the exploit five months later, killing Peralte's successor, Osiris Joseph. Hanneken was awarded the Medal of Honor. In

1929 he captured General Jiron, chief of staff to the Nicaraguan revolutionary chief Augusto Sandino.

Now, a few days after his men had fought off an assault on the ridge behind the Kukum-Matanikau corridor, Hanneken led his battalion into a new engagement. As directed, they had moved by truck to the Ilu and then by foot to Koli Point where they crossed the Nalimbiu. They slogged on three miles to the Metapona River and traversed the sandbar at its mouth under cover of darkness the night of November 2. Having organized a defensive line in the woods facing the beach on the other side, they waited. Soon they saw ships loom up through the rainy night—a cruiser, three destroyers, and a transport, as it turned out. Signal lights flashed from the beach half a mile east of them; they came from Shoji's men. The marines watched in silence as the Japanese, under cover of their naval guns, busily unloaded the ships amid the clatter of gear and chatter of sailors and soldiers. Soaked by rain, Hanneken's radio could not inform Division of this development.*

The fight began at dawn on November 3, when marines fired on a small patrol that trudged unsuspectingly up the beach. The mystifying sounds heard at the CP that morning were the boom of mortars fired by both sides, and of field artillery that the Japanese had brought ashore. To avoid envelopment as the Japanese began a flanking movement Hanneken pulled back, first behind the Metapona, then to the west bank of the Nalimbiu. It was, as noted, two-forty-five in the afternoon before he got through to the division command a message reporting his plight. Division immediately sent reinforcements and air support. Unfortunately the orders to the air command read, "Hit everything east of Koli Point." Hanneken's troops suffered much "friendly" bombing and strafing before they got west of the Nalimbiu.

That night Puller's battalion moved to join Hanneken by

---

*There are conflicting reports, U.S. and Japanese, as to whether the Japanese landed substantial reinforcements on this occasion. Certainly it was an important supply run, for the benefit of Shoji's tattered force. Probably a fresh battalion from the Thirty-eighth Infantry Division also came ashore.

boat. Two battalions of the 164th Infantry began trudging across the grassy coastal plain and jungly river valleys to a point about two miles south of the marines. Artillery joined the eastward move. General Rupertus came over from Tulagi to take over command of the four-battalion effort.

While marines crossed the Nalimbiu near its mouth, soldiers of the 164th Infantry were to wade the swollen river and work northward to outflank the Japanese. But the enemy contingent melted away to the east. Some of them— about 500 as it turned out—dug in at the site of their midnight landing on the 2nd, just east of a sluggish stream known as Gavaga Creek. The mixed Army-Marine force followed. Hanneken got into position east of the enemy beachhead, Puller west of it, along the creek. One of the Army battalions was to move in from the south, to block any Japanese attempt to escape inland.

The climax of this set-to in the east came on the 10th. Marines on either side of the little enemy beachhead began a drumfire of mortar shells against the woods where the Japanese were dug in, to drive them south into waiting Army arms. But the gap along Gavaga Creek had not quite been closed. At least some of the Japanese succeeded in breaking out of the intended trap. After the war Shoji reported that he had been ordered to withdraw inland, toward the upper Lunga, while the Army-Marine flanking maneuver was developing, and had left only a rear guard near Gavaga Creek.

Puller was one of the casualties of the eight-day engagement. He was wounded by mortar fire on the 7th, collecting, as he put it, "a fanny full of shrapnel." When a doctor pinned a casualty tag on him and ordered him evacuated, the colonel shouted: "Evacuate me, hell! Take that tag and label a bottle with it. I will remain in command." But the next day he was ordered to leave and yield command to Major John E. Weber.

On the 11th the American force overran the beachhead. Much booty was captured and destroyed, including artillery pieces, collapsible landing boats, and fifteen tons of rice which the starving Japanese desperately needed. Between four and five hundred of Shoji's rear guard had been killed. His main body was working its way inland to the upper Lunga and Mount Austen, along the track that was now known to Americans as the East-West Trail. Hyakutake had planned to put most of his Thirty-eighth Division ashore in the east and even thought of quickly developing an airstrip on the grassy plain. The American interception beyond Koli Point led him to abandon those plans. The Thirty-eighth, like the Second in October, would land west of the Lunga perimeter.

On November 4 Vandegrift had the equivalent of two regiments west of the Matanikau and a larger than regiment-sized force about fifteen miles to the east. With a major new Japanese effort building up, the division command was anxious about the security of the airfield. Fresh troops were available for Guadalcanal. Indeed, they were on the way. But their destination was not the Lunga perimeter.

Admiral Turner had conceived the idea of building an airfield at Aola, the old headquarters of the district officer, more than thirty miles east of the Lunga perimeter. Again the admiral was showing his fondness for dispersing ground forces when the situation called for their concentration. To build the new strip he would send in 500 Seabees, a battalion of the Army's 147th Infantry (from the Americal Division), detachments of artillery, and Lieutenant Colonel Evans F. Carlson's 2nd Marine Raider Battalion.

No one else in the higher echelons of Navy, Army, and Marine commands in the South Pacific liked the Aola project—no one, that is, except Halsey, who gave his approval. The move deprived the perimeter of needed reinforcements at a time when offensives were under way both to east and to west. The Aola force, too far away to be supported from the perimeter, would be exposed to a counterlanding at a time when the Japanese were again showing a lively interest in the region to the east.

Moreover, the ground around Aola was not fit for an airfield. Clemens, who knew Aola all too well, repeatedly pointed out that the ground was marshy, punctuated by ridges. A scouting party of Marine engineers confirmed his views. No argument deterred Turner. On November 4 the mixed forces of Army troops, Marine raiders, and Navy Seabees came ashore at Aola. They ran into all the predicted construction problems.

---

*November 4.* I went to the beach this morning to see the 8th Marines [commanded by Colonel Richard H. Jeschke] come ashore. What a welcome sight! Three big transports were busily unloading, with cruisers and destroyers hovering around them. The warships gave the Japs a pounding on both sides of us. Pistol Pete opened up on the ships while they were unloading, but our planes think they spotted him. Our 155s laid into his position, and he was quiet the rest of the day.

There was an air raid alert this morning but nothing came over. I suppose the boys are unloading at Aola, too, carrying out the dream of a stubborn naval command. Thomas thinks the entire Aola plan, at this time at least, is a fool's project. Why in God's name do they send a detachment down there, separated from us by thirty miles, when we need all possible reinforcements here? It is heartbreaking.

Re the Aola business: Thomas was talking to Admiral Calhoun this evening [Rear Admiral Calhoun was COMSOPAC's energetic supply officer, regarded by marines as a good friend]. The admiral started telling him "what you need is . . ." Thomas interrupted: "What we need is an end to arbitrary decisions by people who don't know what they are doing." That's the kind of talk I like.

Ira Wolfert of the North American Newspaper Alliance arrived.

*November 5.* We had our first bombing today since October 25—Dugout Sunday. Most of the bombs fell south of our lines.

*November 6.* I spent a good part of the day around the press tent, waiting for Keys to finish an article so that we could get off to the eastern front. We finally got started and bounced along the beach road for ten miles to Sims's command post [Colonel Amor L. Sims commanded the 7th Marines] near the Nalimbiu River. We passed broad grass-covered plains, ideal for really big airfields. It's infuriating to think of Kelly Turner's insistence on the Aola project.

A warning came in that the Japs may attempt another landing near Koli Point. There's nothing to oppose them but dive-bombers and PT boats.

*November 7.* I went over to the 8th Marines this morning, but found the officers in conference. My wait was interrupted by a terrific explosion off the coast. "Torpedo" was my first thought, and torpedo it was. Out at sea a great cloud of smoke was pouring from the *Majaba,* a cargo ship. I rushed up to the beach where boats were bringing in the crew. Miraculously she didn't sink. I watched for forty-five minutes, and she didn't seem to settle at all, only listing slightly to port when I left. Later I heard they were going to beach the ship, so she must have been badly damaged. [The ship was later salvaged.]

The Jap landing at Koli Point, about which we were warned last night, didn't come off. We are slowly pressing eastward, toward the Metapona.

Bob Cromie, just back from Aola, reports he had a fine time down there—good food and a good rest. Early in the morning of the 3rd they [the advance party, including Clemens] lighted their bonfires on the beach to guide in the main landing party. Just at that time the Japs were pulling out after landing beyond Koli, but the Aola boys didn't know it. Lucky they didn't draw a few salvos from the Jap ships.

*November 8.* Norman Lodge (Associated Press) and Foster Hailey *(New York Times)* arrived, just before breakfast.

*November 9.* Bob Brumby (International News Service) arrived—and took over my cot. The influx of reporters is getting on my nerves. I am growing more irascible. They must think me a sour sort. Perhaps it's a reaction from the strain we were under last month. Things are too quiet, and I take that as a bad sign. I expect things will liven up all too soon. Some foolish people seem to think the main bout is over. I don't believe that for a minute.

Henry Keys, Bob Cromie, and I had a good time together—as "good" as life can offer in these conditions. I sort of hate to see the party broken up by new arrivals. Moreover, it means that I won't have any time for writing or doing the work I want to do. I'll be bombarded with questions, requests, and chitchat. Will have no quiet. Will have no transportation. Will have no time to myself.

*November 10.* Henry Keys left this morning. I'm sorry to see him go. He was one of my favorites among the correspondents. He's intelligent, knows what is going on, sees "the big picture" well, is witty, and thinks the Marines are a great outfit—as indeed they are.

———

Things were "quiet" only in the sense that Japanese bombings and shellings had fallen off sharply since the Sendai Division had been crushed, and there had been no assault against the perimeter. The battle around Tetere in the east was reaching its climax. In the west the push toward Kokumbona had been resumed.

What to do in the west when the new threat had appeared in the east had posed an awkward problem for the division command. Should the troops on the Point Cruz line be pulled back? Their main mission—to drive the Japanese beyond six-inch artillery range of the airfield—remained as urgent as ever. But could three regiments be spared outside the perimeter? Vandegrift got conflicting advice.

Edson, whose 5th Marines had been in the lead the first three days of the trans-Matanikau attack, came to the division CP for a conference on the morning of November 4. Usually an aggressive combat leader, on this occasion he opposed continuation of the western offensive. We could expect, he said, Japanese in each draw along the coast. Strongly dug in, they would fight to the last man. The American left flank was wide open.

There were other arguments against continuing a westward push. To an extent not fully known, the Japanese out there had been getting reinforcements almost every night. Two regiments in the Koli Point area could not be counted on for defense of the perimeter. They might even be cut off by landings between themselves and the Lunga position. The stretch of beach between Kukum and the Matanikau was vulnerable to counterlandings. First priority should be given, as it had been given all along, to holding the airfield. Until more was known about what was afoot near Koli Point available forces should be concentrated in the perimeter.

Twining wanted to continue pushing westward. He wanted to keep the Japanese on the defensive. Perhaps the strongpoint Edson's men had just wiped out at the base of Point Cruz was their main point of resistance. It was vital to push the Japanese beyond artillery range of Henderson.

Thomas and Vandegrift decided to halt the western push until more was known about what was developing in the east, but to keep a strong force west of Point Cruz. The 2nd Marines (less the 3rd Battalion) and a battalion of the 164th Infantry were left to hold a beachhead there. For nearly a week they held on, while the Japanese, from higher ground inland, kept them under fire and several times tried at night to break through their little perimeter.

On November 10, with the Japanese threat at Tetere apparently disposed of, Division ordered that the westward advance be renewed. With the newly arrived 8th Marines in reserve, the defenders of the western beachhead were ordered to attack. They were getting deeper into the main Japanese position, which was defended with the usual tenacity. General Hyakutake's command post was near the American target, the Poha River. Some 5,000 Japanese troops, most of them fresh arrivals, were lying in wait in the inland network of ridges and ravines, hoping to cut off and chop up a sizable body of Americans advancing near the shore.

A situation map of Guadalcanal's northern coast at that time was a crazy quilt of red (enemy) and blue (friendly) patches. From the northwestern tip of the island nearly to Point Cruz was solid red; the Japanese were making landings almost nightly and feeding troops eastward to check the American push along the coast. South and southwest of us were other red splotches, where remnants of the Sendai Division and Kawaguchi's brigade held points on Mount Austen and along the east-west trail to Kokumbona.

A fat blue bulge with a narrow streamer out to Point Cruz marked the American perimeter guarding the airfield and its westward extension. A series of blue patches on the other side of the perimeter reached out beyond Koli Point to Tetere. Then a circle of red— the Japanese beachhead at Tetere. There was also a thin moving line of blue marking the path of Carlson's 2nd Raiders in pursuit of Shoji and others who had escaped from the Tetere red patch—a matter to which I will return. And at Aola, some twenty miles further west, a larger hedgehog of blue. Twining smiled wryly as he looked at that motley on the map: "What would the [Marine Corps] Schools make of that!"

It was the red mass in the northern Solomons, the Bismarck Archipelago, and Truk—not on our local situation map—that caused the most anxiety. On November 11, tipped off as to Japanese plans to move that concentration of ships, planes, and troops south, the division command immediately called a halt to the westward push. To strengthen defenses of the airfield against the new threat, the biggest yet, Vandegrift ordered the 2nd and 8th Marines to pull back to the eastern bank of the Matanikau. Not for the first time marines trudged back across ground they had painfully won, this time with Army help, beyond that ill-omened river.

---

*November 11.* William Hipple (Associated Press) arrived.

Something is in the air. I am not sure what it is but can make the obvious guess. Our offensive to the west is being called off. Lincs are being shortened and strengthened. Two waves of Jap bombers came over today—one of dive-bombers, which attacked the ships without success, and another flight of twenty-seven twin-engined bombers (seven were shot down). Reinforcements for us [the Army's 182nd Infantry Regiment, less a battalion] are due to arrive tomorrow—a major movement which Tojo will certainly challenge.

All signs point to increased Jap activity, and soon. I expect it will be a pretty mighty blow—the climax of their efforts to retake this place. They have powerful naval forces to the northwest and have been building up a reserve of planes for more than two weeks. So look out for bombs and fourteen-inch naval shells and artillery. I'll bet they open up with field artillery from the hills.

In short, it looks like a very hot time for the next few days. Operations officers and the command have suddenly become very secretive. There is an undercurrent of excitement in the CP.

*November 12.* I have learned what the Jap plan is. Tomorrow is to be Z-Day, the day of attack. The Japs have shifted large numbers of planes into airdromes in the northwest Solomons, including an Army squadron. Five carriers (three of them apparently small ones) are to join in the attack. A large fleet of combat ships and troop transports will move on Guadalcanal. Yesterday's air raids were the preliminaries. No doubt there will be more today and naval shelling tonight.

However, we have cruisers and destroyers in these waters, and air reinforcements arrive today—dive-bombers, torpedo planes, fighters, and AAF Lockheed interceptors. Our ground reinforcements arrived safely—an Army regiment and Marine replacements. Also more artillery (155s and 105s), ammo, and avgas. Our defense lines have been shortened, the 8th and 2nd Marines pulled back east of the Matanikau.

Our men are doing well out at the Metapona; they have mopped up a battalion of Japs out of the force that landed November 2–3, and are dug in on the west bank of the Metapona. Carlson is chasing another group of Japs (one small battalion and two small companies, he thinks) inland. We are stronger than we ever have been and ready for a showdown.

Later. This afternoon, at 1415, about twenty-five torpedo bombers attacked our shipping; no hits; only one bomber was seen to escape.

Evening air searches were negative, but we have learned not to rely on them too heavily. We still expect a shelling tonight, but this time we have Navy out there to put up a fight.

———————————

The Japanese had indeed planned a "pretty mighty blow." They had originally planned to put most of the Hiroshima

Division ashore near Koli Point. Our reception of their beachhead party had put a crimp in that project; instead, the new division would come in to the west of us. They had been steadily building up their ground strength in that quarter. Operation Rat had been briskly running. On six nights between November 2 and 10 the Guadalcanal Express had brought in fresh troops and supplies.

In one run, the night of the 7th, the advance echelon of the Hiroshima (Thirty-eighth) Division had come ashore at Tassafaronga. On the 9th the division commander, Lieutenant General Tadayoshi Sano, arrived with his headquarters and 600 more troops. These steady accretions were just the beginning.

The Japanese planned to knock out the Cactus Air Force with a combination of heavy aerial bombing and shelling by battleships. Then, before American air power could be replaced, they would ram down the Slot and its parallel routes the main body of Sano's division—some 11,000 strong*—plus 3,000 Special Naval Landing Force troops, in a big convoy of eleven transports. Carrier and other surface forces, including two battleships, would cover this major movement at a distance. The assault would start with a bombardment by two other battleships the night of November 12–13. According to Japanese plans, it was to be mid-October all over again, only more so.

During the lull in Japanese air raids the Cactus Air Force had been reinforced. A fresh Marine Air Group— MAG-11—began arriving on November 1, led by a squadron each of Wildcat fighters and Dauntless dive-bombers. The daily dawn muster roll of flyable aircraft grew moderately from fifty-six on the last day of October to seventy-three on November 10.

On November 7 General Geiger reluctantly yielded local command to his chief of staff, Brigadier General Louis E. Woods, and went to his First Marine Air Wing headquarters in Espiritu Santo. In the absence of major air raids the Cactus Air Force's principal missions were twice-daily

---

*There are wide discrepancies, in both Japanese and U.S. accounts, as to the numbers of troops involved in this major movement. The figures used here accord with the number of ships that took part.

searches for enemy ships coming down the Alley or parallel routes outside the island chain, attacking them when found (if there was time for a strike and if weather permitted, as often it did not), providing air cover for our ships when they came in to unload, trying to locate and eliminate the Pistol Petes, making life miserable for Japanese troops on the western part of the island, and supporting ground troops in their operations to east and west.

As usual, fast Express destroyers, maneuvering violently when under attack, were skillful in evading Cactus strikes— normally only one each afternoon when the ships came within range. More often than not, the strikers scored no hits. Their best afternoon was on the 7th when they went after eleven Rat destroyers and got bombs or torpedoes into two of them. Often, when there was some moonlight, Cactus planes tried to attack the ships as they were unloading, but results were poor and costs high in pilots and planes not equipped for night operations, flying from a field likewise ill-equipped. Even during the lull in aerial combat there were losses almost daily, owing to crack-ups in night landings, stormy weather, exhaustion of fuel in flight, and enemy flak.

When the Japanese master plan and schedule became known on November 11 rear-base commands in COMSOPAC's domain strained to put every plane possible into Guadalcanal. Two more Marine squadrons arrived on the 12th—one of dive-bombers, another of torpedo bombers. At long, long last eight AAF Lockheed Lightnings flew in on the 13th. The partially crippled *Enterprise* sped northward to contribute almost all its air group to Henderson Field. The conglomerate Cactus Air Force was ready for the most fateful day of its career.

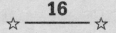
# Decision in November

Between November 2 and 10 the Guadalcanal Express made sixty-five destroyer runs, sometimes augmented by cruisers and seaplane tenders. The ships were laden with troops, munitions, equipment, and supplies. By the 11th a regiment of the Thirty-eighth Division and other units had come ashore. Now the moment had come for the big push—an attempt, after massive bombardment of Henderson Field, to ram through a big convoy of eleven transports.

Aware that the Japanese concentration to the north was on the move, Halsey was gathering what strength he could to oppose it. At the same time he was rushing reinforcements to Guadalcanal. Turner's transports and cargo ships were bringing in Marine replacements and supplies and most of a fresh Army regiment—the 182nd Regimental Combat Team, minus one of its battalions.

The first contingent of three troop carriers arrived safely just before dawn on November 11. Twice air raids interrupted their unloading and damaged all three vessels. The next day another convoy brought in the Army regiment. Again the Japanese pounded the new arrivals from the air. As they had done on August 9, torpedo bombers swung in very low; ack-ack and Cactus fighters brought down all but one. That day American search planes spotted a massive Japanese surface force including two battleships beginning to move toward the island.

Turner ordered his transports and cargo ships to withdraw at nightfall. Admirals Callaghan and Scott, whose combat ships had escorted the reinforcement movement, were to combine their forces and face a much more powerful enemy. Together they mustered five cruisers and eight destroyers. Rushing toward them from the northwest were two Japanese battleships, a light cruiser, and fourteen destroyers.

Both Callaghan, available for reassignment with the departure of Ghormley, and Scott, victor in the October Battle of Cape Esperance, were in the class of 1911 at Annapolis. Although he had never before been in combat Callaghan outranked veteran Scott by a few numbers; he was to be in command of American ships during the coming fracas. It was the dark of the moon, and Callaghan's ships tensely patrolled Ironbottom Sound. They formed a column—four destroyers followed by five cruisers with four more destroyers bringing up the train.

Admiral Hiroaki Abe, avoiding the central Slot, had gathered his ships north of Santa Isabel. After nightfall they began moving toward Savo Island. Abe intended to pound Henderson Field with 14-inch shells. The two battleships that were to deliver these shattering missiles formed the core of his formation, with destroyers protecting their van, rear, and flanks.

At about one-thirty in the morning of Friday, November 13, the two forces nearly collided northwest of Lunga Point. Abe's lookouts spotted the Americans soon after their radar had picked up his own ships. Callaghan was now leading his column north. For some reason he delayed ordering his ships to launch torpedoes or to open fire. As the minutes ticked by—five, eight, ten—the gun crews of Abe's battleships rushed to substitute armor-piercing shells—ship-killers—for the thin-skinned high-explosive bombardment shells with which they had been readied. Callaghan's van destroyer had to swing left to avoid collision with the leading Japanese destroyer, and the whole of Callaghan's column began to turn with her.

At one-fifty the battle started. Having spotted Scott's flagship, the cruiser *Atlanta*, a Japanese battleship and destroyer opened their big searchlights to illuminate her. Japanese turrets swung to pound her. Long Lances were launched. "Friendly" fire, aimed at Japanese ships beyond the *Atlanta*, also raked her. The *Atlanta*'s superstructure was ripped apart, killing Admiral Scott and most others on the bridge. While the American cruiser was returning the fire a torpedo lifted her out of the water and left her a broken wreck, dead in the water. She sank later in the day.

The battleship *Hiei* was now drawing fire from four U.S. destroyers, one of them only 300 yards away, wrecking her superstructure, starting deck fires, and destroying her communications. Admiral Callaghan finally gave orders to fire: "Odd ships commence fire to starboard, even ships to port." But in that inferno the identity of ships on this side or that was not always clear. The American column slashed through the Japanese formation, passing between the battleships *Hiei* and *Kirishima*. By now *Hiei* was so ablaze that she was no longer a threat. *Kirishima*'s big guns were still thundering. At point blank range the battleship's lighter batteries joined other ships' guns to blast the *San Francisco*. They knocked her out of action and killed Admiral Callaghan. At times *Hiei* had been so close to American ships that her shells shrieked loudly but harmlessly over them.

In the donnybrook the fleets were intermingled, friend and foe sometimes indistinguishable, every ship for herself, maneuvering wildly to avoid collisions. Ten minutes after the battle started Abe ordered his two giants to turn away. Their withdrawal decided the issue. The battle was almost over.

But through the rest of the night the flames of burning and exploding ships, sweep of searchlights, and great orange and black blooms from exploding ammunition magazines on stricken vessels illuminated Ironbottom Sound. The sun rose on six ships—five American, one Japanese— dead in the water or barely under way between Lunga Point and Savo Island. Two more ships lay beyond Savo, where *Hiei* had limped during the night. There she was battered unremittingly and finally sunk by planes from Henderson Field and Espiritu Santo.

In the morning only three American cruisers and three destroyers were able to retire eastward through Indispensable Strait, and three of those had been badly wounded. One cruiser, the *Juneau*, did not long survive. At eleven o'clock a Japanese submarine pierced her with a Long Lance and she sank like a plummet, with few survivors.

The cruiser *Portland,* a huge hole in her stern, finished off a crippled Japanese destroyer, and then was nudged to the shelter of Tulagi Harbor.

Two U.S. cruisers and four destroyers had sunk into Ironbottom Sound or nearby waters, either during the night-time slugging match or the next day. The Japanese had lost a battleship and two destroyers, with damage to most other ships. In the totting up of gains and losses the decisive American advantage was that Henderson Field had been spared a devastating bombardment; and that had been an essential element in the Japanese plan. The Night of mid-October was not repeated—not, at least, just yet. The Cactus Air Force was intact.

Groundlings and airmen on Guadalcanal could only watch in awe and anxiety the wild melee at sea which, at enormous cost in lives and ships, had been their salvation. They could only watch and, the next day, play a small part in helping to succor the survivors, many of them burnt, torn by shell fragments and other bits of flying steel, gassed by smoke and noxious fumes, drenched in oil. "It's worse at sea."

Naval tacticians and historians have found fault with the way the U.S. forces had been disposed for the night battle. The ships should not, for example, have been in a column (the formation Scott used in his successful encounter off Savo in October), for destroyers could not rapidly deploy to launch torpedoes. And, it is said, poor use was made of the ships equipped with the best radar, which were not placed in the van. And Callaghan should have had a battle plan, and should have been prompter to order that firing begin. A landlubber may be permitted to suppose that, given the formidable odds against the heavily outgunned U.S. force, its one hope lay in a melee at close quarters, where the 14-inch guns of *Hiei* and *Kirishima* could not be used to full advantage and the Japanese commander was confused. Whether he adequately planned his tactics or not Admiral Callaghan had fought off two battleships and had saved the Cactus Air Force, which was to prove decisive within two days.

Early on the 13th the curtain had rung down on only the first act of a continuing drama. That night the Imperial

Navy was back, and this time there was nothing to oppose them but PT boats. Admiral Mikawa rolled down the back alley, north of Santa Isabel, with six cruisers (four heavy, two light) and six destroyers. His mission was to do what the battleships had failed to do the night before: bombard and knock out Henderson Field. He arrived off Savo shortly after midnight. While the rest of his force patrolled the approaches to Ironbottom Sound, three heavy cruisers pumped more than 1,300 surface-blasting bombardment shells into the Lunga perimeter while Louie the Louse droned overhead.

*November 14.* The Japs shelled us last night, but compared to the performance of a month ago it was a half-hearted effort. A battleship and some smaller ships [actually, three cruisers and two destroyers] started the bombardment at 1:30 in the morning and carried on until about 2:15. They concentrated on the fighter strip; got several hits on the field but did amazingly little damage. Only three planes were knocked out for keeps. About seventeen more Wildcats were slightly damaged but could be quickly repaired. Our torpedo boats tangled with the Japs and apparently drove them off. Certainly this bombardment was trivial compared with what the Japs had planned for us the night before.

It rained hard during the night and I was terribly afraid the field would be so boggy that planes couldn't take off—what few planes, I imagined, had survived the shelling, which sounded worse than it was. But the planes were up at dawn and put in the hardest, most magnificent day's work they have ever been called on to do.

---

The second act, then, had been weak.

The first job for Henderson planes and pilots was to pursue the ships that had shelled us during the night. They caught up with the fleeing Japanese about 140 miles out. Fifteen planes from the *Enterprise* joined in attacking them. In repeated strikes Marine and Navy bombers sank a heavy cruiser and damaged two other cruisers. It was a satisfying morning's work, but greater things lay ahead.

The *Enterprise,* the only U.S. carrier then operating in

the South Pacific, its forward plane-elevator still stuck,
had been undergoing frantic repairs at Noumea. On the 11th
Halsey had ordered the flattop, despite her injuries, to
move toward Guadalcanal, guarded by two new battleships
(*Washington* and *South Dakota*). In the afternoon of the
13th, as Japanese cruisers moved in to bombard Henderson
Field, Halsey had ordered the two battleships to leave the
"Big E" to try to intercept the Japanese cruisers that were
moving in to bombard Guadalcanal. The order came too
late for the battlewagons to close the island that night. But
now, on the 14th, the *Enterprise* was close enough to take
part in the day-long strikes against Japanese ships.

By late morning the main target, the convoy of eleven
big and fast transports, had been found. Shortly before
noon the first flight from Henderson Field—a mixture of
Avenger torpedo planes, Dauntless dive-bombers, and Wildcat fighters, Marine and Navy—roared in on the hapless
troop carriers. Thereafter the flights came over in relays,
as fast as harried ground crews back at Henderson Field
could repair, rearm, and refuel them. Army Air Force
B-17s from Espiritu Santo joined in the assault in midafternoon. Below, where the Japanese transports and their es-
corts milled about, the scene was one of flame, death, and
carnage. The Japanese could provide only skimpy air cover
with Zeros operating at long range from the Rabaul complex and a carrier standing off to the north. The convoy's
main, and grossly inadequate, protection from air attack
was antiaircraft fire from its eleven escorting destroyers.

We have by now many times encountered Tanaka, the
able and tenacious admiral charged with the unenviable
task of moving reinforcements to Gadarukanaru through
much of the campaign. Early in the afternoon of Friday the
13th, as he shepherded the eleven fat transports out of the
Shortlands, he "had a premonition that an ill fate was in
store for us." Later he vividly described the scene as his
charges suffered attack after attack: sticks of bombs wob-
bling down from Flying Fortresses, Dauntlesses screeching
down in steep dives, torpedo bombers in their low runs,
clouds of flame and smoke billowing from sinking transports, destroyers darting about laying smoke screens and
spewing ack-ack and picking up soldiers who leaped from

burning transports, as first one, then two, then more, for a total of seven, were sent to the bottom of the Slot or so damaged that they soon would sink. According to Tanaka, some 5,000 of the embarked troops and crews were rescued by his destroyers, but his estimate seems much too high, given the small number of ships available to pick up survivors.

Despite the carnage Admiral Yamamoto ordered Tanaka to push on toward Guadalcanal with the four remaining transports. An imperial task force built around the battleship *Kirishima*, which had come through the nocturnal brawl of November 12–13 almost unscathed, was speeding south to protect him and to bombard us again. Japanese search planes had reported American "cruisers and destroyers" rushing toward Guadalcanal. The *Kirishima* group was to intercept them. By sunset some of Tanaka's rescue destroyers, bearing survivors from the sunken transports, caught up with him. The admiral felt encouraged. He was further heartened when he saw the *Kirishima* loom far ahead of him about midnight near Savo.

The American "cruisers and destroyers" the Japanese expected to encounter turned out to include two battleships. Rear Admiral Willis A. "Ching" Lee, detached from his daylight duties of protecting the *Enterprise*, had raced toward Savo Island with the *Washington* and *South Dakota* to meet the Japanese battleship. Anxious watchers on Guadalcanal and Tulagi witnessed for the fourth time a major encounter of surface fleets off Savo Island, lighted by flares from floatplanes, brilliant stabs from searchlights, star shells and tracers, flashes of naval guns, and ballooning flames from torpedo and shell hits followed by explosions of magazines and fuel tanks.

Lee's four destroyers took heavy losses. Within fifteen minutes, just after eleven-thirty that night, two were sent to the bottom. A third, her bow shattered by a torpedo, had to be abandoned; she sank the next day. The fourth was damaged and out of action.

An electrical failure took the *South Dakota* out of action for a few crucial minutes. She and the *Washington* were looking for bigger game than the light ships that were smashing Lee's destroyer screen and they soon found Admiral Kondo's bombardment group northwest of Savo. Just after midnight the *Washington* loosed a salvo from her 16-inch guns against the *Kirishima,* followed by one from the *South Dakota,* which had taken more than forty hits during her brief period of helplessness. The Japanese battlewagon was soon aflame, unable to steer, and beginning to sink. Kondo abandoned his plans to bombard Henderson Field, made a smoke screen, and edged northeast while the *Kirishima*'s satellite destroyers took on her crew. Three hours later she was scuttled.

During this fray Tanaka and his convoy had prudently pulled back to the north, where he anxiously watched the battle. He was still under orders to get the four remaining transports unloaded although he was far behind schedule. When the firing dwindled he headed for Tassafaronga. With dawn approaching he decided that his only hope of getting the troops ashore was to beach the ships. After brief soul-searching among his superiors in Rabaul and Truk, one of them approved his plan: "Run aground and unload troops."

---

*November 15.* Our battleships tangled with the Japs last night. The heavy shooting began about 11:30 and went on for half an hour. I still haven't the vaguest idea what happened. I only know that four Jap transports were spotted this morning on the beach to the west of us, unloading. Our artillery set the nearest one afire. Planes disposed of the rest. By the middle of the morning all were flaming. I went down to the beach to see that welcome sight. It was an unreal feeling to see four enemy ships beached and ablaze only a few miles away. I could imagine on that green beach across the bay hundreds of Japs scurrying about, unloading supplies, running for cover when our planes came over, trying to pull themselves together after a really shattering blow. I don't know how many thousands succeeded in getting ashore. It couldn't be anything like the number the Japs hoped to land, and most of their supplies must be destroyed.

We get daily evidence that Jap forces on the island are badly demoralized. Living in the jungle on short rations, decimated several times over during their assaults on us, subjected to daylong air attacks, they must be in pretty bad shape. Their diaries show this. They hate the jungle, the rain, the hardships, bombardments from land, sea, and air, as much as we do, and they are now getting much heavier doses than we are. One diarist cried out in despair: "Where are our friendly aircraft? Where is the might of the Imperial Navy? Have they forgotten we are on this island?" Familiar words.

Today it looks as though we have scored a decisive victory but there are too many uncertainties to permit much optimism. Our fleet suffered heavy losses; have we enough ships left to challenge another Jap thrust on such a large scale? Against this, our planes have performed wonders. And Jap planes have not recently come over in the numbers I expected. Have they run seriously low on planes, or are they on another mission, or are they saving up for another blow? Were Jap losses serious enough to discourage them from another big invasion attempt in a few weeks? We won't know these things for some time. Meanwhile, temporary relief and uncertainty.

---

The victory was indeed decisive. But we did not yet know—in fact, no American knew for two and a half more months—that Tokyo would give up trying to recapture Henderson Field. Few Japanese planes had appeared over Guadalcanal or over its stricken convoy because the Imperial Navy's air arm was crippled by the loss of trained pilots.

Japanese losses in shipping were almost as grievous, and brought on a severe political crisis in Tokyo. U.S. submarines had been taking a heavy toll throughout the western and southern Pacific. On November 15, when news reached Tokyo that eleven precious fast transports had been destroyed at Guadalcanal, IGHQ ordered Hyakutake's Seventeenth Army to hold fast for the time being. The next day they organized a new Eighth Area Army commanded by Lieutenant General Hitoshi Imamura. It was comprised of Hyakutake's army, which was to continue the struggle on Guadalcanal, and a new Eighteenth Army, to fight in New Guinea.

But naval officers on the imperial general staff were

beginning cautiously to whisper about evacuation of Guadalcanal. Heated disputes, on occasion physical brawls, broke out between the Army High Command and the War Ministry in Tokyo over the requisitioning of ships. The Army demanded 300,000 tons of shipping—four times the amount lost in the Slot that flaming November 14—to continue supplying Guadalcanal. Tojo, who was both War Minister and Prime Minister, insisted that the government must take into account the pressing national needs for imports from the newly won resources area to the south. He refused to give in to the Army staff. Eventually Tojo personally assumed the post of Chief of the General Staff in addition to his other posts. He put into key positions on the General Staff officers more amenable to his wishes.

☆ ——— ☆

# Respite and Relief

*November 19.* All quiet—at least fairly quiet. Jap patrols are showing considerable activity. Several small groups were encountered west and southwest of the Matanikau. We are pushing out beyond that river again. Not in a major drive; just sort of feeling our way. There has been no Jap activity in the air or at sea.

General Patch arrived this morning. [Major General Alexander M. Patch, USA, commanded the Americal Division.] Lots of bigwigs are around, many of them Army, all a very welcome sight. Rumors that we will soon leave the island have passed beyond scuttlebutt. I get inklings from many sources that the move may come very soon. The Signal Company is packing up. D-3 is making out a list, which seems to be a roster of the first elements to go. There is a debate as to whether General Vandegrift should leave early or wait until the bulk of the division has moved out. Tarrant [First Lieutenant Guy Tarrant, Vandegrift's aide] is gleeful over some pleasant surprise to be announced on Thanksgiving. Soule says Colonel Buckley has told him to get ready to leave on a moment's notice. Oh happy day!

A recently arrived sergeant-reporter [I still had not heard of combat correspondents] came around this afternoon, very excited, very earnest. Having gone through one naval shelling and two bombings he has decided that war is hell, and that he should write something stark. He showed me a long piece on the terror of men during bombings and shellings, the pain of the wounded, the disease and unpleasantness of this place. It was a gloomy and distorted piece; you would get the idea that every marine on the island is a

terror-stricken, beaten man. I tried to tell him the picture
was badly skewed. Of course, everyone is afraid of bombs
and 14-inch shells. No one likes them except the senders.
Fighting men have to have enough bounce to absorb these
shocks. But he was obviously upset and fired with zeal to
tell the world that war is a nasty business: "Someone has
*got* to do it!"

*November 24.* I spent a lazy afternoon lying on the beach
near the Tenaru. It's the first time I have been in the sea
since August. The water was warm but pleasant. The sky
was cloudless. Lots of planes were overhead—Fortresses,
Hudsons, Wildcats, Lightnings, and Airacobras.

I also visited the assistant division commander's headquarters. There I got one of the men in the intelligence
section to do the reverse of the George Medal. It is now
ready to be cast. I'll undoubtedly be court-martialled.

---

This is the first mention I find of the George Medal. The
diary entry indicates that the project to design and strike
such a "decoration" was well along by November 24. By
now readers will have gathered that marines on Guadalcanal had long felt neglected, almost marooned, poorly
supported by higher Navy commands, and generally put
upon. Such feelings are common enough among exposed
front-line units, who easily persuade themselves that superior headquarters are willing to see them go down the
drain. Whether, in this instance, resentment was more
solidly based than is usually the case, it certainly existed.

"Let George do it" had become a common saying,
referring to an attitude attributed to Navy superiors. Colonel Twining and Captain Donald Dickson, personnel officer for the 5th Marines, were the main progenitors of a
mock decoration to immortalize the sentiment. At some
point I became a party to their plans. Perhaps I contributed
the Latin translation: Faciat Georgius. In any event, that
motto was to go on the face of the medal.

A skilled draftsman whose drawings of Guadalcanal
marines became famous, Dickson drew the picture that
was to appear beneath the motto: a heavily bestriped admi-

ral's sleeve, his hand dropping a hot potato* into the hands
of a crouching marine, with a cactus in the background.

A piece of barnyard humor was to appear on the reverse
side, which I was asking someone at Rupertus's headquarters to draw. There was another common saying among
marines on the island, after a particularly nasty bombing or
shelling or night attack: "Where were *you* when the shit
hit the fan?" The question was illustrated by a cow's
backside presented to an electric fan.

On Vandegrift's urging, Halsey cancelled the Aola venture and ordered the construction units there to move to the
broad plain south of Koli Point, where a new airfield
should have been planned in the first place.

---

*November 25.* I went down the coast to Aola today.
Commander Compton [then commanding the naval operating base], Major Murray, and I set out at 0600. It was a
beautiful morning, with bright skies and a calm sea. Guadalcanal looked fantastically beautiful and I found myself
regretting that I will leave it soon. In less sentimental
moods I know I'll be damned glad to see the last of it. It
took us three and a half hours to make Aola, along a shore
littered here and there with landing boats—ours and Jap—
and past the scenes of many battles.

Aola is a pleasant place. Coconut palms line the shore
and ridges rise steeply behind. The ground troops have dug
in back in the hills and have cut a road through the jungle
leading up to their position. The construction units and
Navy are on the coastal strip. The poor devils have worked
hard to try to develop the place and now it is to be
abandoned. This extra work and wasted month are a mon-
ument to Kelly Turner's stubbornness.

If we at Lunga are George, the Aola group is Little
George. They are pathetically short of manpower, boats,
and equipment to make the move they are called on to

---

*By a coincidence wholly unknown to us at the time, Admiral Halsey
had remarked, upon being appointed COMSOPAC: "This is the hottest
potato they ever handed me." The outline of Guadalcanal is not unlike
that of a Maine or Idaho roaster.

make. I didn't realize what a complicated problem it is until I heard a conference of Navy, Marine, Seabee, and Army officers. There are only six boats here—two tank lighters, two ramp boats, and two T-boats. There's a lot of heavy equipment that will be hard to handle and slow to move. There are not enough men to guard both the Aola area and the new airfield site [behind Koli Point]. Luckily the Japs haven't attacked them. They have an awfully thin line to guard that sprawling area.

We started back early in the afternoon. When we were about six miles from home the engine on our Higgins boat broke down. We drifted about for two hours. The crew consisted of three of the most shiftless, helpless, stupid men I have ever seen. Commander Compton, witnessing at first hand the shameful boat situation, was browned off. Finally he hailed a destroyer, which relayed a message to shore. A boat came out to tow us in.

---

Before we were rescued sunset was approaching and currents were carrying us westward toward Japanese territory. I began to wonder whether I was a jinx for Higgins boats. The two times I had ventured out in them since D-Day the landing craft had broken down.

---

*November 26.* Louie the Louse was over again last night; several lice, I think, for fifteen to twenty bombs were dropped. No damage.

This place will be humming in a few days—I hope—with Army troops pouring in and marines pouring out. I wonder if things will go smoothly. No, that's not the word. They *can't* go smoothly, but I hope we get out of here without a major disaster.

At the CP we are all relaxing now—perhaps too much, for the Japs may pull a surprise. But everyone now knows we will soon leave and inevitably there's a let-up in effort. They can't think of anything but getting out.

*November 28.* I spent another afternoon in the sun on the beach. The supply ship *Alchiba* had been torpedoed. She was lying off Lunga Lagoon, with smoke pouring from her forward hold. Off toward Tulagi destroyers were dashing about, dropping depth charges, and the sky was full of patrol planes looking for the sub. [It turned out that a midget submarine had sneaked through the screen; the *Alchiba* burned for several days but was later salvaged.]

There I was, lying on the beach as though all was peaceful and I was having a vacation at Waikiki. What a change has come over me in the past few months. In August I would have been excited by the happenings at sea and in the sky. Now I just glanced out now and then to watch the ships and planes as a mildly interesting show against a pleasant backdrop.

COMSOPAC, informed about the torpedoing, sent a brusque message to the general saying they assumed the ships were being protected against submarines as well as air attacks. The reply: "Your assumption absolutely correct. There were also four destroyers present." Blame it all on George.

*December 1.* Last night about 2330 a marine stuck his head in Mitchell's tent. [Lieutenant Mitchell was in command of Headquarters Company; I took refuge in his tent when the Press Club was crowded.] He whispered, "Hey, Lieutenant, want to see a naval battle?" There was one going on out toward Savo, but the firing wasn't heavy. I slept right through it until the air raid siren sounded shortly before midnight. There were occasional flashes out to the northwest for more than an hour, with one terrific burst of red flame, and searchlights played up and down the channel.

Later. Last night's naval battle was no triumph for us. One of our light cruisers was sunk, three heavies were badly damaged, with unknown damage to destroyers. Also unknown damage to the Japs. The Navy claims to have intercepted a large force and sunk a lot of ships. But where is the debris and where are the survivors? It's all very obscure.

The press are beside themselves trying to get the story, but I suspect it will be a long time before anything like the truth takes shape.

---

The Guadalcanal Express was still running about every fourth night, to land supplies and a few troops west of us. But the Japanese had developed a new technique, which they hoped would cut down their losses in destroyers. Food, medicine, and other essential supplies were packed in steel drums, which were lashed together and carried on the decks. Tanaka would bring his destroyers close to the shore and cut loose the drums for shore parties to pick up. Then he would hightail to the north, not pausing to bombard Henderson Field, to be as far as possible from the island before the Cactus Air Force took to the skies at first light. And he made the runs only in the dark of the moon.

The night of November 30 Tanaka had eight destroyers in his charge, six of them laden with drums. Rear Admiral Carleton H. Wright, in command of four heavy cruisers, one light, and four destroyers, was to intercept and destroy them. As Tanaka approached Tassafaronga, Wright was steaming toward him past Lunga Point. At about eleven o'clock American ships' radar found Tanaka's lead destroyers, within torpedo range. The two forces were drawing closer to each other, about six miles apart on roughly parallel courses. Before Wright gave orders to launch torpedoes Tanaka's lead ships were already past. The American fish therefore had to chase Tanaka's ships instead of lunging out to meet them. None reached its target.

As the torpedoes began their vain pursuit Wright's cruisers opened fire. Tanaka, taken by surprise, reacted promptly and tellingly. Six of his destroyers cut loose their cargo, turned, and launched their own fish—a breed far superior in speed, accuracy, and striking power to the American variety. Six found their marks. The *Minneapolis* took two and was knocked out of the battle. Another Long Lance hit the *Nev Orleans* and sliced off 120 feet of her bow section; a floating mortuary, it scraped past the main section of the ship.

Yet another torpedo hit the *Pensacola* amidships and set her ablaze. These three cruisers managed to take temporary refuge in Tulagi Harbor, and to return to the fleet within a year after extensive repairs. The fourth cruiser in the American line, the *Honolulu*, escaped the Long Lances' thrust. But two torpedoes ravaged the *Northampton;* she had to be abandoned an hour later and soon thereafter sank.

In about twenty minutes an inferior Japanese force had

cut loose its cargoes, swung to battle stations, and knocked
out four American cruisers—one forever, three for many
months. Tanaka lost one destroyer, sunk by American
shells. This "Little Savo," called the Battle of Tassafaronga,
was the last of five night surface engagements we witnessed from the shores of Guadalcanal: one in August, one
in October, three in November. With the moon waxing,
Tanaka made only two more supply runs early in December, and did not attempt another until January 2. Cactus
fliers continued to greet and to chase the Express whenever
it was within bombing range, with little effect. On the
night of December 3 they did score a hit on one of ten
destroyers.

*December 3.* The press are getting restive, complaining about the lack of information, rebuking me for not
giving them suggestions. To hell with them. The First
Marine Division isn't doing much but patrolling. Their
stories will have to come from Army, Navy, and air.

All the brass has become very secretive lately. I've been
slapped down so often, trying to get information these past
few days, that I'm losing interest in anything but getting
out of here. I am not alone in being rebuffed. I've heard
Twining and Thomas brush off inquisitive colonels, too.

*December 5.* Plans are taking shape to get the 5th Marines and attached units out of here on the 8th or 9th. I'm
to be billeting and liaison officer for the Division HQ
detachment, sailing with the 2nd Battalion on the *Jackson.*
There's apparently not much to it: just find out when what
people are supposed to be where and tell them to be there.

*December 6.* Last minute switches in the embarkation
plans. Now, it seems, the whole of HQ is going, except
for a few unfortunates. This means new ship assignments,
new rosters. The chief of staff is going on the *Adams.* He
wants me with him to work on the history, so I'll be
switched to that ship.

December 7 was the first anniversary of the Japanese
attack on Pearl Harbor. I did not even note the fact in my

diary, but others did not forget. In remembrance General del Valle [the artillery commander had been promoted to brigadier general] arranged a special artillery concentration against positions beyond the Matanikau. He and General Rupertus personally pulled the lanyard on a howitzer whose breech housed shells marked, "Tojo. Dec. 7, 1942." On this anniversary probably no one but a few general staff officers in Tokyo realized that the Japanese now had no grounds for hope of winning the war. The American side was prudently assuming that the enemy would still make another massive effort to recapture Guadalcanal. The Imperial Army was making the same assumption. General Imamura, in his new Eighth Area Army Headquarters in Rabaul, was beginning to gather 50,000 fresh troops for the attempt.

*December 7.* It seems we are going to Brisbane, Australia, instead of Wellington. The change must have been a very sudden one. I hope it doesn't mean that they are going to rush this division into combat again before they have had a proper rest. We'll be under MacArthur's command, of course.

This morning I went, with the press, to see Lieutenant Colonel Carlson and his raiders, who just got back to the perimeter after roaming the jungle for a month. We found him in an unpleasant mood. The 2nd Raiders had been forty-eight hours without food or water. They arrived at Lunga about four o'clock this morning feeling, quite justifiably, that they were being badly used by Division.

Carlson, who was trying to take a nap, said he wasn't interested in anything this morning except looking after his boys—"the best in the world." But he soon thawed. He and his officers gave a good account of their adventures the past month. What a great bunch of soldiers they are.

Lieutenant Colonel Evans F. Carlson had been for most of his adult years a Regular, commissioned in the Marine Corps after serving in the Army in World War I. In Nicaragua, and later in China, as an Observer of Mao Tse-tung's army, he developed the guerrilla tactics for which he became known. He served three tours of duty in

China, studied the languages, and formed a strong attachment to the Chinese. He came to regard Mao's army as the one effective Chinese force in fighting the armies of the Rising Sun. Increasingly agitated by the growing Japanese military threat to Asia and the Pacific, Carlson resigned his commission in 1939, to be free to speak out. Among old China hands, who admired his spirit, some thought his hopes for a unified, democratic China to be naively unrealistic. Within the Corps he was widely regarded as an able officer but also a romantic or a "pinko," or both. At the very least he was seen as a friend of President Roosevelt (as indeed he was) in an officer corps not noted for New Deal tendencies.

Back in uniform after Pearl Harbor, Carlson was put in command of the 2nd Raider Battalion. Forty-five years old at the time of the Guadalcanal campaign, he was a lean, intense man with graying hair and a memorable beak of a nose. Two companies of his raiders, it will be remembered, had been among the units landed at Aola in Turner's abortive effort to build an airstrip there. When the 7th Marines and 164th Infantry went out to the Metapona to deal with the Japanese beachhead, Vandegrift persuaded Turner, who had kept Carlson under his own control, to release the battalion for an attack on the beachhead from the east.

On November 6 two raider companies set out from Aola while the four remaining companies in the battalion headed for Guadalcanal to join them. When it became clear that the main body of Japanese had already moved inland, Carlson was ordered to pursue. Colonel Shoji, who so recently had led his bedraggled regiment down the Metapona to receive supplies and reinforcements near Koli Point, was now retracing his steps. On November 11 Carlson's men, pushing up the river valley, began to run into Shoji's rear guard, and took some casualties. Pressing on, along both banks of the river, raiders surprised an enemy party at a ford—some swimming, some passing supplies across the stream—and killed more than a hundred.

By the time Carlson had moved up additional companies, Shoji's men had gone farther south and crossed to the west side of the river. And thus the pursuit continued, marked by frequent small engagements as the Japanese withdrew toward Mount Austen and Carlson followed, finding and disposing of scattered enemy pockets in bivouac areas. The little detachments were, for the most part, survivors of Maruyama's futile and costly effort to overrun Henderson Field from the south in the last week of October.

The 2nd Raiders were by now going over the same rugged ground traversed and retraversed by the enemy in their east-west movements south of the airfield. Wooded riverbanks and grassy fields gave way to steep coral ridges and rain-forested gullies. By November 29 they had reached a precipitous, narrow ridge that separates the upper courses of the Lunga and Ilu. Struggling, in a rainstorm, with the help of ropes, across this slippery razorback, they found beside the Lunga what had been a major Japanese base—a bivouac area large enough for a regiment. A second encampment, deserted, was found, and then a third, occupied by about a hundred Japanese troops. Caught with most of their weapons stacked in the center of the clearing, the Japanese lost most of their number when a raider squad stormed in with automatic weapons blazing.

Carlson's battalion established its own bivouac on the southern slopes of Mount Austen. Patrolling from that point, the raiders found Japanese stragglers but no sign of a major movement from the west along the trail. They did find a strong but unoccupied Japanese defense position in the tangle of ridges near the top of Mount Austen. When an enemy combat patrol approached a spirited fire fight began, with both Carlson and his opponent trying to outflank the other. The enemy patrol was wiped out. The 2nd Raiders spent the night, without any water, in the enemy's caves and dugouts.

The next day they began making their way down the northern side of the mountain, carrying their wounded. They took more losses when they ran into an ambush, but made their way back to the perimeter without further encounters. "We smelled Japs all the way down," said a raider. But if a substantial number were on the mountain, as Carlson suspected, they were not in a mood to attack.

During their month on the trail the 2nd Raiders had taken a substantial toll of Japanese soldiers, weapons, and supplies. They had demonstrated that well-trained, jungle-wise troops, living on light rations (raisins, bacon, tea, and rice), disposing of heavy automatic firepower, could operate independently and with deadly effectiveness away from an established supply base. Colonel Twining, for one, was convinced that marines in general could learn much from the practices and tactics of Carlson's Raiders.

December 9, departure day, arrived at last. It was departure day, that is, for the 5th Marines and attached units, and for division headquarters. The 1st Marines and 7th Marines would soon follow. The 2nd Marines were organically part of the Second Marine Division, which was assembling as a unit on Cactus. They had to stay until the middle of January and still faced some grueling combat. They, too, had been in the area since D-Day, and now they watched with bitterness the departure of their luckier brethren. But they did not "watch"; as the 5th Marines were embarking, the 2nd, far from the Lunga beaches, were moving into the Point Cruz line.

On December 9 General Vandegrift turned over the command of forces in the Guadalcanal-Tulagi area to the Army's General Patch. With a few of his staff the Marine general flew to Brisbane, where his new chief, MacArthur, was headquartered. Those of us leaving with the 5th Marines embarked in the ships that had brought in the Army's 132nd Infantry, the third and last of the Americal Division's regimental combat teams to reach the island.

On this occasion, "raggedy-ass marines" was a fitting name for the weary, disease-ridden, bedraggled troops who filed into the landing craft and then hauled themselves, sometimes with difficulty, up the cargo nets to the decks of transports. They were dressed in frayed green dungarees or dirty khaki, stained with Cactus sweat and muck. Socks had become a luxury; many had long since rotted away. Boondockers were run down at the heels, tied up with knotted laces or bits of string. Almost everyone had lost many pounds. Hundreds had malaria.

In the two days before the embarkation medical officers examined "one regiment" (unspecified in their report, but presumably the 5th Marines) to determine how many were fit for further combat. In the doctors' opinion, one-third of the entire regiment were unfit. The number would have been even higher if 400 recent replacements had not been included in the survey.

─────────────

*December 9.* We got under way about 1500, under the stimulus of an air raid alert. We shoved off when word came that unidentified planes were thirty minutes out, and we didn't go back when the alert ended.

Loading and embarkation of troops went smoothly, on the whole. Division HQ, as usual, got fouled up—each man, each staff section, for itself. Everyone seemed to be so afraid of missing the boat that they all dashed down to the beach before they got the word as to where they were to assemble. It complicated my job because I couldn't find many of my charges. But they got aboard with a minimum of confusion, much to my surprise.

I hung around the beach herding strays into boats, then went out to the ship about 1030. My first act was to take a hot and cold shower. I felt really clean for the first time in four months. I have a bunk with a spring mattress, and electric lights. Such luxury! For noon chow they gave us weiners, sauerkraut, boiled potatoes, and rice pudding.

It's strange; I do not feel nearly as elated at leaving Guadalcanal as I thought I would. It seems quite normal to be aboard ship again and it is hard to realize we are still in a danger zone. I find the memory of those four months fading rapidly; can't believe I was actually on Guadalcanal or remember the times we went through. My mind refuses to accept that we are in the midst of war. We had two air raid alarms during the afternoon; I sat in my cabin and read, feeling no concern.

I suppose all of us are glad to be leaving Guadalcanal, but none is gladder than Dr. Brown [Captain W. T. Brown, USN (MC), the division surgeon]. He has always been the gloomiest man around HQ. I saw him topside after the first alert. He asked me what foreland we were approaching. I said it was Taivu Point. Then he asked, hopefully, if that was near the end of the island. I replied: "No, sir, it's just about halfway down. We've forty miles to go." He sighed and turned away. He can't be happy until we have seen the last of that island.

# 18

☆ ─────── ☆

# Malaria Down Under

*December 13.* We arrived in Brisbane this afternoon, pulling up to the dock about 1500. We are getting no liberty tonight, no movies either. Everyone is wandering aimlessly about the ship with nothing to do and feeling very sore about it. But we have lights. It's strange not to have a blackout.

Vandegrift, Thomas, and Twining [who had flown to Brisbane] were on the dock to greet us. The rest of the senior officers got off and disappeared into town, getting a head start, of course, on the rest and relaxation that is now supposed to be our due.

*December 14.* Troops disembarked today. Our camp— Camp Cable—is about forty miles from Brisbane, which disappoints everyone. There was chaos when we got there. No one knew where we were supposed to be. We finally settled down in the Army division headquarters area. The general and senior staff are staying in town at Lennon's Hotel. Thinking they might be planning to set up temporary HQ there, Col. Snedeker, Ray Schwenke [of the operations section, formerly personal aide to Vandegrift], and I rode back into town to see for ourselves. Lennon's is elegant; at least it seems so after four months in the wilderness. The staff was resplendent in clean khaki and we felt very conspicuous in our soiled and rumpled trousers and shirts, without field scarves [neckties]. I got several disapproving once-overs from the rank.

It turned out that only the senior staff officers will stay in town, and no offices will be set up there. After lunch we came back to camp. Everyone is irritable and bitter about being stuck out here in the boondocks.

*December 16.* I went into town with Ray Schwenke. I haven't been able to lay hands on any clean khaki trousers. The pair I saved for five months just for this occasion was stolen aboard ship. So I went in far-from-clean khaki. I called on Col. [Lloyd] Lehrbas, one of MacArthur's public relations officers. He kept me standing throughout our brief conversation. I wonder if that sort of thing is typical of the Army.

---

Lehrbas was no more an Army officer than I was a Marine; we both were civilians in uniform. Happily for me, that was the one encounter I had with the courtiers around MacArthur.

---

*December 18.* The Rear Echelon arrived from Wellington today, disgustingly fat and sleek and red of face from high living. They are feeling very sorry for themselves because they had to leave New Zealand just before the Christmas holidays.

What a messed-up situation. There has been no division CP for the past week. The staff is living in style at Lennon's and shows no concern about what is going on at Camp Cable. The rest of HQ is out in the boondocks with nothing to do, and nothing to do it with. The 5th Marines have the job of assigning bivouac areas to units, making arrangements for liberty, leave, pay, and so on.

Col. Farrell [the headquarters commandant] dropped me off at the 5th Marines CP today, where he was supposed to go for a conference on liberty. He decided it didn't become his rank to stay for such a piddling matter, and told me to stick around and get the dope, then took off in the car leaving me stranded. "Oh, you'll get a ride."

After I had hitchhiked back Farrell showed no interest in the liberty rules. I pointed out that even if he wasn't interested the men undoubtedly were. So he said, All right, tell the men. All the NCOs said it was no affair of theirs, and Major Lynch [c.o. of the headquarters company] said it didn't affect him. I gave up. Semper Fidelis!

*December 23.* I went into town today and tried, among
other things, to have the George Medal made. Everything
went nicely, all arrangements were apparently made, when
I learned that the firm of engravers couldn't take on the job
unless an official request was made. The engraver said he
might otherwise get into trouble with the manpower board,
because his men are exempted from the draft on the ground
that they are doing war work. No Marine officer in authority is likely to want his name associated with the
project. Colonel Twining, who has been the most ardent
promoter of the George Medal, said he couldn't sign a
request. He suggests we let the matter rest for a while, but
by no means give it up. [The medal was eventually struck
and has become a collector's item.]

————————————

The myriad things to bitch about in so unpromising a
place for "rest and rehabilitation," and later for training,
were trivial compared to the division's overriding problem—
malaria.

The spread of that debilitating disease to uninfected
human beings depends on three things. The parasite must
be in the bloodstreams of people nearby—"reservoirs" of
infection. Certain man-biting species of *Anopheles* mosquito must be within flying range both of the living reservoirs and victims-to-be. And there must be suitable breeding
grounds for the mosquito.

Guadalcanal abundantly provided all three requisites.
Among Solomon Islanders malaria was endemic. Villages
near the Lunga perimeter were deserted, but native scouts
and labor battalions were nearby. The division surgeon had
strongly protested the use of native labor but was overriden;
all available hands were needed.

Mosquitoes of the right kind flourished on Guadalcanal.
Six of the fifty-odd man-biting species of *Anopheles* were
found there. The one that caused the most damage bred in
stagnant pools of fresh water, amply found, before our
arrival, in lagoons, sluggish streams, swamps, and jungle
pools, and, after our arrival, in shell-holes, bomb craters,
and rutted roads.

A month after D-Day the Marine command, on the
advice of the Navy malaria control unit, ordered all hands

to begin treatment to suppress malaria. Everyone was supposed to take a prescribed dosage of Atabrine, a synthetic antimalarial drug developed by the Germans after World War I. But it was hard to persuade troops—or their officers, for that matter—that malaria was a serious menace. Atabrine discipline varied from unit to unit. And by the time dosage began the first few cases of malaria were beginning to turn up in sick bays and the field hospital.

By the end of October the incidence had reached epidemic proportions. More than 2,000 men with malaria had been admitted to the field hospital. In November it was worse; with accurate figures for the last week missing, the number was over 3,200. Some of these, of course, were repeaters. There are no figures on the men with malaria who did not check into the hospital. And no one knew, at that stage of the war, how many suppressed cases would flare up when men were taken off Atabrine. The number proved to be enormous.

The Melanesian malarial belt in the South and Southwest Pacific included New Guinea, the Bismarck Archipelago, the Solomons, and the New Hebrides—all of them important battlegrounds or bases. Malaria was a continuing problem in all. Scarcely any progress in controlling the disease was made until the middle of 1943. Malaria control units of the Army and Navy then began spraying mosquito breeding grounds with diesel oil and destroying them with landfills and drainage. Commanding officers at all levels began to enforce strict antimalaria discipline—the taking of Atabrine and keeping exposed skin covered at night with clothing and nets.

Even so, it remained hard to convince commanders of combat troops, whether they were generals or platoon leaders, Marine or Army, that it was as important to make their men use mosquito nets and take Atabrine as it was to make them clean and oil their rifles. There was a stock joke on Guadalcanal: "I'm going to let my arm hang outside the net tonight and get myself evacuated." Probably it was not always a jest.

By mid-November the division command was ready to let malaria control units, earlier rejected, come to the island. Army medical accounts report the attitude of one "high-ranking officer" on Guadalcanal (name, rank, and service unspecified): "We're here to kill Japs; to hell with the mosquitoes."

The First Marine Division's Final Report on the Guadalcanal Operation has a long section on "Lessons and Conclusions." It sums up the hard-won lessons that its writers wanted to pass on to others. On medical matters it emphasizes the importance of foot care. It makes specific recommendations as to the minimum gear troops should carry in jungle warfare. Nothing is said about carrying mosquito nets. Indeed, not a word is said about the crucial importance of anti-malaria measures and discipline. That is left to the medical annex. And yet malaria caused far more losses in manpower on Guadalcanal than Japanese weapons. It took time for malaria to be recognized as a major problem, not only for medics, but for field commanders.

The malaria problem moved with the First Marine Division from Guadalcanal to Australia.

---

*December 24.* Still fighting mosquitoes. They are everywhere, all the time. Guadalcanal was never like this. Our being here at all is absurd. With almost 100 percent of personnel infected by malaria, we are sent to an anopheles-ridden area to recuperate! A child could realize that this division will not be restored to fighting form so long as it is here. *Surely* we'll be moved.

---

MacArthur's Army Surgeon had assured the Marine command that the area was free from *Anopheles*. It was not. The problem was not only one of the division's infecting replacements fresh from the States; it involved the good folk of Queensland, threatened by a reservoir of malarial parasites in their midst.

Two days before Christmas the division surgeon, backed by at least one doctor on MacArthur's staff, reported that *Anopheles* was prevalent in our corner of Queensland, and recommended removal of the division southward, to more salubrious climes. The province's medical authorities added their note of alarm. They asked Vandegrift what he proposed to do to relieve Queensland people of the threat of infection—a query the general passed on to MacArthur.

Marines explored possible sites for the division around
Sydney and Melbourne.

On New Year's Day 1943 MacArthur reluctantly authorized a move to Melbourne. But he added that no rail
transportation was available; all facilities were needed to
move men and supplies to his northern combat zone.
Vandegrift then wrote a personal, hand-delivered letter to
Halsey in New Caledonia, followed by an official dispatch, asking if he could help. In reply, Halsey arranged to
send the *West Point* (in prewar days, the liner *America*),
which would deliver other contingents of the First Marine
Division en route from Guadalcanal to Melbourne, then
pick up the Brisbane units and take them to the same
destination.

Years later Vandegrift said, about MacArthur's apparently grudging consent to the move: "That thing stuck in
my craw—that thing about we could go, but we couldn't
use any rail transportation." But MacArthur did in fact
have a major campaign on his hands. December was a
month of grueling combat in New Guinea. Probably the
general needed every railroad car he could lay hands on to
move men and supplies over lines which grew exiguous
and inadequate as they reached toward Brisbane and points
north.

MacArthur was carrying out his part of the Joint Chiefs'
plan, promulgated on July 2, to roll the enemy back in the
Solomons and New Guinea, aiming finally at the seizure
of Rabaul. The Japanese drive on Port Moresby in August,
let us recall, had deflected imperial strength from a poten-
tial counterattack on Guadalcanal at a time when the American hold on that island was precarious. In September
IGHQ had shifted its sights from New Guinea to Guadalcanal as the main immediate target.

Thereafter MacArthur had moved to the offensive. Australian troops pushed the Japanese back across the Owen
Stanley Range. Other MacArthur forces had occupied Milne
Bay and held it against the enemy's own attempt to capture
the tip of the turkey's tail and to outflank Port Moresby.

Now, in December 1942, MacArthur was trying to capture the Buna-Gona area on the northern coast of Papua.
Australian troops overran Gona on December 9, the day

the 5th Marines were delivered from Guadalcanal. On December 12, the day before we arrived in Brisbane, American troops moved into Buna village. The fighting in Papua went on for another six weeks, while the First Marine Division was trying to settle down in Australia.

---

*December 28.* Major Murray informed me casually at lunch that HQ in Washington has ordered me back there. I'm so filthy sick that I can't feel elated. [For several days I had kept to my tent in the bogs of Camp Cable with a fever, gobbling quinine in case it turned out that I had malaria.] Hurlbut will go, too, and is overjoyed.

Later I saw Murray alone and he opened up somewhat. He and the general, he said, take a very poor view of my recall; the general is writing a letter to ask that I be reassigned to the division before it starts another operation. I feel flattered, and think that I sincerely do want to return to the division. I suspect that after a few months in Washington I'll forget the unpleasant side of life in the field, that it will seem only exciting and adventurous, and that I'll be eager to get out of the Washington atmosphere. We'll see.

---

It was January 16 before I got away. Meanwhile the division had moved to Melbourne and I had three days in that pleasant city before sailing home on the *West Point*. I never got back to the First Marine Division. In 1943 I spent eight months stateside, writing a history of the division's Guadalcanal campaign and doing the talk circuit— war-bond and Red Cross rallies, defense plants, armed-service training schools, and the like. Then came a year in the European theater, based in London: more talks about Guadalcanal to largely uninterested British audiences (who, understandably, had Hitler on their minds), D-Day off Normandy with the Royal Marines, and D-Day off southern France aboard the battleship *Nevada*. And then came a final year back in the Pacific, on the staff of the Tenth Army (a joint Army-Marine organization), in Oahu and Okinawa.

Here, then, my diary ends and, it no longer being my duty to keep records, I never started another during the war. And here ends the account of Guadalcanal based on personal experience and observation. That campaign, however, went on for two grueling months after our departure, and its impact on the whole course of the war only became clear later on.

# 19

☆ ───────── ☆

# The Final Push

One of the last familiar landmarks we saw, as ships carried us away from Lunga Roads on December 9, was Mount Austen, looming over Henderson Field. The eminence had seemed to menace us for four months. To the Army, now taking over responsibility for ground action on Guadalcanal, it appeared an intolerable threat so long as the Japanese had access to it.

Mount Austen (or Mambulo, as islanders called it) is a jumble of grassy ridges and jungly ravines, with rain forest also on some of the upper slopes. The uppermost of several peaks on the massif is 1,500 feet high. From its northern ridgetops the Japanese had a splendid view of the airfield and the open parts of our perimeter. Within ten days of our landings they were beginning to report movements within our position and the location of our artillery batteries. They could report when our planes, and how many, of what types, were taking off and landing. If they had been able to move enough artillery and ammunition to Austen's heights they could have made the airstrip unusable. Fortunately for us, the rugged island terrain over which they had to move heavy weapons spared us that threat.

On a visit to Guadalcanal in November General Harmon (commanding, it will be recalled, all U.S. Army forces in the South Pacific Area) asked Vandegrift—with, we may assume, a hint of reproach—when he proposed to occupy Mount Austen. The Marine general had replied, "At the earliest opportunity." With the forces available to him, he felt no more able to expand his holdings to the south than

251

he could to the west, where the threat was far graver. When the Army took over responsibility, Harmon and Patch decided to do something about Mount Austen. It was necessary to safeguard that flank before making a major push beyond the Matanikau. The undertaking proved to be a major one.

For the first few weeks of his new command General Patch had only about the same number of troops at his disposal that Vandegrift had had upon being relieved. The two Army regiments that landed in December were relief, not reinforcements, for the departing marines. Until substantial additional troops came in, Patch would be pretty much confined to the same perimeter Vandegrift had held—with the important exception of Mount Austen. Enemy raiders, apparently coming out of jungle cover at the base of Austen, managed to reach the new fighter strip at Kukum the night of December 12 and destroyed a P-39 fighter. This foray gave an added sense of urgency to driving the enemy off Austen.

Patch assigned the task to the newly arrived Illinois National Guardsmen of the 132nd Regimental Command Team—troops who had never been in combat and were not yet acclimated to the dank heat. The attack began on December 17. Lieutenant Colonel William C. Wright, commanding the lead battalion (the 2nd), died of wounds received on the third day.

By Christmas Eve soldiers of the 2nd Battalion reached the edges of the "Gifu," named after a prefecture in Japan. This was the most stubbornly defended enemy position that American troops would encounter on the island. In the rain-forested ravines, scoured by watercourses that feed the Matanikau on the western slopes of Austen, the Japanese had built a series of forty-five or more mutually supporting pillboxes and emplacements. At first thought to be a horseshoe-shaped line, the Gifu was later found to form a fully enclosed ring.

Another battalion of the 132nd Infantry was committed to the effort to reduce the stronghold. By the end of December the two battalions had taken 182 casualties and 131 more troops had been evacuated as sick, but the Gifu held out. Many of the attacking Americans were fatigued, ailing with malaria and other diseases, and dispirited. Their commander was among the sorely afflicted; he asked to be relieved. The attack continued. By the night of January 3 the two battalions had enveloped the Gifu on three sides. In twenty-two days they had suffered 385 casualties, and many others had been evacuated on the sick list.

The attack on the Gifu was then held up until fresh troops could relieve the 132nd. The Japanese had been driven from their observation posts on Austen and hundreds had been killed. But reduction of the redoubt would take two more weeks from the time the attack was resumed by units of the Twenty-fifth Infantry Division. That division, commanded by Major General J. Lawton Collins, had come directly from Hawaii, and landed at intervals between December 17 and January 4. Resistance in the Gifu finally ended the night of January 22–23, when twenty-five Japanese officers led a suicidal charge—the first of many that the emperor's troops would stage during the Pacific War as final hopeless gestures. All in all, five Army battalions were committed to the capture of Mount Austen and the struggle lasted five weeks.

Meanwhile, Patch was making plans for a general drive to the west as soon as he had built up enough strength. His target date for beginning the offensive was January 15. In Rabaul and on intermediate islands the Imperial Army was also gathering strength through December for another assault on the American position. Their target date, too, was mid-January.

By the second week of the month General Patch had three divisions on Guadalcanal—nearly 42,000 officers and men. His command also included about 5,000 in naval and 1,500 in air units. In addition to the Army's Americal and Twenty-fifth Infantry Divisions he had the Second Marine Division. The 6th Marines, the last of its regiments to arrive, landed on January 4. For the first time the Second Marine Division was united. Patch became commander of the XIV Corps, activated January 2, comprised of the three divisions and supporting units.

By the end of 1942 the Cactus Air Force was also much stronger than it had been when the Japanese sent down their big convoy in November. The original airstrip was now fully covered with perforated steel mats and could be used in all weather. A new fighter strip—Fighter No. 2—was completed near Kukum in December. A new bomber field was abuilding on the grassy plains behind Koli Point. The day after Christmas the Second Marine Air Wing, Commanded by Brigadier General Francis P. Mulcahy, began to come in to relieve the veteran First. AAF heavy bombers were again staging through Guadalcanal and some twin-tailed Lightnings were at last available to escort them on long-range missions to the north.

A new and important target had appeared for Cactus planes and flights from rear bases. Under cleverly rigged palm-frond camouflage the Japanese had built an airstrip at Munda Point on New Georgia Island, only 175 miles from Henderson Field. Its use would free their Zero fighters from the need to carry belly-tanks of fuel for return trips from the Rabaul complex and fields on Bougainville to Guadalcanal and back. But it also brought an airbase within range of the light planes used by Marine and Navy fliers. American airmen subjected it to a steady drubbing.

As earlier mentioned, General Imamura's new command at Rabaul, the Eighth Area Army, included two field armies—the old Seventeenth Army, earlier battered on Guadalcanal and still earmarked to recapture the island, and the Eighteenth Army, for operations in New Guinea. Hyakutake was still on Guadalcanal, at a command post near Kokumbona, trying to rally the remnants of his command for another effort when heavy reinforcements arrived. American estimates as to how many enemy troops were still on the island, concentrated west of the Matanikau and along the ridge system that linked their base with Mount Austen, varied from 9,000 to 16,000. Postwar Japanese estimates place the number at about 25,000. Whatever their actual numbers, most were in wretched condition. Americans who were feeling sorry for themselves were well off by comparison. Many Japanese had starved to death, and many more were starving. Only rice, and little of that, was available for food. Men in the front line were worse off than those near the beach, who pilfered what small amounts came ashore. In one group fighting men were put on one-quarter rations, others on one-twelfth. When a medical station moved, only those able to walk went along. Those too sick or wounded to move wasted away in their holes.

Operation Rat failed to deliver even the minimum in rations and medical supplies needed for bare survival. Only about a third of the lashed-together drums reached their targets; the rest floated out to sea, or were shot up by American fliers, or both. The only hope for the Japanese lay in massive reinforcements. And these were gathering—50,000 strong, as I have mentioned—in Rabaul and in the northern Solomons through December. But how were they to get to the island?

Facing a foe so reduced in numbers and circumstances, Americans on Guadalcanal could be confident of final victory, unless the Japanese successfully mounted a combined effort on a scale even larger than that attempted in November. Hyakutake's remaining troops on the island were incapable of another major offensive on their own. But they were still formidable on the defense, as American soldiers and marines learned during the last few weeks of combat.

When the Japanese invasion convoy headed for Guadalcanal in mid-November, we will recall, the Marine command had ordered troops who had fought their way beyond Point Cruz to return east of the Matanikau, to strengthen the perimeter against the massive new threat. When the convoy had been sunk and the Imperial Navy driven off, Vandegrift had ordered a new drive west of the river, to begin on November 18. My diary entry for the 19th referred to the effort, much too casually, as "Not a major push—just sort of feeling our way." It turned into a bitter fight.

Soldiers from Massachusetts (the 182nd Infantry), and later North Dakotans of the 164th Infantry and the 8th Marines, had run into increasing resistance as they met head on an enemy pushing in the opposite direction, trying to regain the Matanikau. The battle ended in a stalemate on a line running from a point just west of Point Cruz along connecting ridges to Hill 66, a mile and a half inland. With the First Marine Division about to depart the Americans could not throw in enough men to push further, nor could the Japanese, unless they received reinforcements. For seven weeks, after November 23, Americans and Japanese confronted and harassed each other across the ravines lying just west of the Point Cruz–Hill 66 line. In preparation for his January drive, Patch had supply roads built as far southwest as Hill 66.

The January offensive began on the 10th. Jumping off from the Mount Austen area, General Collins's 25th Division was to sweep farther inland than American troops had yet ventured. One Regular Army regiment, the 27th Infantry, began an attack on a massive ridge system, called (because of its shape as seen in aerial photographs) the Galloping Horse. In four days the soldiers cleaned out enemy pockets in that area, hooked up with American forces farther north, and lengthened the XIV Corps line running two and a half miles southward from the coast.

Another of Collins's Regular Army regiments, the 35th Infantry, drove even farther south. Leaving a battalion to reduce the Gifu, as already noted, the 35th's sweep carried it four miles in six days, against relatively light resistance but through the densest jungle Americans had yet encountered. Meanwhile the Second Marine Division had jumped off from the Point Cruz line, in the sector closest to the coast, on January 13. The division, commanded by Brigadier General Alphonse de Carre, was fighting as a unit for the first time. Strong Japanese defenses in the coastal belt, which had stopped the American westward push in November, held the division to an advance of less than a mile in five days.

By January 18, then, XIV Corps held positions on ridges extending about three miles from the coast from a point three-quarters of a mile west of Point Cruz. There it paused while fresh units replaced some of those who had been carrying the burden. The push westward was resumed on the 22nd. This time a composite division of Army and Marine regiments continued to the west in the coastal belt, where enemy defenses were strongest, while the 25th Division, angling northwestward, quickly moved along the ridges leading to Kokumbona, to cut off enemy troops remaining between that village and the composite division advancing along the coast. On the 23rd, Collins's advance

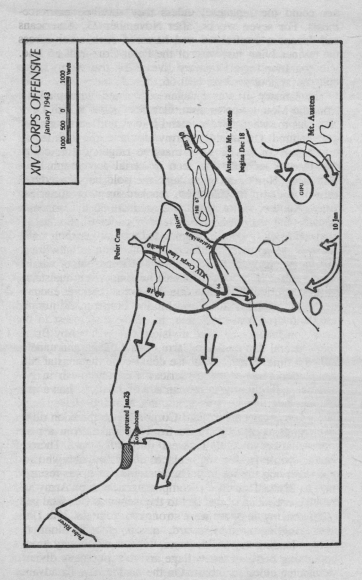

XIV CORPS OFFENSIVE
January 1943

1000  500  0       1000
                   Yards

Poha River

Kokumbona
captured Jan 23

Point Cruz

XIV Corps Line Jan 10

Hill 66

Hill 67

Jan 18

Jan 10

Matanikau River

10 Jan

GIFU

Attack on Mt. Austen
begins Dec 18

Mt. Austen

units entered the village, joined the next day by men of the composite division. At last Kokumbona and the east bank of the Poha nearby to the west were in American hands, five and a half months after the Marines had landed.

In the two-week westward sweep by the XIV Corps Japanese resistance had been scattered, but intense and stubborn where it was encountered. Even weakened as they were, the emperor's soldiers and naval troops held their caves and emplacements of logs and earth to the death of the last man able to fire a machine gun or rifle, or to toss a grenade. They were stirred to suicidal zeal not only by a sense of honor and do-or-die-for-the-emperor spirit astonishing to the occidental mind but also by a conviction that if they held on, reinforcements would soon arrive. Another factor was the fear, instilled by Japanese officers, that they would be killed if captured. So far as Japanese soldiers knew, officers and men alike, their mission was still to recapture Guadalcanal. Even as they drew back the troops were rallied by their officers, one of whom told his men: "Do not expect to return, not even one man, if the occupation [of Guadalcanal] is not successful. Everyone must remember the honor of the Emperor. We must ease the Sacred anxiety."

Poised on the banks of the Poha, "Lightning Joe" Collins ("Lightning" was the field-code name for his headquarters) was eager to pursue the enemy toward Cape Esperance. Beginning in the middle of January, however, alarming intelligence was beginning to reach Halsey and Patch. Let us remember that Imamura had gathered 50,000 fresh troops as reinforcements for Hyakutake. A series of troop-laden convoys left Truk and Rabaul for the Shortland Islands; the area at the southeastern tip of Bougainville had long since become an important complex of bases second only to Rabaul itself. U.S. intelligence supposed the eventual destination of that large movement was Guadalcanal.

CINCPAC began warning that Tokyo Express runs, or even a major move by a big convoy, as in November, might begin as early as January 20. There was bound to be support for such a move from Japan's big navy. Fleet intelligence detected three carriers and the new battleship

*Musashi* at Truk. Enemy submarines began concentrating southeast of Guadalcanal late in the month. Other I-boats, a cruiser, and an unusual number of freighters were spotted in the Marshall and Gilbert Islands—obviously, it seemed, a diversionary gesture. The big move on Guadalcanal seemed about to start. A task force from Truk was scheduled to sail from there on January 30.

As a precautionary measure in the face of the new threat, Patch ordered the 25th Infantry Division back to the perimeter, to protect the airfields—much to Collins's disappointment and disapproval. One Army regiment, with artillery attached, was given the task of attacking toward Cape Esperance. This they carried out, slowly and cautiously, their main resistance coming from a special battalion the Japanese had sent to retard the advance. Patch also dispatched one of the Illinois battalions to land on the other side of the island, near the tip, on February 1. They came ashore at Verahue, about ten miles from Cape Esperance as the crow flies, twice that far along the coast. The plan was to catch the last remnants of the Japanese garrison between the two American columns as they converged on the Cape.

Fleet radio intelligence had picked up, in intercepted Japanese radio traffic, references to a new "Operation KE," which they thought referred to a reinforcement movement. On February 1 the Imperial Navy changed its radio call system, making it impossible for American radio snoopers to know who was sending messages, and to whom they were addressed. But a bulletin of February 2 reported: "Continued references [in Japanese messages] to 'Reinforcement Force, as well as a number of associations involving Guadalcanal make it reasonably certain that reinforcement of Guadalcanal by the Japanese has not been abandoned."

A big Tokyo Express run down the Slot the night of February 1–2 was opposed only by Cactus fliers and PT boats, without effect. Halsey, having assembled his major naval forces south of the island, was waiting for bigger game; he expected his opposite number to move down from Truk at any moment.

\*          \*          \*

The Japanese, however, were not sending in more troops; they were evacuating all they could. After the destruction of the big reinforcement convoy in the middle of November, Tokyo planners had begun to have thoughts previously unthinkable: perhaps they must give up Guadalcanal. Staff officers voiced their doubts more boldly as December wore on. The government crisis in Tokyo brought on by the November shipping losses has already been mentioned. The Imperial Navy could not undertake to move Imamura's 50,000 fresh troops to Guadalcanal. IGHQ canvassed the top field and fleet commands about the possibilities of continuing the struggle; headquarters was not reassured. On New Year's Eve, with the greatest reluctance, the Army and Navy chiefs of staff had informed Emperor Hirohito that Guadalcanal must be given up. They would pull back to other islands in the Solomons and there stop the American advance.

On January 4 IGHQ issued its orders:

The troops in the Solomon Islands will give up the task of recapturing Guadalcanal Island and will withdraw to the rear. After withdrawal, they will hold New Georgia Island and the Solomon Islands from Santa Isabel north, including the Bismarck Archipelago.

The Imperial Navy was ordered to provide destroyers (the initial number was twelve, later increased, it seems, to twenty) which were to go to Guadalcanal on three specified nights and pick up a total of 600 evacuees each.

It remained to inform the Army and Navy commanders in Rabaul, and Hyakutake and his senior officers on Guadalcanal, of the grim news. Griffith has reconstructed the painful scenes that ensued. With difficulty IGHQ's emissary, a major general, persuaded General Imamura and the senior admiral at Rabaul to carry out Tokyo's orders. Admirals and generals alike realized that the withdrawal was more than recognition of a humiliating defeat, Japan's first in the Pacific war; it also marked a strategic turning point in the war, with Japan now going to the defensive and facing ultimate defeat.

On January 14 Imamura dispatched a lieutenant colonel

to Guadalcanal, to deliver and explain the orders to Hyakutake and his staff and senior commanders. Again the emissary found disbelief and defiance among his listeners. Their first reaction was that the Army could not obey the orders without dishonor; it would be far better to throw themselves against the enemy in one last sacrificial assault. But they were finally persuaded to obey orders that had the emperor's sanction.

Unbeknownst to the Americans, their last drive, beginning on January 22, had been against an enemy who was executing a planned withdrawal toward the northwest tip of the island, fighting only delaying actions in the hope that the main body of men still able to walk could reach the embarkation points, get aboard ships, and depart this island of death.

The Japanese plans were efficiently executed. On the night of February 1–2 the remnants of the Thirty-eighth Division climbed into landing barges and collapsible boats to be ferried out to waiting destroyers. The Second Division's turn came on the night of February 4–5, and other units left three nights later. Cactus fliers were able to inflict some damage on two destroyers out of the twenty that made the three nighttime runs. Halsey's surface fleet— waiting, as I have said, for bigger game—did not interfere.

The two American forces converging on Cape Esperance —one along the northern coast, one from the south—met in the village of Tenaro on February 9, finding, in their progress, much abandoned equipment but no Japanese troops except those who had been left behind. That evening General Patch reported to Admiral Halsey: "Total and complete defeat of the Japanese forces on Guadalcanal effected 1625 [4:25 P.M.]. . . . Tokyo Express no longer has terminus on Guadalcanal."

The triumph would have been headier if 10,500 Japanese troops (one Japanese report says 13,000) had not escaped. Militarily speaking, few actions became the Japanese effort on Guadalcanal so much as their departure. It was a brilliant maneuver, ruefully acknowledged as such by Admiral Nimitz: "Only skill in keeping their plans disguised and bold celerity in carrying them out enabled the Japanese to withdraw the remnants of the Guadalcanal garrison."

# 20

☆ ───── ☆

# Fruits of Victory

On the last day of August 1942, it may be recalled, the U.S. navy's commander of land-based aircraft in the South Pacific had sent from Guadalcanal an urgent plea that two squadrons of fighter planes be sent immediately to the beleaguered island: "With substantially the reinforcement requested Guadalcanal can be a sinkhole for enemy air power and can be consolidated, expanded, and exploited to the enemy's mortal hurt."

Admiral McCain's message turned out to be prophetic. No fresh fighter squadron had flown in until September 11, when Ghormley released twenty-four Wildcats from the stricken *Saratoga* to help counter a new Japanese offensive. But Henderson Field had then been held and, as we have seen, had survived even graver crises, becoming indeed a sinkhole for enemy air power.

With final victory on Guadalcanal early in February 1943 came the opportunity to consolidate, expand, and exploit the air base, and these things were done, to the enemy's mortal hurt. The drain on Japan's best-trained air crews, and on her planes and ships, would continue in the Solomons for another year after the great clash of mid-November 1942. Guadalcanal, the unsinkable aircraft carrier, became the major base for the Allied drive toward Rabaul up the Solomons.

Shortly after the First Marine Division left the island, fighter planes began to fly from the new hard-surfaced airstrip by the sea, near Kukum. Engineers were constructing a large new airdrome, able to serve as a base for the AAF's heavy bombers, in the broad grassy plain south of

Koli Point. In February U.S. forces occupied the Russell Islands, some thirty miles northwest of Cape Esperance, and quickly built two fighter strips there.

In the same month Halsey and Turner began Operation DRYGOODS, a massive build-up of logistic support for future operations—tens of thousands of tons of supplies and equipment, including a tank farm for fuel. Guadalcanal's code name was changed from CACTUS to MAINYARD.

Along the north coast of Guadalcanal tent cities replaced the early primitive bivouac areas. Point Cruz was cleared of trees. Quays and warehouses were built there. Machine shops, repair facilities for vehicles and aircraft, supply depots sprang up. Tulagi harbor teemed with combat ships, transports, freighters, and landing craft. The beaches, coves, and inland ridges out toward Cape Esperance became training grounds for Army and Marine troops engaged in landing exercises. In Robert Sherrod's phrase, Guadalcanal was growing up.

A remarkable hybrid air force, known as AirSols (Aircraft, Solomons), gathered in numbers that Cactus fliers of an earlier day would have found unbelievable. Made up of Marine, Navy, AAF, and New Zealand units, AirSols officially came into existence on February 15, 1943. The command, initially held by a rear admiral, would be rotated from time to time among the Navy, Marine Corps, and AAF. AirSols took over the task of neutralizing Japanese air bases to the northwest, attacking enemy shipping, coastal barges, and landing craft, and providing close air support for American landings on other islands.

Meanwhile, the Japanese, having taken the humiliating decision to evacuate Guadalcanal, were busily digging in on islands further up the Solomons chain. They built new airstrips, expanded old ones, reinforced island garrisons, trying to strengthen a defensive shield around their major bastion at Rabaul. Munda was the new airfield most immediately troublesome to the victors of Guadalcanal. Only 175 miles northwest of Henderson Field, Munda provided a springboard for Zero fighters, which could accompany bombers toward the new American base. Heavy and medium bombers of the AAF and Royal New Zealand Air Force, and Marine and Navy light bombers kept up a steady round of attacks on Munda. Only the heavies could reach other Japanese airstrips.

On December 9, 1942, the day when General Vandegrift had turned over command to General Patch, Admiral Nimitz was meeting with Admiral King in San Francisco, in one of their periodic conferences. King had been thinking of a daring shift in strategy. The seizure of Guadalcanal, we will recall, was the first phase of a two-pronged Allied move toward Rabaul. King had grown impatient during the long struggle for Guadalcanal. Were further advances toward Rabaul going to be as slow as this hard-fought campaign seemed to indicate, one embattled island after another?

King now made a bold proposal—much too bold, in the opinion of his subordinate commanders in the Pacific: skip past the other Solomon Islands, bypass Rabaul itself, seize the Admiralty Islands west of that stronghold, and from there render the New Britain base useless by unremitting aerial bombardment. Nimitz and Halsey thought this a poor idea. The United States would be reaching deep into Japanese-held territory, its line of communication and its fleet exposed to attack from Truk and islands to its east, on the one hand, and on the other, from the chain of mutually supporting enemy bases on Bougainville, New Britain, and New Ireland.

In the opinion of the top naval commanders in the Pacific, U.S. forces ought not to make any move that would take them beyond the range of land-based fighter planes. And the next advance must await the buildup of Allied strength on its newly won base at Guadalcanal. King yielded, and endorsed their strategy. Moreover, at the end of 1942, only two U.S. aircraft carriers had survived the Guadalcanal campaign—the damaged *Enterprise* and twice-torpedoed *Saratoga,* now back in service after repairs. The new *Essex*-class carriers would not be coming into service until the middle of 1943. Nimitz intended to hold them at Pearl Harbor until he had enough to begin his drive across the central Pacific. Land-based aircraft would have to cover the push up the Solomons.

King accepted the views of his Pacific commanders. On March 21, 1943, the Joint Chiefs of Staff approved a new directive for operations in the South and Southwest Pacific, superseding that of July 2, 1942. In preparation for the final assault on Rabaul, Allied forces were to seize the Solomons up to the southern part of Bougainville and to drive the Japanese out of their bases in much of New Guinea and in western New Britain. MacArthur was to be in strategic command, coordinating all operations. Halsey would direct seaborne and air forces in the Solomons.

During the fight for Guadalcanal the Cactus Air Force had won control of the air within a radius of roughly two hundred miles of Henderson Field. That was the effective range of Marine and Navy dive-bombers, torpedo planes, and Wildcat fighters, which were the mainstay of the local air arm. The same limitation had dictated the range at which carrier engagements had been fought, although Japanese planes could reach considerably farther than their enemy's. A like team of light naval aircraft remained the chief Allied air weapon in the advance toward Rabaul in 1943, except that two formidable new fighter planes began to replace the sturdy Wildcat (F4F). One was the F4U, or Vought Corsair, faster and longer-ranged than its predecessor. By midsummer all Marine fighter squadrons were equipped with the Corsair. For flying from carriers, the Navy preferred a new Grumman fighter, replacing the Wildcat; this was the F6F, or Hellcat. AAF bombers, protected by the few available long-range Lightnings, or P-38s, could reach Japanese airfields at both ends of Bougainville. AirSols' combined power, however, was most effective when concentrated within a radius of 200-300 miles.

The task of amphibious forces—ground troops, ships and other craft that convoyed and supplied them, and fighting ships in the supporting screen—was to seize and hold plots of island acreage in the Solomons suitable for airfields. Thereby the most effective combat radius for aircraft could be shifted northwestward in a series of overlapping circles. It was as if a row of dimes, the edge of each covering that of the one behind, was stretched across an appropriately scaled map.

The first major offensive in the renewed Solomons

campaign began late in June 1943. Its major target was the Munda airfield on New Georgia. Munda was defended by a strongly emplaced Japanese garrison, which could be readily reinforced by barging troops from a larger garrison on New Georgia's immediate neighbor to the north, Kolombangara. By now AirSols could put 455 planes into the air to support the attack. Two bomber airdromes on Guadalcanal—Henderson Field and the new field south of Koli Point—and four fighter strips, including two in the Russells, were now usable.

The New Georgia operation was a complex one, which I will not describe here. Suffice it to say that it took three Army divisions five weeks to capture Munda. As the Japanese had learned on Guadalcanal, Americans learned here, and in MacArthur's attack on Buna, how costly it is in men, materiel, and time to try to capture a well-defended air base.

From then on, in the Solomons, U.S. forces followed a different strategy: seize an undefended, or lightly defended piece of land where airfields could be built, establish a strong defensive perimeter around it, construct an airstrip as fast as possible, and let the enemy, if inclined and able to bring in troops for counterattacks, wear himself out in assaults on the cordon.

On August 15, ten days after Munda was finally taken, the circle of airpower was moved forward again. Bypassing Kolombangara, an island defended by 10,000 Japanese, Halsey's forces seized a beachhead on lightly defended Vella Lavella Island, where engineers quickly developed an airstrip. The Japanese expected, and the Americans initially planned, that the next Allied target would be at the southern tip of Bougainville. The cluster of Japanese airfields, anchorages, and shore installations at that point— the Shortland-Faisi-Buin-Kahili complex—was a major base, defended by a large garrison. The Japanese had about 40,000 troops on Bougainville, concentrated at the two ends.

Halsey and his senior commanders, however, decided to bypass the forbidding concentration at the southern end. An assault there, even one limited to outer islands, would be extremely costly. Moreover, airfields at the southern tip of Bougainville would still not bring AirSols within range of the ultimate target—Rabaul. Halsey decided instead to seize a beachhead in Empress Augusta Bay, about halfway up the west coast of Bougainville, the largest of the Solomons. There the Japanese garrison was relatively small— only about 2,000, as it turned out, scattered near the landing site. L-Day was set for November 1, 1943.

Major General Nathan F. Twining, a brother of the First Marine Division's operations officer on Guadalcanal, had become commander of AirSols late in July. He was the first AAF officer to hold a top operational command in the South Pacific. For the Bougainville operation he could muster more than 650 combat planes.

In the narrow coastal strip seized by marines, engineers rapidly hacked out space for a landing strip that could serve as a staging base for aircraft headed north. Inland lay a swamp. The landing force had to push much farther inland than the original plans called for, against mounting opposition, to occupy enough solid ground for two more substantial airstrips to be built. The first could not be used until January 5, the second January 17. Meanwhile, Rabaul was being thoroughly drubbed.

The Japanese had reacted furiously, by air and sea, to each advance by Halsey's forces. They had tried to stop the northward push before it even started. They had bombed the new complex of American bases on and around Guadalcanal intermittently through the first half of 1943. The biggest Japanese effort came early in April. To about 200 planes of the Eleventh Air Fleet at Rabaul Admiral Yamamoto added 155 from his aircraft carriers. In two days of raids on the Tulagi-Guadalcanal-Russells area fifty-nine of the attacking aerial armada were lost, while they sank three Allied ships.

When Halsey's forces moved against Munda and other positions on New Georgia, Japanese carriers again contributed elite squadrons to reinforce air strength in the Shortlands-Buin area. Twining reported that the combined Japanese air fleets had lost 358 planes in the thirty-seven days of that operation. When Americans seized the beachhead in Empress Augusta Bay in November, the imperial fleet again lent Rabaul carrier planes to oppose the advance.

No more than their American counterparts did Japanese admirals like to strip their flattops of aircraft and highly trained air crews in order to reinforce land bases. But IGHQ was determined to hold Rabaul. Accordingly they tapped their last remaining reservoir of elite airmen to defend their bastion in New Britain. The consequences were mortal.

In August 1943, meeting at Quebec, British and American leaders had decided there was no need to undertake the capture of Rabaul, which would have been an extremely costly venture. Instead, Allied forces operating from New Guinea and the Solomons would throw a ring of bases around the Japanese bastion and, by bombing, render it useless. The main object of the Bougainville operation was to add bases from which AirSols could attack Rabaul.

MacArthur's Fifth Air Force, commanded by Lieutenant General George C. Kenney, assisted the Bougainville landings (and MacArthur's own operations in New Guinea) by knocking out as many planes, ships, and installations as possible at Rabaul. In a series of raids beginning on October 12, pushed through whenever weather permitted, Kenney did considerable damage. Although it was not as heavy as his extravagant communiques claimed,* Kenney's October and early November raids undoubtedly eased Halsey's problems in Empress Augusta Bay. With considerable anxiety about so close an approach to Japanese airfields, Halsey also brought his two carriers—the *Saratoga* and light carrier *Princeton*—into the waters southwest of Bougainville. Their planes joined in the L-Day air strikes against the landing area.

Halsey then became concerned about a Japanese cruiser force assembling in Rabaul's Simpson Harbor, which the Japanese intended to throw against Allied shipping off

_____

*Reporting the results of the first big raid the official Army Air Force historian later chided: "In this and other instances, the [MacArthur] GHQ policy of basing the daily communique on premliminary reports rather than photo-interpreted figures caused later embarrassment."

Bougainville. On November 4 his two carriers sent nearly a hundred planes to attack the ships at Rabaul, with highly satisfactory results—seven cruisers damaged. A week later, three additional carriers, borrowed temporarily from the vast American armada then moving toward Tarawa in the Gilbert Islands, joined the other two in hitting Rabaul again. The Japanese lost forty-one planes in a futile attack on the carriers. Nimitz was later to write that, in this venture, the carrier groups "had settled once and for all the long-debated question as to whether carriers could be risked against powerful enemy bases."

During two months, beginning December 19, 1943, AirSols took over the task of pounding Rabaul. Long-range bombers and fighters began the assault. Then, as the three new airstrips within the Bougainville perimeter came into use, shorter-ranged Marine and Navy dive-bombers, torpedo planes, and fighters joined in the attacks. AirSols was now under the command of Marine Major General Ralph J. Mitchell. In January 1944 his bombers—heavy, medium, and light—made more than a thousand sorties against the Japanese bastion, and fighter planes almost twice that number. Resistance continued strong. On some days eighty to ninety Zeros rose to meet the attackers. At the end of the month nearly a hundred more Japanese planes flew in from Truk as reinforcements for Rabaul.

In the first nineteen days of February, AirSols bombers made more than 1,300 sorties, and fighters nearly 1,600. On the 19th, twenty-three out of fifty Japanese fighters that rose to meet 145 American light bombers and fighters were shot down, according to AirSols reports. That was the last day Rabaul offered significant fighter defense. The remnants of its air force were withdrawn to Truk, which the Navy's carriers had just massively raided. Thereafter only a few planes, and usually none at all, came up from any of Rabaul's five airfields to oppose Allied bombers. Japanese shipping had already virtually ceased to venture into Simpson Harbor; fighting ships avoided it after Halsey's carrier raids against the cruisers in November, merchant shipping after AirSols bombers had sunk 40,000 tons in two raids in the latter half of January.

February 19, 1944, is regarded as victory day in the long

siege of Rabaul. Allied planes continued to attack the
fortress throughout the war, to make certain that it remained knocked out. But the Solomons bases had served
their purpose. The continuing Allied watch over the 100,000
Japanese in Rabaul, marooned but well supplied from stocks
earlier built up, was mounted mainly from islands to the
northwest, north and east—islands seized by MacArthur's
and Halsey's forces in March and April, completing the
ring around Rabaul and its major satellite, Kavieng.

A year and a half after the landings on Gaudalcanal the
objective of the operations begun with WATCHTOWER had at
last been achieved. Fortress Rabaul had been eliminated as
the main bastion of Japan's outer defense perimeter. Japan's IGHQ had chosen to expend, in vain, the elite of the
empire's airmen in its defense. That fact had a profound
effect on the remainder of the war in the Pacific.

As the war moved up the Solomons, the northern coastal
strip of Guadalcanal and the nearby Russells became a
quiet rear area—a place for rest, rehabilitation, and training,
and a staging area for troops that would move closer to
Japan's heartland. After its campaign in Cape Gloucester,
on the western tip of New Britain, beginning at the end of
1943, the First Marine Division returned "home." This
time it was encamped at Pavuvu in the Russells, thirty
miles from "the 'Canal." From there it embarked for its
grueling and bloody campaign at Peleliu, which cost it
6,000 casualties.

Again, in October and November 1944, the First returned to the Russells. At last, most of its veterans of the
original landings on Tulagi and Guadalcanal were able to
return home. Nearly 6,000 officers and men had served in
the Pacific thirty months. Most of the enlisted men went
Stateside for the duration of the war. But few of the
officers could be spared and had to be content with a
thirty-day home leave (a month with family and friends in
addition to travel time).

Eight thousand replacements had to be trained in four
months before the First embarked for its final campaign of
World War II. They went from the Russells to Guadalcanal for landing exercises and maneuvers in January 1945

and again early in March. Then, on March 15, the First embarked at the Russells for Okinawa.

The Sixth Marine Division, also destined for Okinawa, was assembled for the first time as an organic unit in September 1944 at Guadalcanal. It was made up largely of veteran units—raider battalions that had taken part in the march up the Solomons and others who had fought at Eniwetok and Saipan. Their command chose Tassafaronga Point, west of Point Cruz, as the division's campsite.

These later inhabitants of Guadalcanal—Marine, Army, and Navy—had brought under control the scourge of earlier American forces on Guadalcanal and many other islands in the South Pacific. Antimalaria measures had begun to be effective in the middle of 1943. Spraying of breeding sites—first with diesel oil, later with DDT—kept down *Anopheles,* and men had learned the merits of nets and Atabrine.

Another Marine division, the Third, had gathered in New Zealand early in 1943 and moved to Guadalcanal in July. Tetere, where a Japanese beachhead had been broken up in November 1942, was the site of their encampment. They were destined for Bougainville, the campaign which marked the end of the march up the Solomons. After that operation, in January 1944, the Third had returned to Tetere for rest and renewed training before their attack on Guam in July 1944.

With the departure of two Marine divisions for Okinawa in 1945 Guadalcanal became a backwater of the war. And with the unexpectedly early end of hostilities in September, only a few troops, mainly Army, remained to mind, and to liquidate, the stores. The last Army contingent left in 1950.

☆ ——— ☆

# Guadalcanal
# in Perspective

The struggle for Guadalcanal began as a significant but small eddy in the Pacific war. On August 7, 1942, neither the United States nor Japan foresaw what a raging vortex it would become, sucking in larger and larger forces. It grew in fury because the Japanese decided to stake the elite of their naval air power on an effort to throw back the first American offensive.

U.S. war leaders probably would not have undertaken the venture if they had known the ultimate dimensions of the Japanese reaction. As we have seen, the American leadership was torn between a desire to launch an offensive and an anxious concern, in that first year of the war, to preserve scarce assets. After some wavering, the United States, too, decided to take great risks. Classic naval doctrine on both sides, premised on massive fleet engagements in which the enemy would be decisively defeated, gave way before the demonstrated need for complex air-sea-land operations.

The Japanese Army lost nearly three-fourths of the men it committed to Guadalcanal. One historian who made a careful survey estimates that out of roughly 36,000 troops who reached the island, more than 14,800 were killed or missing and 9,000 died of disease. About 1,000 were taken prisoner. Thousands more, victims of air and sea attacks on transports and barges, never got to Guadalcanal. As we have seen, at least 10,000, and possibly more, were evacuated.

In comparison with those heavy losses, American ground troops got off lightly. Of about 60,000 men, Army and

Marine, who were on the island during part of the six-month campaign, the Japanese killed about 1,600 and wounded more than 4,200. The First Marine Division suffered most heavily: 774 killed and 1,962 wounded, for a total of 2,736 casualties. In addition uncounted thousands were knocked out of action by diseases, mainly malaria; the precise number is elusive because many who checked into hospitals were repeaters, but Navy doctors estimated that some 75 percent of the division was infected when it left the island.

Many more lives were lost in the U.S. Navy than in American ground forces. From official tables it is impossible to reckon, with any confidence, just what the correct figures are, but it appears that nearly a thousand officers and men were killed in each of two major actions—the Battle of Savo Island and the mid-November battles. Many more were lost in other actions, including the two carrier engagements and blockade-running attempts, that took place during the Guadalcanal campaign. One historian's estimate, based on a study of action reports of the ships and other craft involved, places the Navy's toll in dead at about 5,000.

Japanese troop losses were a painful blow to the empire, but, in cold strategic reckoning, not a factor significantly affecting the course of the war. Fortunately for both the Japanese and Americans, the main bulk of their armies never met in combat; it was primarily a naval and air war.

Japanese air losses at Guadalcanal, on the contrary, had a profound impact on the course of the war. Reports, both American and Japanese, vary widely as to losses by the Eleventh Air Fleet based at Rabaul and by carrier squadrons that flew either from their own ships or from land bases. We might suppose that Japanese records, becoming available after the war, would provide an accurate check on U.S. estimates, which were almost always exaggerated and sometimes wildly so. But those who have studied the records have found so many inconsistencies and gaps that the Japanese figures cannot be regarded as reliable.

Several factors account for the undependability of estimates, by both sides, of Japanese plane and air-crew losses. For reasons of morale, or out of national or armed-service pride, or from honest mistakes in reporting made in the melee of combat, the commands on both sides announced exaggerated claims, some services being more inaccurate than others. We can only make a rough stab at the actual figures.

Marine Corps airmen claimed to have shot down 1,520 enemy planes in the Solomons campaigns, ending with the air battles over Rabaul. After the war the Department of Navy put the figure a thousand higher, or 2,520, for Japanese planes lost to Navy and Marine fliers in the South Pacific—mainly from the Cactus Air Force and AirSols—during roughly the same period. If we divide that number by two—a somewhat arbitrary but, in the light of world-wide experience during the war, not unreasonable rule of thumb—then South Pacific aviators destroyed about 1,250 Japanese aircraft during the seventeen months between the landings on Guadalcanal and the reduction of Rabaul.

One American estimate, based on cross-checking American and Japanese reports, placed the number of Japanese aircraft that fell to U.S. planes or antiaircraft fire during the period of most intense aerial combat in the Guadalcanal campaign—from August 20 to November 15, 1942—at 263, while Cactus fliers lost 101 planes and 35 pilots in combat. The ratio of about five to two in plane losses (Japanese aircrew losses were proportionately much heavier) was vastly improved, in favor of the United States, as the war wore on; the war-long average, according to Navy Department claims, was about one American loss to seventeen Japanese.

While the numbers will always remain in doubt, the effects of steady attrition of Japanese air strength during the Solomons campaigns do not. As noted earlier, Japanese naval air commanders from time to time fed into their bases in the northern Solomons and Bismarcks elite air groups from their carriers, at costs that proved to be prohibitive. It was the loss of these highly trained and, as it turned out, irreplaceable naval pilots that crippled the Japanese air arm.

When the U.S. fleet began its drive across the central Pacific with the invasion of the Gilbert Islands in Novem-

ber 1943, no Japanese carriers could come out to challenge
it; the enemy was waiting for newly trained pilots. Captain
Tashikazu Ohmae, chief of staff of the Southeastern Fleet
and chief naval planner at Rabaul for the Solomons operations, put it this way:

> First we lost our best carriers at Midway, then our
> pilots in the Solomons. Due to our reduction of [aviation]
> fuel, we were unable to properly train replacements,
> even though we were able to produce carriers. In the
> Marshalls-Gilberts campaign we were unable to risk a
> fleet action without air cover. The defense of those
> islands was made by a few land-based planes and the
> military garrison. You moved too quickly for us to
> replace our losses. The same thing happened in Mari-
> anas and the Philippines.

After the Battle of the Santa Cruz Islands in October
1942, the Imperial Japanese Navy's flattops did not again
go into battle until the American invasion of the Marianas
in June 1944. By then the U.S. Navy's carrier-based airpower
was overwhelming. Against fifteen American carriers (seven
large, eight light) bearing 956 planes, the Japanese could
muster twelve (five heavy, four light) with 473 aircraft.
What mattered even more than the two-to-one difference in
numbers of planes was the poor quality of Japanese pilots.
On the average they had trained only 275 hours in the air—
half as much as their proud predecessors or the American
pilots who now opposed them. The difference quickly
showed. In addition to losing two carriers to U.S. submarines in the Battle of the Philippine Sea, about 400 of
Nippon's "sea eagles" were shot down. American naval
fliers dubbed the engagement the "Marianas Turkey Shoot."

From then on the aerial slaughter was fearsome. Four-
fifths of Japan's air losses came in the last two years of the
war, when huge American carrier fleets were attacking
land-based planes and their airdromes, mostly in the Philippines, Formosa, the Ryukyus, and Japan itself. But nearly
half of U.S. Navy and Marine losses during the entire war
came in the Solomons campaigns. Japan did not again
become a serious threat in the air until she resorted to the

suicidal tactics of the *kamikaze,* beginning with the long struggle for the Philippines.

The First Marine Division's Final Report on the Guadalcanal Operation remarks, as may be recalled, that "seldom has an operation been begun under more disadvantageous circumstances." It notes the brief time that elapsed between first notification of the targets and D-Day, the skimpy intelligence available about the Guadalcanal-Tulagi area, the difficulties of hasty combat-loading, lack of opportunity for rehearsal, and especially the lack of time for coordinated planning among all the forces involved. The division command had to draw up operational plans

Without detailed knowledge of the plans of higher and supporting commanders. . . . The direct consequence of this unilateral planning was the absence of a complete meeting of the minds of commanders concerned. For example, from the landing force point of view, the undertaking was planned and executed as a normal amphibious operation premised upon firm control of sea and air by our naval forces. The latter however regarded the enterprise more in the nature of a large-scale raid or hit and run operation as in fact it proved to be.

The words, written by Colonel Twining, were endorsed by General Vandegrift. The basic question, masked by impersonal military officialese, seems, in blunter terms, to be this: if the three aircraft carriers were meant to provide air cover for only thirty-six hours, then why did U.S. commanders send their few available transports into exposed waters, put ashore a division of 19,000 men, and leave them without the equipment and supplies needed to hold on against major counterattacks? As we have seen, different commanders at different levels had different views of the operation's purpose and of the actions they should take to achieve that purpose.

The Joint Chiefs of Staff, acting for their commander-in-chief, at the urging of their Navy member, gave what seems at first sight a forthright directive: seize and occupy Tulagi and "adjacent positions" and the Santa Cruz Islands. Their immediate aim, as stated, was to deny the islands to the enemy, their longer-term objective to seize Rabaul.

But what was to be gained by occupying Tulagi, a naval anchorage and seaplane base, unless it could be held? And how could it be held without a strongly defended air base on land nearby—much nearer than the Santa Cruz Islands, 350 miles to the east? Florida, the most obvious "adjacent position," was unfit for airfield construction; it was too hilly. Guadalcanal, it will be remembered, came into the plan only when it was learned that the Japanese were already building an airstrip there; immediately it became the prime target.

As we have seen, those charged with the responsibility for carrying out the Joint Chiefs' plan gave varying interpretations to their orders, and quite different degrees of zeal and determination to carrying them out. Admiral Ghormley, the Area commander, whose own position in the command structure was ambiguously defined, made it clear—in his decisions, official dispatches, and later writings—that keeping open the line of communication with Australia had, is his own interpretation of his orders, priority over a successful continued occupation of Guadalcanal. Long insistence on the occupation of Ndeni, at the expense of possible reinforcements for Guadalcanal, and understandable reluctance to strip rear bases of their garrisons, stemmed from his responsibility for protecting the rear and securing fallback positions if the Japanese recaptured Guadalcanal. These defensive concerns and pessimism over the outcome at Guadalcanal, and what would happen if it fell, held him back from giving full support to the active fighting front. Under Halsey's aggressive leadership and willingness to take great risks, American fortunes changed dramatically.

Admiral Fletcher, nominally in command of the whole expeditionary force, acted as though there were really two distinct forces, each with its own job: the carrier groups, which should give close support only briefly, then withdraw to minimize risk to scarce assets; and the amphibious force of ships and troops which would seize the target. Responsibility for the longer, larger mission apparently rested, in his view, on Admiral Turner, commander of the amphibious force, the war-planner with no combat experience, fresh from Washington, who had concocted this chancy operation and sold it to Admiral King.

Among the top naval commanders in the area, Turner and McCain (and his successor as commander of land-based aviation in the South Pacific, Rear Admiral Aubrey Fitch) gave their best efforts to make the operation succeed. Notwithstanding some costly errors in judgment and meddling in ground-force affairs, there was no reason to doubt that Turner was determined from the outset to hold Guadalcanal. He became the Navy's leading master of amphibious warfare.

General Vandegrift, who had no voice in the decision to go to Guadalcanal, managed to maintain at least an outward appearance of optimism and confidence, which is, after all, an important part of a commander's job. We will probably never know what doubts and discouragement he must at times have felt; he was not given to speaking of such things in public, even after his retirement.

Vandegrift's half-trained Marine division, led by able officers, did its job well; it seized and doggedly held the port and airfield that were the prizes of the long struggle. The Marines' prewar development of amphibious skills had made it possible for them to move to the attack from New Zealand on dismayingly short notice. If the Navy had not had its own "army," ready to move without argument on the Fleet's orders, Guadalcanal could not have been seized when it was.

Everyone was going to school in the Guadalcanal campaign, getting a painful on-the-job education. For the Marine Corps it was their first division-sized (later a corps-sized) operation in wartime. Bearing by far the heaviest responsibility in the Pacific war, the Navy had most to learn. Fortunately it learned quickly and well. Perhaps the most important lesson was the need, in the advance across the Pacific, for closely knit teamwork of sea, air, and land forces, working in mutual support and shared trust. The magnificent fleets marching across Alfred Thayer Mahan's "great common" would be one element—a crucially im-

portant element, but only one—in the combination needed
for victory over Japan.

In naval circles the argument over the proper role of
aircraft carriers in support of land operations continued
long after Guadalcanal was secured. It became acute before and after the operations at Tarawa, Saipan, and Leyte,
even when U.S. carrier fleets had become overwhelmingly
dominant. Should flattops be "tied down," deprived of
their precious mobility, to give close support to ground
forces during a landing operation? Or should they be free
to roam the seas, seeking out enemy fleets and air groups
and, beginning late in 1943, destroying his land-based
aviation? Guadalcanal held some lessons, and the yen to
roam was curbed. By the end of 1943 it had become clear
that the carriers' major role would be to attack the enemy's
land bases in support of the general advance.

"I do not have the tools to give you" to carry out your
task, King had told Ghormley in the spring of 1942. And
not many more were available in mid-summer, when King
ordered the attack on the lower Solomons. But Americans
are reputed to be adept improvisers; their skill and ingenu-
ity had full scope at Guadalcanal. Somehow the necessary
forces were patched together, and repatched to meet crisis
after crisis. And somehow, despite lapses in leadership,
they bulled through. Ernie King's bold gamble paid off—
handsomely. Because it did, the war was much shorter
than it would otherwise have been.

Thus ends my personal exploration of the Guadalcanal
campaign. The road from a Washington club to Bloody
Ridge was short compared to the one since traveled in an
effort to find out what happened that I could not myself
observe, and why, and what it signified. The one journey
took four months, the other four decades—although at a
far more leisurely pace, over ground much less rocky, with
long and frequent pauses and a sprint only at the end.

I had put Guadalcanal out of my mind many years ago.
Now and then, as some new book brought out new facts,
memories revived and interest flickered. It began to be
clear that I had witnessed not only a local victory, one that
put the Japanese on the defensive, but one of the decisive

actions of the war. Other things became evident. Bombs and shells exploding on Henderson Field caused tremors, and ships sinking into Ironbottom Sound had set up waves, that spread all the way to Tokyo and Washington, with a fascinating complex of vibrations along their paths.

Mild interest quickened into intense curiosity only recently, when I again read my diary and notes of those days. I decided to seek the answers to some lingering questions. To seek does not ensure finding; some of the answers have undoubtedly gone, with their possessors, to the grave, and some may elude the civilian mind. This book is the result of the search.

# Epilogue:
# Country Belong You-Me

After the war, Guadalcanal would never be the same. "Savage" Melanesian islanders had seen slaughter and destruction on an unimaginable scale. They had also seen material goods and construction—of airfields, roads, warehouses, wharves, tank farms, repair shops—beyond anything they could dream of. They had had job opportunities beyond anything they had earlier known, and beyond their needs. They had served as scout-guides for the Americans, members of the defense forces, carriers, cargo-handlers, dock workers. Four decades after the war had engulfed them, however, many islanders still looked upon employment for cash wages as only an occasional occupation, necessary in order to get those few necessities or luxuries that only money could buy. "Real" life was still in the village.

In March 1943, a month after the Japanese had taken their soldiers from Guadalcanal, the first U.S. Army black troops began to arrive on the island. Others followed, including two aviation engineer battalions that had spent the first year of the war building airfields in New Caledonia. These helped to construct the bomber airdromes south of Koli Point. Through the remainder of the Solomons campaigns black American troops were stationed on Guadalcanal or staged through on their way to other islands.

The islanders noted with great interest that Americans as dark-hued as themselves wore the same uniforms, ate the same food, slept in the same kind of tents, and did many of the same jobs, as white troops did. Visible and tangible signs of American power, wealth, approachableness, generosity, and racial diversity left their mark, with results unwelcome to the islands' British rulers. Even while battles continued in the central and northern Solomons, an independence movement began to take shape. It was called Marching Rule, a name apparently derived from "marsinga." The word means "brotherhood" in one of the languages of Malaita Island, where the movement was strongest. Adherents built their own fenced-in villages, set up their own police and courts, and collected their own taxes. Apart from Malaita, Guadalcanal and Florida Islands became Marching Rule's chief strongholds.

The movement was in part a cargo cult of the kind known in other parts of Melanesia, especially in New Guinea. People built huts to hold the presents that Americans would shower upon them. They posted lookouts for ships that would bring such bounty—rice, meat, bolts of cotton cloth, twists of tobacco, and everything else one could desire.

In 1947 protectorate authorities began cracking down on Marching Rule, imprisoning some of the chief agitators and ordering people to pull down the palisades they had erected around their villages. Some prominent figures associated with the movement, including Vouza, were treated more gently; Vouza was sent to Fiji for training in local government. The movement petered out, but the idea of independence did not.

Other leaders and movements emerged. The most influential, led by a self-styled prophet named Moro, grew in the late 1950s. Moro preached a return to old customs, including traditional rules for landholding—a matter on which British and Australian plantation owners were particularly sensitive. Rumors spread that Moro was backed by black Americans, who would return with shiploads of goodies for his followers. In 1965 he offered the district commissioner two thousand slowly accumulated Australian pounds for independence.

Meanwhile British policy was changing. Intent upon reasserting colonial rule immediately after the war, the British government had painfully come to the conclusion in the 1950s that the empire must be liquidated. They began preparing the Solomon Islanders, like colonial peoples elsewhere, to take on more responsibility for their own governance and economic support. There was the familiar progression from grudging concession to local demands for a greater voice in government to the granting of full autonomy and, finally, of independence.

Britain gave funds and guidance for more widespread education, better health services, and greater economic self-sufficiency. Foreign-exchange earnings were improved through expansion of copra production and development of new export industries in timber and fish. Not surprisingly, export of scrap iron was a major earner of foreign exchange immediately after the war. At first, islanders were indignant at, but came to accept, deals with the Japanese for the expansion of fisheries. To the old subsistence agriculture—the growing of taro, yams, other root vegetables, fruit, and a few pigs—were added grain crops and cattle herds in the grassy plains once studded with airdromes and other military installations. In 1960 colonial officers began a serious effort to control malaria, and over the years almost eradicated the disease.

On July 7, 1978, the protectorate came to an end and the new nation of Solomon Islands came into existence. Among widely scattered islanders whose interest and trust in prewar years had seldom extended much beyond their own villages, the Solomons south of Bougainville became "kantri bilong yumi"—"our country." In expressive Pidgin, the only common language throughout the chain, the new constitution was known as "as lo bilong gavman" —the "ass," or fundamental, law of [belonging to] government. Parliament was, appropriately, in the Solomons as elsewhere, the "Tok Tok House."

The new nation's first prime minister was the Right Honorable Peter Kenilorea, a thirty-seven-year-old native of Malaita, who had been to school in New Zealand. Most of the new rulers were men who had been children or not yet born when the Japanese, and then the Americans, came to Guadalcanal in 1942. Some had been educated at the new technical college in Honiara or the new University of the South Pacific in Papua. The old rulers did not forget old friends. The Solomon Islands' most famous citizen gained new honors; in 1979 he was awarded the Order of the British Empire and knighted, becoming Sir Jacob Vouza.

After the war the British protectorate's seat of government was no longer in Tulagi. Instead, the colonial administration sensibly took advantage of American military construction in the Point Cruz area, with its wharves, warehouses, other buildings, and water and power systems. A new capital city named Honiara (or "Naho ni ara"—The Face of the East Wind) rapidly developed there. On an island that had never boasted a village larger than a few hundred, Honiara, by independence day, had grown to nearly 18,000, and continued to expand thereafter. It was served by an international airport, still bearing the name Henderson Field. The old coastal trail past the base of Point Cruz had become the broad principal thoroughfare of the new city. Australian cruise ships, coming in through waters still known as Ironbottom Sound, tied up to the Point Cruz wharves in the Down-Under winter.

Honiara was established on ground that had been the most bitterly fought over, for the longest time, in the Guadalcanal campaign. Two ridges immediately inland from Point Cruz early became the favored residential district for important officials and foreign and local managers of banks and business enterprises. On the western of those two rises Puller's battalion of the 7th Marines had nearly been encircled and wiped out on September 27, 1942. Two weeks later, in a ravine behind that same ridge, Puller's men had almost destroyed a Japanese battalion bivouacked there. Early in November part of Edson's 5th Marines had eliminated a Japanese strongpoint at the foot of the eastern ridge, where Point Cruz joins the mainland. For nearly two months—from mid-November 1942 to mid-January 1943—the two enemies had faced and fought each other across the jungly gulch between the two hills, the Japanese dug-in on the western prominence, Americans on the eastern. Across that divide and along Honiara's boulevard American troops had begun their final push as part of the XIV Corps offensive in January 1943.

Honiara stretched eastward to the Matanikau, across ground even more soaked in American and Japanese blood, and beyond. The Kola Ridges, overlooking the shore east of the river, became a fashionable suburb. There Hanneken's battalion of the 7th Marines had fought off a Japanese assault on the night of October 25, 1942. "The Valley" into which John Hersey had descended with a weapons company earlier that month became the thoroughly domesticated site of a housing development. Kukum was developed as a center for light industry. The two towns of Honiara and Kukum almost merged as ribbon development began to fill up the coastal corridor in between.

The last known survivor of Hyakutake's army to be seen on Guadalcanal was apprehended in Honiara in 1947, while stealing vegetables from the police-barracks garden.

# Glossary

AA—antiaircraft

AAF—Army Air Forces (U.S.)

AirSols—Aircraft, Solomons

AK—cargo ship; AKA—attack cargo ship

Amtrac—amphibian tractor

AP—transport; APA—attack transport

APD—fast transport, or destroyer-transport (World War I destroyer converted to carry about 175 troops)

BB—battleship

B.S.I.P.—British Solomon Islands Protectorate

CA—heavy cruiser

CACTUS—code name for Guadalcanal

CG—commanding general

CINCPAC—Commander in chief, Pacific (Fleet and Ocean Area)

CL—light cruiser

CNO—Chief of Naval Operations

C.O.—commanding officer

COMAIRSOPAC—Commander, Aircraft, South Pacific

COMAMPHIBFORSOPAC—Commander, Amphibious Force, South Pacific

COMINCH—Commander in chief, U.S. Fleet

CP—command post

Crudiv—cruiser division

C/S—chief of staff

CTF—Commander, Task Force (with numerical designation)

CTG—Commander, Task Group

D-1—division personnel officer, or personnel section

D-2—division intelligence officer, or intelligence section

D-3—division operations officer, or operations section
D-4—division supply officer, of supply section
DD—destroyer
Desron—destroyer division
HQMC—Headquarters, U.S. Marine Corps
I-boat—Japanese submarine
IGHQ—Imperial General Headquarters
IJN—Imperial Japanese Navy
JCS—Joint Chiefs of Staff (U.S.)
MAG—Marine Air Group
MAW—Marine Air Wing
MP—military police
NOB—Naval Operating Base
PRO—public relations officer
PT—motor torpedo boat
RINGBOLT—Code name for Tulagi
SNLF—Special Naval Landing Force (Japanese)
T-boat—Higgins boat (named after designer and builder,
    Andrew Higgins); landing craft without ramp
TF—Task Force
TR-boat—Higgins boat with ramp
VMF—Marine fighter squadron
VMSB—Marine scout- or dive-bombing squadron
WATCHTOWER—Code name for the Guadalcanal operation
YP, or "Yippie boat"—small Patrol craft, converted from
    tuna-fishing boats and similar craft

AIRCRAFT TYPES (U.S.)

B-17—"Flying Fortress," four-engined AAF heavy bomber,
    made by Boeing
B-24—"Liberator," four-engined AAF heavy bomber, made
    by Martin
F4F—"Wildcat," Navy and Marine fighter, made by
    Grumman
F6F—"Hellcat," improved fighter, made by Grumman
F6U—"Corsair," Navy and Marine fighter, made by Vought
P-38—"Lightning," twin-engined, twin-tailed, long-range
    AAF pursuit, or fighter, plane, made by Lockheed
P-39—"Airacobra," single-engined AAF fighter, made by
    Bell

P-400—"Airacobra," export model
SBD—"Dauntless," Navy and Marine single-engined scout- or dive-bomber, made by Douglas
TBF—"Avenger," Navy and Marine torpedo-bomber, made by Grumman

# Appendix:
# Excerpts from
# Operations Orders

*Joint Chiefs of Staff Directive, 2 July 1942*

For offensive operations in the Southwest Pacific Area the United States Chiefs of Staff have agreed on this joint directive:

1. Objective: Offensive operations will be conducted with the ultimate objective of seizing and occupying the NEW BRITAIN–NEW GUINEA–NEW IRELAND area.
2. Purpose: Denying the area to Japan.
3. Tasks:
    a. Task One. Seize and occupy SANTA CRUZ ISLANDS, TULAGI, and adjacent positions.
    b. Task Two. Seize and occupy the remainder of the SOLOMON ISLANDS, LAE, SALAMAUA, and the northwest coast of NEW GUINEA.
    c. Task Three: Seize and occupy RABAUL and adjacent positions in the NEW GUINEA–NEW IRELAND area.

August 1st is tentatively set as a target date for planning purposes.

4. . . .
5. Forces:
    a. Those now under command of Southwest Pacific.
    b. At least two CVs [aircraft carriers] and South Pacific Amphibious Force with the necessary transports.
    c. Marine air squadrons, all available land-based air in South Pacific.

    d. The utilization of Army occupational forces in the
       South Pacific Area to garrison TULAGI and adja-
       cent island positions; troops from Australia to pro-
       vide other required garrisons.
Command:
    a. Task One. CINCPAC will designate TF [Task Force]
       commander. . . .
[To the Navy dispatch communicating this directive to
Nimitz and Ghormley, COMINCH (King) added: "It is as-
sumed Ghormley will be made TF commander at least for
Task 1 which he should command in person, in operating
area. He should also have conference with MacArthur]

*Dispatch from CINCPAC (Nimitz) to COMSOPAC (Ghorm-
ley) on 9 July 1942:*

You are hereby designated Task Force Commander for
Task One. "Operating area" is to be interpreted to be
initially NEW CALEDONIA–NEW HEBRIDES. You will
exercise strategic command in person. [List of Task Forces
assigned for the operation, including three aircraft-carrier
groups] With the forces under your command you will,
commencing about August 1, 1942, seize and occupy the
SANTA CRUZ ISLANDS, TULAGI and adjacent positions, in order to deny that area to Japan.

CTF [Commander Task Force] Sixty-One [Expeditionary
Force] U.S.S. Saratoga, Flagship Operation Order No.
1-42. At sea July 28, 1942

[Addressed to the two components of TF 61: Air Support
Force (three carrier groups) and Amphibious Force] This
force will seize, occupy and defend (1) TULAGI and
adjacent positions, (2) the SANTA CRUZ ISLANDS. The
purpose of these operations is to deny these positions to
enemy forces and prepare bases for our own future offensive operations.

*Air Support Force*
Proceed to TULAGI area in tactical support of Amphibious
Force. On D day and subsequently (1) cooperate with

Commander Amphibious Force by supplying air support, (2) protect own carriers from enemy air attacks, (3) make air searches as seem advisable or as ordered.

*Amphibious Force*
(1) [Deals with rehearsal in the Fiji Islands] (2) On D day seize and occupy TULAGI and adjacent positions, including an adjoining portion of GUADALCANAL suitable for the construction of landing fields. Initiate construction of landing fields without delay. Defend seized areas until relieved by forces to be designated later. (3) On departure of carriers call on Task Force 63 [shore-based air units at rear bases] for special aircraft missions. (4) Occupy and defend NDENI [in the Santa Cruz Islands]. Initiate construction of landing field without delay.

CTF 62 [Commander Amphibious Force] July 30, 1942

Para 2. This force will, on D-Day, capture and occupy TULAGI, GAVUTU, and GUADALCANAL ISLANDS, and subsequent to the main operations will destroy enemy minor forces in outlying positions on FLORIDA and nearby islands. The purpose of the operation is to deny these positions to enemy forces and to prepare bases for our own future offensive action.

First Marine Division Operation Order No. 7-42
Wellington, New Zealand    20 July 1942

1.  . . .

2. This division will attack and destroy the hostile garrison of TULAGI, GUADALCANAL, GAVUTU, and MAKAMBO by simultaneous landings on D day. It will then organize and defend those islands. . . . [Specific orders to units follow. The complete operations order, less the annexes, can be found in an appendix to Hough-Ludwig-Shaw, *Pearl Harbor to Guadalcanal*.]

# Notes

About a dozen dependable accounts of air, sea, or ground operations (in some cases, all three) in the Guadalcanal campaign are available. Most of these describe unit actions in details usually in the context of broader strategy. Although there are discrepancies among them, they can be regarded, on the whole, as reliable. Most of these basic accounts are documented, and I have not considered it necessary or helpful to note here the sources for statements that are generally agreed to be accurate.

The following notes refer to sources of direct quotations; to dispatches that are quoted or paraphrased; to sources not readily found in other accounts; and, in selected instances, to inconsistencies among two or more other reports.

For abbreviations or short-form references used in these Notes, see the Glossary and Bibliography.

In the six-digit numbers identifying radio dispatches, the first two digits refer to the day of the month, the last four to the hour when the message was sent. The hour may be local Guadalcanal time or Greenwich time (generally used in the Navy messages; Guadalcanal time minus eleven hours). The Japanese always used Tokyo time.

CHAPTER 1. INITIATION

The first part of the chapter (up to the embarkation for New Zealand) is based on letters in the author's possession and on his memory. The account of events on the voyage to Wellington is based mainly on the loose-leaf notebook referred to in these Notes as the Black Book; of events in New Zealand, on the HCM Diary.

For the beginnings of the combat correspondents' program, see also: Benis M. Frank, *The Story of Marine Combat Correspondents, Photographers, and Artists* (Washington: Marine Corps Combat Correspondents Association, 1967); and the oral history of Brigadier General Robert L. Denig, Marine Corps Historical Center, Oral History Section.

## CHAPTER 2. THE BIG PICTURE

For the background, in strategic planning and decisions, to the Guadalcanal campaign, see: Dyer, *The Amphibians Came to Conquer*, vol. 1, pp. 245–53 (Admiral R. K. Turner's role in planning the Solomons offensive); Hayes, "Pearl Harbor through Trident," pp. 194–237; Matloff and Snell, *Strategic Planning for Coalition Warfare*, pp. 147–78 (allocation of Army forces to the Pacific in 1942); J. Miller, *Guadalcanal*, chap. 1; Morison, *History of U.S. Naval Operations*, vol. 4, chap. 12.

23 Excerpt from the *Dominion*. Merillat, pp. 11–12.

27 King-Marshall exchange concerning Army garrisons for U.S. Island bases. Matloff and Snell, pp. 151–53, 161–64; King and Whitehill, p. 382.

28 King to Ghormley, "I do not have the tools . . ." Ghormley MS, p. 1; Morison, vol. 4, p. 251.

29 JCS directive of July 2, 1942. CSP-WD, July 4: COMINCH to CINCPAC, 022100. See Appendix.

29 King-Marshall exchange. Dyer, pp. 285–86; Hayes, 205–8; Morison, vol. 4, pp. 258–60; J. Miller, pp. 11–14.

29 King-Ghormley exchange. CSP-WD, July 11, COMINCH to COMSOPAC, 102100; COMSOPAC reply, 1 12000; Ghormley, pp. 52–54.

30 Joint Ghormley-MacArthur message urging delay. CSP-WD, July 9: COMSOPAC to COMINCH, 080102–081020; Dyer, pp. 285–86; Ghormley, pp. 46–52.

31 Reports of airfield construction by Japanese. Dyer, pp. 273–76.

CHAPTER 3. A WOBBLY WATCHTOWER

40   "The decision of the United States . . ." First
     Marine Division Final Report on the Guadalcanal
     Operation, Phase V, p. 1.

45ff.  Reports of the conference aboard the *Saratoga*
     on July 26. Dyer, pp. 300–3; Ghormley, pp.
     64–67; Vandegrift, p. 120.

46   "I was desirous of attending this conference . . ."
     Ghormley, p. 64.

46   Ghormley's problems with censorship of the
     Free French. CSP-WD, entries for July 18–23;
     Ghormley, p. 61.

46   Ghormley and the New Zealand government.
     Ghormley, pp. 98–103.

46   Doubts of Nimitz and King concerning Fletcher.
     Buell, *Master of Sea Power*, pp. 194–99; Nimitz
     Papers, Nimitz letters of May 29 and June 13;
     Potter, *Nimitz*, p. 86.

47   Fletcher's sensitiveness about carrier losses. Dyer,
     p. 384; Morison, vol. 4, p. 28; Potter and Nim-
     itz, p. 694, fn. 2.

47–48  Fletcher's promotion over Noyes. Dyer, p. 293.

48   Nimitz instructions to Ghormley, and Ghormley's
     interpretation, ibid., pp. 303–4; CSP-WD, May 9.

48   King appoints Ghormley as task force command-
     er; Nimitz gives Ghormley "strategic command."
     CSP-WD: COMINCH to CINCPAC, 022100, July 2
     (see Appendix); CINCPAC to COMSOPAC, 190633,
     July 19; Dyer, pp. 304–4; Ghormley, p. 55.

49   Ghormley's understanding of "strategic com-
     mand." ZDC, Zimmerman interview of Ghorm-
     ley, Feb. 8, 1949.

49   Turner letter to Fletcher concerning need for air
     cover. Dyer, p. 307.

49   Vandegrift at the conference on the *Saratoga*.
     Vandegrift, p. 120.

40–50  Peyton and Kinkaid accounts of the *Saratoga*
     conference. Dyer, p. 301.

50   Callaghan report on the *Saratoga* conference.
     Ghormley, pp. 65–66.

CHAPTER 4. THE FIRST DAYS

53    "The climate is abominable; . . ." Dull, p. 181.
55    Congestion on Beach Red. Final Report, Phase
      II p. 11; Dyer, pp. 350–53; Hough-Ludwig-
      Shaw, pp. 257–58; Zimmerman, pp. 46–47.
58    "Sluggish" progress of 5th Marines. Thomas
      Oral History, p. 281; Vandegrift, pp. 125, 127.
58    "It looks like Nicaragua . . ." Merillat, p. 33.
61    Varying estimates of Japanese troop strength in
      the Tulagi area. Final Report, Phase II p. 8
      (1,000); Hough-Ludwig-Shaw, p. 271 (750–800);
      J. Miller, p. 67 (about 500); Morison, vol. 4
      (about 1,500); Ohmae ("some 180 riflemen at
      Tulagi").

CHAPTER 5. PERIL ON THE SEA

The account of the Battle of Savo Island is based on
Morison, vol. 5, pp. 17–64; Dull, pp. 184–93; Gill (from
an Australian point of view), pp. 133–55; Ohmae (from a
Japanese point of view).

64–65   Turner blames McCain for lack of information on
        air searches. Dyer, pp. 368–69.
65      Crutchley's removal of HMAS Australia from
        the western screen. Dyer, p. 378; Morison, vol.
        5, pp. 31–35; not mentioned in Gill.
67–68   Navy casualties. Morison, vol. 5, p. 63 (number
        includes eighty-four dead and fifty-five wounded
        on HMAS Canberra).
68      ". . . the blackest day of the war." Buell,
        Master of Sea Power, pp. 222, 579. The re-
        marks as quoted are almost identical with those
        reportedly made by King in an interview appear-
        ing in the New York Times, October 22, 1945,
        p. 5.
68      Lack of censure. Dyer, 357–74 (concerning
        Turner's and McCain's roles); Morison, vol. 5,
        pp. 61–63.
68–69   Fletcher's message concerning withdrawal. CSP-
        WD, CTF 61 to COMSOPAC, 080708 (1808 local
        time), August 8; Morison, vol. 5, pp. 27–28.

69  Fletcher's task force, but not Fletcher personally, gets word of the engagement off Savo. Dyer, p. 395.

69  Ghormley's report of withdrawal to Nimitz. CSP-WD, Aug. 9, COMSOPAC to CINCPAC, 090834.

69  Fuel levels in Fletcher's task force. Dyer, pp. 393–94; Morison, vol 5 p. 28.

70  "All knew that the enemy could arrive . . ." Ghormley, p. 93.

70  "Am informed you plan to withdraw . . ." CSP-WD, Aug. 2, COMSOPAC to CTF 61, 020210.

70  Fletcher's later explanations of his decision to withdraw. Dyer, pp. 384–86, 391–95.

71  Special instruction. Buell, *Quiet Warrior*, p. 121; Dyer, p. 384; Potter, p. 87.

72  Fletcher (CTF 61) operation order. See Appendix.

72  Nimitz comments on August 23. CINCPAC to CO-MINCH, "Preliminary Report—Solomon Islands Operation," Serial 02576, Aug. 25.

72–73  Nimitz comment on August 27. CINCPAC to CO-MINCH, Report on "Solomon Islands Campaign—Action of 23–25 August," Serial 02827, Aug. 27.

CHAPTER 6. TWELVE DAYS IN LIMBO

74–75  Defense plans for Lunga perimeter. Final Report, Phase III, pp. 1–2; not shown to Turner until last minute, Thomas Oral History, p. 269.

76  Snedeker, on radio station and shortage of telephone wire. Snedeker Oral History, pp. 49–53.

76–77  Rations available to the Guadalcanal garrison. The following are entries in CSP-WD:

Vandegrift to Turner 120945 (Aug. 12). ". . . essential that vessels containing food arrive here earliest possible date."

Radio Noumea to Tulagi 140640 [Turner's reply]. "Transport records indicate following landed your area: . . . Rations, Guadalcanal, 567,000 [more than fifty days' supply]."

Tulagi to Auckland 151015 [Vandegrift's rejoinder]. "From rations on hand and con-

sumed to date estimate about twelve days'
rations landed Guadalcanal. Further loss due
to weather and handling reduced this to ten
days. No opportunity should be lost to forward
rations to this command.''

77    ''. . . the major essentials of battle . . . were
always present.'' Dyer, p. 417. ''. . . 100 percent
of the logistic support ashore . . .'' ibid., p. 353.

78    Nonessentials put ashore: ''fancy cheese,'' ibid.,
p. 352; tennis equipment, ibid., p. 433.

78–79   Lack of logistics planning. Ibid., pp. 403–8,
412–19, 433.

80–82   Higgins boats intercepted by submarine on way
to Tulagi. Black Book; Griffith, pp. 72–73;
Tregaskis, pp. 74–78, 92–94.

84    Japanese ''estimate of the situation'' and map
dropped on August 14; in possession of the author; translated in part by Captain Sherwood F.
Moran on Guadalcanal.

85–87   Goettge patrol. Final Report, Phase III, p. 6, and
Phase III D-2 Report, pp. 9–11; MacMillan, pp.
52–55 (interview with a survivor); Vandegrift, p.
136; ZDC, Whaling letter of Jan. 26, 1949.

88–89   Jacob Vouza. Clemens, pp. 56–57, 137.


CHAPTER 7. THE VIEW FROM RABAUL

90    Tulagi radio messages. Several versions of these
messages appear in the literature. The texts quoted
here, from an intercept by the Fleet radio intelligence unit at Pearl Harbor, were supplied by
Captain E. T. Layton, Fleet Intelligence Officer
in 1942. ZDC, Layton letter, March 3, 1950.

90    Reactions in Rabaul. Jap. Mono., Southeast Area
Naval Operations, part 1, pp. 10–12; Ohmae,
''Battle of Savo Island.''

91    American and Japanese designs on northern
Papua. Jap. Mono., Southeast Area, pp. 8–9,
15–18; Milner, pp. 34–70.

92    Japanese movements from Rabaul to Papua. Ibid.,
pp. 68–69.

95–96    Japanese codes. Holmes, pp. 16–19, 108–10, 118; Kahn, pp. 562–603; Potter, pp. 63–68.

96    Changes in Japanese naval code in August. Radio Intell: SRH-012, vol. 4, part 1, pp. 5–11, 69.

97    Japanese messages concerning the Ichiki Detachment. Ibid., p. 13; vol. 4, part 2, no. 530 of August 14.

98–99    Methods of receiving and handling radio intelligence on Guadalcanal. Letters to the author from Merrill B. Twining (July 14, 1981) and Sanford B. Hunt (Aug. 8, 1981).

99    Warning from Vandegrift to Rupertus. Final Report, Phase III, Annex E (Operations Daily Journal).

## CHAPTER 8. THE FLY AND THE TORTOISE

100    Origins of the Brush patrol. Final Report, Phase III, p. 9; Griffith, p. 81; Hough-Ludwig-Shaw, p. 285; author's interview of Gerald C. Thomas, Jan. 13, 1981; ZDC, Brush letter of Jan. 15, 1949.

101    Beginnings of the Cactus Air Force. Sherrod, pp. 73–74, 79–80.

104    Accounts vary as to where Ichiki committed suicide. Gen Nishino, a Japanese war correspondent who accompanied Japanese forces later on Guadalcanal, is reported to have said it took place on the battlefield. Toland, p. 367.

108–110    The account of the Battle of the Eastern Solomons is based on Dull, pp. 197–207; T. Miller, pp. 41–52; Morison, vol. 5, pp. 79–107.

109    "What saved Guadalcanal . . ." Sherrod, p. 90, fn. 28.

109–110    ". . . like a housefly attacking a giant tortoise." Tanaka, "The Struggle for Guadalcanal," p. 56.

## CHAPTER 9. PREPARING FOR THE NEXT ROUND

113    Army reluctance to add to forces in the Pacific. Ghormley, pp. 71, 75–76; Pogue, pp. 382–97 (points out, at p. 397, that by the end of 1942

Army allocations of forces to the Pacific far exceeded those planned earlier in the year).

114   McCain plea for fighter planes. CSP-WD, COM-AIRSOPAC to CINCPAC, 310402, Aug. 31.

117   Fletcher's wound on the *Saratoga* and subsequent relief. Action Report on Torpedoing of USS *Saratoga*, Aug. 31, 1942, Navy Operational Archives; Potter, *Nimitz*, p. 185.

117   Switch in Japanese priorities from New Guinea to Guadalcanal. Japanese sources, both Army and Navy, report that the decision to give temporary priority to Guadalcanal was made at the end of August: Hayashi, p. 59; Jap. Mono. Army High Command, p. 65; SE Area Naval Ops., pp. 9, 19; Milner, p. 98. Orders were then issued to suspend the drive on Port Moresby. The shift in priorities became more evident in mid-September.

124   Remarks concerning Raider battalions, at the Nimitz-King conference. King Papers, conference records. COMINCH staff officers who recorded these periodic conferences did not always separate chaff from substance; the remarks referred to here should probably be regarded as chaff.

125   Dispute over formation of Raider battalions. Dyer, pp. 450–51; Hough-Ludwig-Shaw, pp. 261–62; Isely and Crowl, p. 154. See also Robert E. Mattingly, "The Worst Slap in the Face the Marine Corps Ever Was Given," *New Aspects of Naval History* (Annapolis: Naval Institute Press, 1981), pp. 373–85, and Charles L Updegraph, Jr., *U.S. Marine Corps Special Units of World War II* (Washington: HQMC Historical Division, 1972), pp. 14–17.

CHAPTER 10. THE RIDGE

127   "Centipede Hill." Translation of Col. Furumiya's diary, Final Report, Phase V, Annex I (Intelligence). The translation gives "Centipede Plateau"; I have substituted "Hill."

133–134    Rabaul requests for information about the airfield
           and instructions for signals. Radio Intel: SRNS
           0151–0153, Sept. 11–13, 1942.

    134    Scene at Edson's CP. Grifith, pp. 116–17.

    135    "But because of the devilish jungle, . . ." Ibid.,
           p. 117.

    135    Air reinforcements. Sherrod, p. 90.

    137    "Totsugeki." Toland, p. 380 (quoting a Japanese
           war correspondent who was with Kawaguchi).

    138    "Now march it . . ." Merillat, p. 99.

    140    Ghormley's pessimistic estimate of the situation,
           brought by Turner. Vandegrift, p. 152; author's
           interview with Thomas, Jan. 13, 1981. Twining
           later said his secret emergency order called for
           withdrawal eastward along the coast—in order,
           if possible, to keep in touch with the Navy (Twin-
           ing lecture).

140–141    "Had it been a successful assault, . . ." Vande-
           grift Draft Oral History, p. 798.


CHAPTER 11. AFTER THE RIDGE

144–145    Turner report on the delivery of the 7th Marines.
           COMPHIBFORSOPAC to COMSOPAC, serial 00195,
           Sept. 27, 1942, "Report of operation for rein-
           forcement of Guadalcanal Island forces by the
           7th Marines (Reinforced)."

    145    Turner "suggestions." Vandegrift, pp. 169–70.

    151    Theft of Geiger's whiskey. Vandegrift, p. 149.

    157    Whaling's Scout-Snipers. Black Book.


CHAPTER 12. MATANIKAU—SINISTER RIVER

    159    Spanish discovery of the Solomons. Amherst,
           pp. xxvii-xxxv, 6, 31, 38, 175–76, 309; Guppy,
           pp. 192–220.

    159    Guadalcanalese not cannibals. Woodford, p. 32.
           Headhunting elsewhere in Solomons, ibid., pp.
           153–57; Guppy, pp. 16–17, 35–39, 67–71.

    160    Discovery of Point Cruz. Amherst, pp. 38,
           175.

161 Patrol to Kokumbona. Final Report, Phase IV, pp. 4–5; ZDC, comment from Major M. V. O'Connell, Feb. 8, 1949.

165 Varying views of Matanikau plans. Final Report, Phase V, p. 8; Davis, pp. 134–41; Griffith, pp. 134–37; Twining lecture.

CHAPTER 13. OCTOBER CRISIS: FIRST PHASE

172–173 The full text of the Harmon letter is found in J. Miller, Appendix A.

174 Vandegrift and Morgan remarks upon hearing artillery. Merillat, p. 142.

175 The scene "baffled description, . . ." Tanaka, p. 62.

176 "It is almost beyond belief that we are still here, . . ." *Time* magazine, Nov. 16, 1942, p. 47.

178 Macklin's search for aviation gasoline. HCM Diary, and Merillat, pp. 151–52.

179 Evacuation of the last pilot of VMSB-232. Sherrod, p. 96, fn. 6.

179 New Japanese fighter-sweep tactics. T. Miller, pp. 101–6.

180 "Little Navy" running blockade. Morison, vol. 5, pp. 179–81.

183–184 Estimates of Japanese strength, mid-October. J. Miller, p. 139 and fn. 13.

185 Nimitz: "It now appears that we are unable . . ." Dyer, p. 414; Morison, p. 178.

185 Vandegrift message to COMSOPAC. CSP-WD, Oct. 15.

186 Nimitz letter to wife. Potter, p. 197.

186 Halsey remarks. Bryan, p. 109.

186 Ghormley's abscessed teeth. Buell, *Master of Sea Power*, p. 222; Potter, 225.

CHAPTER 14. OCTOBER CRISIS: SECOND PHASE

189 American failure to find Maruyama Trail. J. Miller, p. 154.

189   Failure of Japanese Communications concerning postponement. Griffith, pp. 166–67; J. Miller, p. 157.

192   Puller's outpost. Davis, pp. 153–54; Merillat, pp. 167–68, 170–77.

199   D-3's warning message to the air command. Black Book.

199   Furumiya diary. Final Report, Phase V, Annex I.

199   Twining Comments. Black Book.

202   Japanese and U.S. carrier planes in the Battle of the Philippine Sea. Morison, vol. 8, p. 233.

203   Command arrangements in Vandegrift's absence. Author's interview of Gerald C. Thomas, Jan. 13, 1981.

203   Halsey promises support. Bryan, p. 117; Vandegrift, p. 184.

203–204   President Roosevelt's note to the JCS. Holograph reproduced in Sherwood, following p. 624.

204   AAF promises more planes. Craven and Cate, vol. 4, pp. 51–52.

CHAPTER 15. TWO FRONTS

205–206   Twining and Thomas remarks. Black Book.

207   Intelligence report of expected enemy landing at Koli Point. Black Book.

208   Paul Moore wounded and George Mead killed. Merillat, pp. 92, 162.

210   Conflicting reports as to what the Japanese put ashore at Tetere. Griffith, p. 185; J. Miller, p. 196 and fn. 9.

211   Puller's remarks after being wounded. Zimmerman, p. 139; Merillat, p. 205.

215–216   Conflicting advice on the continuation of action beyond the Matanikau. Black Book. (Final Report, Phase V, p. 28 notes, rather too optimistically, that there was "every prospect of capturing Kokumbona [until] the threat in the east developed.")

216   2nd Marines beyond the Matanikau early in November. Final Report, Phase V, Annex V (Rec-

ord of Events, 2nd Marines Reinforced); ZDC,
Cornelius P. Van Ness's comments, Jan. 12,
1949; John M. Arthur's comments, Feb. 1, 1949.

216   Japanese plans to attack American flank. Cronin,
pp. 66–67; J. Miller, p. 205.

219   Number of Japanese troops in the mid-November
convoy. Griffith, p. 192 (11,000 Army troops
and about 3,000 SNLF personnel were embarked);
Sherrod, p. 116, fn. 10 ("another estimate says
. . . a total of 7,700''); USSBS(P), *Campaigns
of the Pacific War*, p. 125 (10,000 troops of the
Hiroshima Division and 3,500 SNLF personnel
were embarked).

CHAPTER 16. DECISION IN NOVEMBER

The main sources for the account of naval and air actions,
November 12–15, are: Dull, pp. 240–47; T. Miller, pp.
181–205; Morison, vol. 5, pp. 225–87; Sherrod, pp. 114–17.

224   Criticism of Callaghan's tactics. Morison, vol. 5,
p. 237.

226–227   Tanaka remarks. Tanaka, p. 66.

227   Varying estimates of Japanese troop losses in the
convoy. Final Report, Phase V, p. 32 ("possibly
more than 18,000" lost); J. Miller, p. 188 (about
4,000 landed safely); Jap. Mono. Southeast Area
Naval Operations, p. 45 (2,000 survivors landed);
Sherrod, p. 116, fn. 10 ("another estimate says
3,000 landed, 3,000 drowned, and 1,700 picked
up, out of a total of 7,700''); Tanaka, p. 66 (400
killed, 5,000 rescued).

229–230   Crisis in Tokyo over the allocation of shipping
for Army use. Hayashi, pp. 62–64; Jap. Mono.,
Army High Command, p. 71 (reports Army need
for "3,000,000" tons of shipping; evidently a
misprint for "300,000").

CHAPTER 17. RESPITE AND RELIEF

239   For varying appraisals of Carlson, see: Barbara
Tuchman, *Stillwell and the American Experience
in China* (New York: Macmillan, 1970), pp.

175, 184, 189; James Roosevelt, "Evans Carlson: A Personal Memoir," and Comments by Benis M. Frank, in *New Aspects of Naval History*, edited by Craig L. Symonds (Annapolis: Naval Institute Press, 1981).

239–241   Operations of Carlson's 2nd Raiders. Final Report, Phase V, pp. 30–31; Merillat, pp. 217–27.

241   Physical condition of a Marine regiment. Final Report, Phase V, Annex T (Medical), p. 10.

## CHAPTER 18. MALARIA DOWN UNDER

General sources used in the discussion of malaria in Guadalcanal and elsewhere in Melanesia are: *Communicable Diseases: Malaria*, pp. 2–7, 398–479; "Malaria and Epidemic Control in the South Pacific, 1942–1944" (HQ, South Pacific Base Command. Mimeographed. Army Center of Military History).

246   Incidence of malaria in the First Marine Division. Final Report, Phase V, Annex T (Medical), pp. 5–7.

247   ". . . to hell with the mosquitoes." *Communicable Diseases: Malaria*, p. 426.

247   Crisis over malaria in Brisbane; the move to Melbourne. Vandegrift, pp. 205–7; Vandegrift Draft Oral History, pp. 807–15.

248   "That thing stuck in my craw, . . ." Ibid., p. 815.

## CHAPTER 19. THE FINAL PUSH

Sources consulted for the account of operations under General Patch's command, from December 9, 1942, to February 9, 1943: Collins, pp. 144–67; Cronin, pp. 72–99; Hough-Ludwig-Shaw, pp. 359–71; J. Miller, pp. 211–350; ZDC, comments of Col. John M. Arthur, Feb. 1, 1949.

254   Estimates of Japanese forces on Guadalcanal. Hough-Ludwig-Shaw, p. 364, and Morison, vol. 5, p. 344 (25,000); Griffith, p. 212 (30,000, including naval personnel; citing Jap. Mono. 17th Army Operations, Vol. 2, p. 51); J. Miller, pp.

228–29 (9,100 to 16,000; citing local 1942 and 1943 U.S. Army intelligence estimates).

258 ". . . do not expect to return . . ." Cronin, p. 98.

258–259 CINCPAC intelligence estimates concerning expected Japanese efforts to reinforce Guadalcanal. Radio Intel: SRNS 0294–0302, Feb. 1–9, 1943.

260 Reports of number of Japanese destroyers involved in the evacuation. Dull, p. 259; Jap. Mono. Army High Command, Eighth Area Army, and Southeast Area Naval Operations; Dull (also notes one destroyer was sunk by a U.S. mine off Savo Island the first night).

260–261 IGHQ orders for withdrawal. Jap. Mono. Eighth Area Army.

260–261 Notification of evacuation plans to Japanese commanders at Rabaul and on Guadalcanal. Griffith 233, 238–41.

261 Patch's victory message. J. Miller, p. 348.

261 Nimitz comment on Japanese evacuation. Morison, vol. 5, 370.

CHAPTER 20. FRUITS OF VICTORY

Principal sources for the campaigns in the central and northern Solomons and in New Britain, and the final neutralization of Rabaul: Craven and Cate, vol. 4, chaps. 7, 8, and 10; Morison, vol. 6, *Breaking and Bismarcks Barrier;* Shaw and Kane, *Isolation of Rabaul;* Sherrod, chaps. 9, 10, 12, and 13.

262 McCain dispatch. See second note, Chapter 9.

263 Operation DRYGOODS; code name MAINYARD. Dyer, p. 498.

263 Beginnings of AirSols. Sherrod, 131; Craven and Cate, vol. 4, pp. 210–12.

264 King's plan to bypass Rabaul and Nimitz-Halsey reaction. Potter, *Nimitz,* p. 210.

264–265 Summary of JCS directive of March 29, 1943. Morison, vol. 6, pp. 95–96.

266 New bypass and perimeter strategy. Potter and Nimitz, pp. 718–22.

268    Kenney's exaggerated claims. Craven and Cate,
       vol. 4, p. 319, fn. 26.
269    Nimitz: ". . . settled once and for all . . ." Pot-
       ter and Nimitz, p. 727.
269    Air sorties against Rabaul in January and Febru-
       ary 1944. Craven and Cate, p. 353.
269    Japanese air losses on Feb. 19, 1944. Sherrod, p.
       200.


CHAPTER 21. GUADALCANAL IN PERSPECTIVE

272    Japanese losses on Guadalcanal: Griffith, p. 244
       (8,500 killed in action, more than 12,300 dead
       of wounds, disease, or starvation; cites corre-
       spondence with Miyazaki, Hyakutake's chief of
       staff); J. Miller, p. 350 (more than 14,800 killed
       or missing in action, 9,000 dead of disease,
       1,000 taken prisoner; cites interrogations of
       Hyakutake, Miyazaki, and Maruyama); ibid.,
       footnote 69 (total deaths from battle and disease
       given as 21,600 in Jap. Mono. 17th Army Opera-
       tions, II; 28,580 casualties, according to U.S.
       Army Forces in the South Pacific; 24,330, ac-
       cording to Americal Division).
272–273 American casualties (not including Navy losses at
       sea). Final Report, Phase V, Annex X: for pe-
       riod Aug. 7–Dec. 9, 1,318 killed or died of
       wounds in all units, 10,635 hospitalized for dis-
       eases and injuries in First Marine Division alone;
       J. Miller, p. 350, 1,600 dead in whole campaign.
273    Navy casualties. *The Statistics of Diseases and
       Injuries*, Appendix Table 14. Vol. 3 of *The His-
       tory of the Medical Department of the United
       States Navy in World War II* (Washington: Gov-
       ernment Printing Office, 1950). Estimate of 5,000
       Navy dead from a work in progress by Richard
       B. Frank.
274    Marine claims of 1,520 enemy planes. OpNav,
       Marine Air Intelligence Bulletin, Aug–Sept 1945.
274    Navy Department's estimates of Japanese air
       losses. Naval Aviation's Air Combat Record, a

mimeographed departmental report released May
9, 1948.

274 Japanese air losses during period of heaviest air
combat at Guadalcanal. T. Miller, p. 209.

275 "First we lost our best carriers . . ." USSBS(P),
*Interrogations,* p. 474.

275 Japanese and U.S. carrier-plane strength in June
1944. Morison, vol. 8, *New Guinea and the
Marianas,* p. 233.

275 Reduction in hours of Japanese pilot training.
USSBS(P), *Japanese Air Power,* pp. 35–36, 40,
42.

## EPILOGUE: COUNTRY BELONG YOU-ME

The main general sources consulted for this chapter:
BIS, *Solomon Islands;* Colonial Office, Annual Report on
the British Solomon Islands Protectorate for 1948; Kent,
*The Solomon Islands;* Luke, *Islands of the South Pacific;*
Trumbull, *Tin Roofs and Palm Trees.*

281 Black Army troops in the Pacific. Ulysses Lee,
*The Employment of Negro Troops* (Washington:
Department of the Army, 1966), pp. 450, 471–72,
497–500, 594–99.

282 "Marching Rule." B.S.I.P. Annual Report for
1948 pp. 26–28; Kent, pp. 143–49; Luke, p.
134; Trumbull, pp. 64–65.

282 Prophet Moro. Kent, pp. 152–54.

285 Last Japanese soldier found on Guadalcanal. Kent,
p. 137.

# Bibliography

BOOKS AND ARTICLES

Works are cited in the Notes by reference to the last names of the authors.

Amherst, Lord, of Hackney and Thomas, Basil. *The Discovery of the Solomon Islands*. 2 vols. London: Hakluyt Society, 1901. Kraus Reprint, 1967. Translations, with comments and notes, of records and reports by members of the Spanish expedition that discovered the Solomon Islands in 1568.

Arnold, Henry H. *Global Mission*. New York: Harper and Brothers, 1949. The autobiography of the Chief of Staff, U.S. Army Air Forces, during World War II; includes accounts of his differences with commanders in the Pacific and Admiral King over allocation of AAF groups to the Pacific and of his visit to the area in September 1942.

Buell, Thomas B. *Master of Sea Power: A Biography of Fleet Admiral Ernest J. King*. Boston: Little, Brown & Co., 1980. Provides interesting sidelights on the planning phase of Guadalcanal campaign and on the principal Navy commanders there involved. The campaign itself, after the Battle of Savo Island, is dealt with in only one page.

————. *The Quiet Warrior: A Biography of Admiral Raymond A. Spruance*. Boston: Little, Brown & Co., 1974. Although Spruance was not directly involved in the Guadalcanal campaign, some of his instructions and decisions throw light on naval decisions in that campaign.

Bureau of Yards and Docks, Navy Department. *Building the Navy's Bases in World War II*. 2 vols. Washington: Government Printing Office 1947. Volume 1 includes descriptions of the work of Navy Construction Battalions (Seabees) in the construction of air bases, naval operating bases, and other facilities on Guadalcanal during and after the campaign.

Collins, J. Lawton. *Lightning Joe*. Baton Rouge: Louisiana State University Press, 1979. The autobiography of the Commanding General, 25th Infantry Division (later in his career, Chief of Staff, U.S. Army); includes an account of his division's operations in the final two months of the Guadalcanal campaign.

*Communicable Diseases: Malaria*. Preventive Medicine in World War II, vol. 6. Washington: Surgeon General, Department of the Army, 1963. A study of the incidence of malaria, and measures to combat it, in World War II theaters of operations; includes valuable material on joint Army-Navy efforts to control the disease in the Solomons.

Craven, Wesley Frank, and Cate, James Lea, eds. *Guadalcanal to Saipan*. Chicago: University of Chicago Press, 1950. The volume of the official Army Air Forces history covering AAF participation in the Guadalcanal and related campaigns. Chapter 1 ("New Guinea and the Solomons"), by Richard A. Watson and Kramer J. Rohfleisch; chapters 2 ("The Battle for Guadalcanal"), 3 ("The Thirteenth Air Force"), 7 ("The Central Solomons"), and 8 ("Bougainville"), by Kramer J. Rohfleisch; chapter 10 ("Rabaul and Cape Gloucester") by Capt. Bernhardt L. Mortensen.

Cronin, Francis D. *Under the Southern Cross*. Washington: Combat Forces Press, 1951. The unit history of the Americal [America-New Caledonia] Division, including an account of its operations on Guadalcanal.

Davis, Burke. *Marine!* Boston: Little, Brown & Co., 1962. A biography of General Lewis B. Puller, commanding officer (as a lieutenant colonel) of the 1st Battalion, 7th Marines, on Guadalcanal.

Dull, Paul S. *A Battle History of the Imperial Japanese Navy (1941–1945)*. Annapolis: Naval Institute Press, 1978.

Describes engagements of the IJN in World War II, drawing on the author's translations of (1) microfilms of Japanese unit reports and (2) parts of the monumental history of World War II (known in abbreviation as the BKS) being prepared by the History Section, Japanese Defense Agency.

Dyer, George C. *The Amphibians Came to Conquer: The Story of Admiral Richmond Kelly Turner*. 2 vols. Washington: U.S. Government Printing Office, 1971. An annotated biography of Admiral Turner, with emphasis on his career in World War II. Volume 1, which covers the Guadalcanal campaign, is particularly valuable for its presentation of Turner's (and, to a lesser extent, Admiral Fletcher's) views on many issues, based on the documentary record and interviews with the principals. Only Volume 1 is cited in this book.

Feldt, Eric A. *The Coastwatchers*. Oxford: Oxford University Press, 1946. An authoritative report on the organization and operations of the coastwatchers (code name: FERDINAND) in the Solomons and neighboring islands, who, with the help of friendly natives, observed and reported, by radio, on Japanese air, sea, and ground movements. Unfortunately, the book is often inaccurate in its accounts of miltary operations in the islands.

Gill, G. Hermon. *Royal Australian Navy 1942–45*. Canberra: Australia War Memorial, 1968. Includes accounts, from the Australian point of view, of events in the first few days of the Guadalcanal campaign, including the Battle of Savo Island.

Gillespie, Oliver A. *The Pacific*. Wellington: War History Branch, Department of Internal Affairs, 1952. A volume in the Official History of New Zealand in the Second World War; includes a description of movements by New Zealand units, particularly its 3d Division Brigade, in support of the Allied effort on Guadalcanal, and later, participation in campaigns in the upper Solomons and beyond.

Griffith, Samuel B., II. *The Battle for Guadalcanal*. Philadelphia: J. B. Lippincott Company, 1963. The best comprehensive account of the Guadalcanal campaign, ranging from high strategy and major command decisions to small-unit actions; carefully researched and read-ably written; contains material, based on interviews and correspondence, with both Japanese and American offi-cers, not available elsewhere.

Guppy, H. B. *The Solomon Islands and Their Natives.* London: S. Sonnenschein, Lowry & Co., 1887. De-scription of the Solomons by a nineteenth-century natu-ralist and explorer; contains a translation of the diary kept by the chief pilot of the Spanish expedition that discovered the islands in 1568.

Halsey, William F., and Bryan, J., III. *Admiral Halsey's Story.* New York: Whittlesey House, 1947. Reminis-cences of his World War II experiences by the admiral who served as Commander, South Pacific, during much of the struggle for Guadalcanal.

Hayashi, Saburo. *KOGUN: The Japanese Army in the Pacific War.* Translated and annotated by Alvin D. Coox. Quantico: Marine Corps Association, 1959. An IGHQ Army staff officer, during most of the Pacific war, wrote this terse, authoritative account of the Jap-anese Army's role in that war; written originally for Japanese readers.

Hersey, John. *Into the Valley.* New York: Knopf, 1943. A vivid story of a small-unit action in the Guadalcanal campaign, written by one who participated as a war correspondent.

Holmes, Wilfred J. *Double-Edged Secrets: U.S. Naval Intelligence Operations in the Pacific during World War II.* Annapolis: Naval Institute Press, 1979. A description of the work of the CINCPAC radio intelligence unit, which decrypted and translated intercepts of Japanese naval radio messages; deals only briefly with radio intelli-gence that directly affected the Guadalcanal campaign, but provides interesting background.

Horton, Dick C. *Fire over the Islands.* Sydney: Reed, 1970. The recollections of a district officer for Guadal-canal (Clemens's predecessor) who served as a guide and adviser to the 1st Raider Battalion.

Hough, Frank O., Ludwig, Verle E, and Shaw, Henry I., Jr. *Pearl Harbor to Guadalcanal.* Washington: Histori-cal Branch, G-3 Division, HQMC, 1958. Part VI of this official Marine Corps monograph covers the Guadalcanal campaign, from its conception in strategic planning to the Japanese evacuation of the Island.

Isely, Jeter, and Crowl, Philip A. *U. S. Marines and Amphibious War*. Princeton: Princeton University Press, 1952. A study of the U.S. Marine Corps's development of equipment, doctrine, and training for amphibious operations and their use in World War II; includes a brief account of the Guadalcanal operation.

Johnson, Richard W. *Follow Me!* New York: Random House, 1948. The unit history of the Second Marine Division; includes an account of its operations and experience on Guadalcanal.

Kahn, David. *The Codebreakers*. New York: Macmillan, 1967. A comprehensive historical review of cryptanalysis, including a valuable section on U.S. and Japanese efforts to break each other's codes and ciphers, with material directly pertinent to the Guadalcanal campaign; written before detailed materials on radio intelligence were declassified late in the 1970s.

Kenney, George C. *General Kenney Reports*. New York: 1949. An account of Fifth Air Force operations in MacArthur's area, including aerial attacks on Rabaul in support of U.S. operations in New Guinea and the Solomons; written by the Force's commanding general.

Kent, Janet. *The Solomon Islands*. Harrisburg: Stackpole Books, 1972. A handbook of information on the Solomon Islands, including material on political, economic, and social developments since World War II.

King, Ernest J., and Whitehill, Walter Muir. *Fleet Admiral King*. New York: Norton, 1952. A biography of the wartime Commander-in-Chief, U.S. fleet; includes material on the planning of the Guadalcanal operation, but nothing on the campaign itself.

Lord, Walter. *Lonely Vigil: Coastwatchers of the Solomons*. New York: The Viking Press, 1977. An American writer's account of the officials, planters, traders, clerics, and others who remained on Japanese-held islands in the Solomons to collect and report intelligence on enemy plane and ship movements.

Luke, Harry G. J. *Islands of the South Pacific*. London: 1962. The British Governor of Fiji and High Commissioner for the Western Pacific (1938–1942) looks at the Solomon Islands and other British island possessions in the South Pacific before, during, and immediately after World War II.

MacMillian, George. *The Old Breed*. Washington: Infantry Journal Press, 1949. The unit history of the First Marine Division in World War II, from its organization in North Carolina to its duty as part of the occupation force in China after the Japanese surrender.

Matloff, Maurice, and Snell, Edwin M. *Strategic Planning for Coalition Warfare, 1941–42*. Washington: Office of the Chief of Military History, Department of the Army, 1953. An authoritative account of strategic decision making in the first year of the Pacific war, among the Allied Combined Chiefs of Staff and the U.S. Joint Chiefs of Staff; discusses allocations of Army forces to the Pacific areas, before and during the Guadalcanal campaign.

Merillat, H. L. *The Island*. Boston: Houghton Mifflin Co., 1944. An on-the-scene report of operations of the First Marine Division, Reinforced, during the Guadalcanal campaign, by the press officer and in-house historian assigned to the division; useful for its accounts of major ground actions based on interviews of unit commanders.

Miller, John, Jr. *CARTWHEEL: The Reduction of Rabaul*. Washington: Office of the Chief of Military History, Department of the Army, 1959. The volume in the official Army historical series that covers post-Guadalcanal campaigns in the Solomons, New Guinea, and New Britain.

———. *Guadalcanal: The First Offensive*. Washington: Historical Division, Department of the Army, 1949. The official Army monograph dealing with the Guadalcanal campaign; valuable and generally reliable as to operations under the Marine command in the first four months; includes a detailed report on operations under Army command thereafter. Cited as "J. Miller."

Miller, Thomas G. *Cactus Air Force*. New York: Harper & Row, 1969. An excellent account of air operations—from Henderson Field and aircraft-carriers—during the

Guadalcanal campaign; well researched, with an appendix on sources, but not annotated. Cited as "T. Miller."

Milner, Samuel. *Victory in Papua*. Washington: Office of the Chief of Military History, Department of the Army, 1957. The official Army study of the Papuan campaign in New Guinea; notes shifts in Japanese strategy that affected the Guadalcanal campaign.

Morison, Samuel Eliot. *History of United States Naval Operations in World War II*. 15 vols. Boston: Little, Brown and Company, 1947–62. The monumental and classic account of naval operations, unofficial but generally authoritative; less reliable as to ground operations. Three volumes are of particular interest in connection with the Guadalcanal and later Solomons campaigns:

   Vol. 4. *Coral Sea, Midway, and Submarine Action*. 1964 (first published in 1949). Pages 245–96 deal with planning, composition of forces, and landing phase in the Guadalcanal operation.

   Vol. 5. *The Struggle for Guadalcanal*. 1964 (first published in 1949).

   Vol. 6. *Breaking the Bismarcks Barrier*. 1964 (first published in 1950).

——. *The Two-Ocean War*. Boston: Little, Brown & Company, 1963. A summary of the fifteen-volume work. The author has sometimes revised earlier reports and opinions, criticizing more severely, for example, some of the decisions made by Turner and Fletcher during the Solomons campaign.

Morton, Louis. *Strategy and Command: The First Two Years*. Washington: Office of the Chief of Military History, Department of the Army, 1962. A valuable study of developments in strategic thinking and command relationships, U.S. and Japanese, from the beginning of the Pacific war and initial U.S. buildup in the Pacific through the campaigns for Guadalcanal, the other Solomons, New Guinea, and Bismarck Archipelago.

Ohmae, Toshikazu. "The Battle for Savo Island." *The Japanese Navy in World War II*. Annapolis: U.S. Naval Institute, 1969, pp. 74–85. A report on the Battle of Savo Island from a Japanese point of view; written by a Japanese naval officer who was chief of staff to the commander of the Eighth Fleet at Rabaul in 1942, and, toward the end of the war, Chief, Operations Section, Naval General Staff in Tokyo.

Pogue, Forest C. *George Marshall: Ordeal and Hope 1939–42*. New York: Viking Press, 1965. The second volume of Pogue's classic biography of the wartime Army Chief of Staff; includes a discussion of Marshall's thoughts and decisions affecting the Guadalcanal campaign.

Potter, E. B. *Nimitz*. Annapolis: Naval Institute Press, 1967. A biography of Admiral Chester W. Nimitz, CINCPAC from late December 1941 through the remainder of the Pacific war; authorized by the admiral's family.

————, ed., and Nimitz, Chester W., assoc. ed. *Sea Power: A Naval History*. Englewood Cliffs, N.J.: Prentice-Hall, 1960. Standard history of the world's navies, edited by a leading naval historian at the U.S. Naval Academy with the active participation of Admiral Nimitz; includes a brief but useful summary of the Guadalcanal operation. Nimitz once said, "Everything I have to say about World War II is in *Sea Power*."

Reynolds, Clark G. *The Fast Carriers: The Forging of an Air Navy*. Huntington, N.Y.: Krieger, 1978. A review of Navy strategy, tactics, operations, and personalities in the Pacific war from the point of view of naval aviation officers, who were often at odds with their nonaviator peers; includes a brief account of earlier operations during the Guadalcanal campaign.

Shaw, Henry I., Jr., and Kane, Douglas T. *Isolation of Rabaul*. Washington: Historical Branch, G-3 Division, HQMC, 1963. The official Marine Corps monograph on operations by Marine units in the central and northern Solomons and on New Britain that helped to reduce the major Japanese base at Rabaul.

Sherrod, Robert. *History of Marine Corps Aviation in World War II*. 2nd ed. San Rafael, California: Presidio Press, 1980. The classic account of Marine aviation during the war, with chapters covering operations during the campaigns in the Solomons, at Guadalcanal, and later.

Sherwood, Robert E. *Roosevelt and Hopkins*. Rev. ed. New York: Harper & Brothers, 1950. An examination of strategic planning at the highest political and military levels of the United States and Great Britain; includes some important references to the Guadalcanal campaign.

Tanaka, Raizo. "Tbe Struggle for Guadalcanal." *The Japanese Navy in World War II*. Annapolis: U.S. Naval Institute, 1969, pp. 52–73. As a rear admiral, with special experience in command of destroyer squadrons and in night flghting, the author was responsible for the movement of Japanese reinforcements to Guadalcanal during much of the campaign.

Toland, John. *The Rising Sun*. New York: Random House, 1970. Part 4, "The Island of Death," deals with ground operations in the Guadalcanal campaign, as seen through Japanese eyes.

Tregaskis, Richard. *Guadalcanal Diary*. New York: Random House, 1943. This account of the first six weeks on Guadalcanal, by a war correspondent, has become a minor classic of World War II.

Trumbull, Robert. *Tin Roofs and Palm Trees*. Seattle: University of Washington Press, 1977. A report on developments in the Pacific islands since World War II, by a *New York Times* correspondent with long experience in Asia and the Pacific.

Vandegrift, A. A., with Asprey, R. B. *Once a Marine*. New York: Norton, 1964. The "as-told-to" autobiography of the Marine general who commanded U.S. forces on Guadalcanal during the first four months of the campaign and later became commandant of the Marine Corps; provides information on the Guadalcanal campaign of a kind uniquely available to the commanding general.

Willoughby, Malcolm F. *The U.S. Coast Guard in World War II*. Annapolis: U.S. Naval Institute, 1957. The Coast Guard, incorporated into the Navy in wartime, participated in the Guadalcanal campaign by providing many of the crewmen for landing craft and by manning one of the transports, the *Hunter Liggett*.

Woodford, Charles Morris. *A Naturalist among the Headhunters*. London: George Philip & Son, 1890. A description of the Solomon Islands and their people, from first-hand observation and experience, by the man who became the first resident commissioner of the British Solomon Islands Protectorate.

Yokoi, Toshiyuki. "Thoughts on Japan's Naval Defeat." *U.S. Naval Institute Proceedings*, 86: 68–75 (Oct. 1960). The author, a pioneer aviator in the Imperial Japanese Navy, served as chief of staff to the Fifth Air Fleet during the Okinawa campaign.

Zimmerman, John L. *The Guadalcanal Campaign*. Washington: USMC Historical Division, 1949. The first official Marine monograph reporting the Guadalcanal campaign; valuable for its detailed description of Marine unit operations, particularly on the ground.

OFFICIAL DOCUMENTS AND ARCHIVAL MATERIAL

Abbreviations appearing in the left-hand margin below are used in the Notes.

| | |
|---|---|
| BIS | British Information Service, Reference Division. *Solomon Islands*. London: HMSO, 1978. Reviews postwar political, economic, social, and educational developments in the British Solomon Islands Protectorate up to 1978. |
| Black Book | One of the notebooks in which the author kept notes during the Guadalcanal campaign. In the author's possession. |
| Cates | Cates, Clifton B. My First at Guadalcanal. Unpublished manuscript based on a diary kept by Colonel Cates, then commanding officer of the 1st Marines, on Guadalcanal. Marine Corps Historical Center, Personal Papers Section. |
| Clemens | Clemens, Martin. A Coastwatcher's Diary. Unpublished manuscript. The diary of the district officer for Guadalcanal, in the government of the British Solomon Islands Protectorate, recounting his experiences as a coastwatcher before the U.S. landings and as director of native scouts' activities thereafter. Photostat copy in Marine Corps Historical Center, Library. |

| | |
|---|---|
| CSP-WD | COMSOPAC War Diary. Operational Archives, Naval Historical Center. Includes copies of important communications between COMSOPAC and other commands. |
| Final Report | First Marine Division, Final Report on the Guadalcanal Operation. In five Phases, with annexes. Marine Corps Historical Center, Archives. A basic source for information concerning the operations of ground forces during the first four months of the Guadalcanal campaign; written during the half year following the departure of the division from the island and not always accurate in detail. |
| Ghormley | Ghormley, Robert L. The Tide Turns. Unpublished manuscript. Photocopy in Operational Archives, Naval Historical Center. An account of the author's stewardship as Commander, South Pacific, including the texts of many important communications with other commanders. |
| Hayes | Hayes, Grace P. History of the Joint Chiefs of Staff in World War II: The War Against Japan. 2 vols. Volume 1, "Pearl Harbor through Trident." Mimeographed manuscript, Navy Operational Archives. An official report of the deliberations of the JCS concerning the war in the Pacific; classified "Secret" until 1971; a basic source of information on the strategic background and allocation of forces to operations in Pacific areas in 1942 and early 1943. |
| HCM Diary | A diary in which the author kept notes during the Guadalcanal campaign. In the author's possession. |
| Jap. Mono. | Japanese Monograph Series, prepared in the Military History Section, U.S. Army Far East Command [General MacArthur's Headquarters]. In general, former Jap- |

anese officers compiled the material and wrote the reports in Japanese, which were then translated and rewritten in English. Since the early postwar monographs were prepared, much more information on the Japanese side of the war has become, and is becoming, available.

Monographs of particular interest in connection with the Guadalcanal campaign are:

History of the Eighth Area Army.
IGHQ [Imperial General Headquarters] Army High Command Record.
17th Army Operations.
Southeast Area Naval Operations. Part 1.

King Papers          *King Papers.* Operational Archives, Naval Historical Center. Contains Admiral King's official correspondence during the war and records of his periodic conferences with Admiral Nimitz.

Nimitz Papers        *Nimitz Papers.* Operational Archives, Naval Historical Center. Includes the admiral's daily Command Summaries and file of official dispatches and letters.

Malaria              Malaria and Epidemic Control in the
in SoPac             South Pacific, 1942–44. HQ, South Pacific Base Command. Unpublished report. U.S. Army Center of Military History. A report on Army efforts to control malaria on Guadalcanal and elsewhere in the South Pacific.

OH                   Transcripts of oral histories of Marine officers. Marine Corps Historical Center, Oral History Section. I have consulted transcripts of interviews with the following:

General Clifton B. Cates
Lieutenant General E. W. Snedeker
General Gerald C. Thomas
General Pedro del Valle
General A. A. Vandegrift

Radio Intel:    U.S. National Archives records of radio intelligence activities in World War II; include the following materials bearing on the Guadalcanal campaign:

SRH-012    "The Role of Radio Intelligence in the American-Japanese Naval War." National Archives, NSA/CSS Control No. SRH-012. Summaries and interpretations of decrypted Japanese naval radio dispatches and texts of decrypted intercepts.
vol. 1—August 1941–June 1942 (pp. 162–283 missing).
vol. 3—The Solomon Islands Campaign (background of the Battle of Savo Island)
vol. 4—The Solomon Islands Campaign (background of the Battle of the Eastern Solomons) includes Japanese dispatches relating to the Ichiki Detachment.

SRH-036    "Radio Intelligence in World War II. Tactical Operations in the Pacific Ocean Area." January 1943. National Archives, NSA/CSS Control No. SRH-036. Review of CINCPAC dispatches, based on radio intelligence, sent to subordinate commanders; reports indications of a new Japanese offensive early in 1943.

SRNS 0016-0302    Summaries of Japanese Naval Activities. From 7 August 1942 to 9 Feb. 1943. National Archives, NSA/CSS Control No. SRNS 0016-0302. Daily summaries of radio intelligence prepared by Chief of Naval Operations and distributed in seven copies only: White House, COMINCH, Vice CNO, and certain sections of naval war plans and operations. Some contain information bearing directly on operations on Guadalcanal.

Twining    Twining, Merrill B. "Guadalcanal: The Commander and His Staff." A presentation to the Marine Corps Schools, Quantico, by General Twining, then Commandant of the Schools, on November 4, 1957 (an adaptation of a lecture first given at the Schools in 1943); a discussion of the senior staff officer's role, illustrated by the writer's experience as operations officer on the First Marine Division staff.

USSBS(P)    *U.S. Strategic Bombing Survey (Pacific).* A study, by a specially appointed U.S. official group, of the effects of U.S. strategic bombing on enemy war efforts. With regard to Japan, the Survey investigated not only strategic bombing but the entire U.S. air effort. Despite some inaccuracies and evidences of service bias, these reports contain much useful information on the campaigns in the Solomons.

*Summary Report (Pacific War).* Washington, 1946.
Report No. 1.
*Japanese Air Power.* Military Analysis Division, 1947. Report No. 62.
*Air Campaigns of the Pacific War.* Military Analysis Division, 1947. Report No. 71a.
*Interrogation of Japanese Officials.* 2 vols. Naval Analysis Division, 1946. Report No. 72.
*The Campaigns of the Pacific War.* Naval Analysis Division, 1946. Report No. 73.
*The Allied Campaign against Rabaul.* Naval Analysis Division, 1946.

ZDC    Zimmerman Draft, Comments on. Marine Historical Center, Archives. Many officers who had served on Guadalcanal were asked to comment on a draft of the monograph written by John L.

Zimmerman. The letters and comments received in response, written within a few years of the campaign, are valuable for the detail they add and the corrections they offer, to official unit reports.

# Index

Abe, Hiroaki, 222
Admiralty Islands, 264
Aircraft, Solomons (AirSols), 263, 266, 269
Air losses: Japanese, 57–58, 115, 179, 202, 267, 269, 273–275; U.S., 62, 274
*Alchiba*, 234–235
*Alhena*, 109
Allies, combined planning and conferences, 24–25, 203, 268
*Amberjack*, 180
Aola, 87, 88, 208, 212–213, 217, 233–234, 239
*Argonne*, 186
Army Air Forces (U.S.), 25, 27, 31, 102, 109, 114, 204, 218, 220, 226, 254, 262–264, 267
Army units (Japanese)
  armies: Eighth Area Army, 229, 238, 254; Seventeenth Army, 91, 92, 169, 183–184, 229; Eighteenth Army, 229
  divisions: Second (or Sendai) Division, 141, 165, 183, 190–199, 205, 215, 216, 261; Thirty-eighth (or Hiroshima) Division, 183, 209, 210n, 212, 218–219, 221, 261
  brigades and detachments: Ichiki Detachment, 93, 118, 129–130, 133–135, 137–139, 183, 216; Kawaguchi Detachment, 93, 118, 129–130, 133–135, 137–139, 183, 216; Oka Detachment, 118, 138–139
  regiments: 4th Heavy Field Artillery, 184; 4th Infantry, 166, 169, 184, 190; 28th Infantry, 98, 107; 29th Infantry, 190–192, 195; 41st Infantry, 92; 144th Infantry, 92
Army units (U.S.)
  XIV Corps, 253, 256, 258, 284
  divisions: Americal, 209, 212, 231, 241, 253; 25th Infantry Division, 209, 253, 256, 259
  regiments: 27th Infantry, 256; 35th Infantry, 256; 132nd Infantry, 241,

# WORLD WAR II
## Edwin P. Hoyt

**BOWFIN**                                     69817-X/$3.50 US/$4.95 Can
An action-packed drama of submarine-chasing destroyers.

**THE MEN OF THE GAMBIER BAY**          55806-8/$3.50 US/$4.75 Can
Based on actual logs and interviews with surviving crew members, of
the only U.S. aircraft carrier to be sunk by naval gunfire in World War II.

**STORM OVER THE GILBERTS:**            63651-4/$3.50 US/$4.50 Can
**War in the Central Pacific: 1943**
The dramatic reconstruction of the bloody battle over the Japanese-
held Gilbert Islands.

**TO THE MARIANAS:**                     65839-9/$3.50 US/$4.95 Can
**War in the Central Pacific: 1944**
The Allies push toward Tokyo in America's first great amphibious
operation of World War II.

**CLOSING THE CIRCLE:**                  67983-8/$3.50 US/$4.95 Can
**War in the Pacific: 1945**
A behind-the-scenes look at the military and political moves drawn
from official American and Japanese sources.

**McCAMPBELL'S HEROES**                  68841-7/$3.95 US/$5.75 Can
A stirring account of the daring fighter pilots, led by Captain David
McCampbell, of Air Group Fifteen.

**THE SEA WOLVES**                       75249-2/$3.50 US/$4.95 Can
The true story of Hitler's dreaded U-boats of WW II and the allied forces
that fought to stop them.

**THE CARRIER WAR**                      75360-X/$3.50 US/$4.50 Can
The exciting account of the air and sea battles that defeated Japan in
the Pacific.

**LEYTE GULF**                           75408-8/$3.50 US/$4.50 Can
**The Death of the Princeton**
The true story of a bomb-torn American aircraft carrier fighting a
courageous battle for survival!

**RAIDER 16**                            75449-5/$3.95 US/$4.95 Can
The gripping story of the deadliest of the German surface marauders
that preyed on Allied supply lines and her legendary captain.

## FROM PERSONAL JOURNALS TO BLACKLY HUMOROUS ACCOUNTS

# VIETNAM

**DISPATCHES**, Michael Herr
01976-0/$4.50 US/$5.95 Can
"I believe it may be the best personal journal about war, any war, that any writer has ever accomplished."
—Robert Stone, *Chicago Tribune*

**M**, John Sack
69866-8/$3.95 US/$4.95 Can
"A gripping and honest account, compassionate and rich, colorful and blackly comic."
—*The New York Times*

**ONE BUGLE, NO DRUMS**, Charles Durden
69260-0/$4.95 US/$5.95 Can
"The funniest, ghastliest military scenes put to paper since Joseph Heller wrote *Catch-22*"
—*Newsweek*

**AMERICAN BOYS**, Steven Phillip Smith
67934-5/$4.50 US/$5.95 Can
"The best novel I've come across on the war in Vietnam"
—Norman Mailer